Steer
Clear

Driving Skills

Manual and Logbook

Monica Schaefer

Irish Drivers Education Association Ltd

First published by
Irish Drivers Education Association Ltd
IDEA House
Killarney Road Business Park
Bray
Co. Wicklow
www.steerclear.ie
Phone: 01 202 2428

© Irish Drivers Education Association 2008
Reprinted 2010

Editing team
Sorcha McDonagh, Denise Sweeney, Máire Daly,
Brian Murphy, Monica Schaefer, Mark Loughran

Director of operations
Brian Murphy

Design and production
Mark Loughran (Identikit Design Consultants),
Tani Pratchayaopak and Anneke Calis (Tanika Design)

Illustrations and photography
William Siddall, Carla Tome, VW (Motor Distributors Ireland),
Volvo Car Ireland, Mini Ireland, Dave Leahy (Big Bad Wolf Animation)

Author
Monica Schaefer

Printing
Printed and bound in Dublin, Ireland by Plus Print

All rights reserved. No part of this publication may be reproduced
or transmitted in any form or by any means electronic or mechanical including
photocopying, scanning, recording or in any other form of storage or retrieval
system without the prior written permission of the publishers.

While every effort has been taken to ensure that all information contained
in this publication is correct and in accordance with Irish standards and laws, readers
should apply their own skill and judgement when using the information contained
within it. The author and publishers assume no responsibility for any injury,
loss or damage caused or sustained as a consequence of the
use and application of the contents.

Foreword

'New drivers face an increased risk of loss of control and collision over the first few months of obtaining a driving license. Research shows that young drivers typically underestimate the demands of the driving task and overestimate their capability. To be effective as a safety measure, driver training needs to develop not only competence in vehicle handling skills but also an ability to read the road ahead, to relate speed to the prevailing conditions and to maintain an adequate safety margin at all times. For this, graduated training and extensive mentored driving practice are needed. But even these alone are not enough. The safe driver needs in addition to embrace attitudes of care, courtesy and consideration for all road users, including his or her passengers.

This state-of-the-art, comprehensive and beautifully illustrated programme is designed with these goals in mind and should prove of immense value to novice drivers, instructors and mentors alike and make a significant contribution to safety on our roads.'

Professor Ray Fuller,
School of Psychology,
Trinity College Dublin

Contents

Instruction

Training record

Practice

How to use this book

In line with International best practice and the Road Safety Authority's (RSA) latest guidelines and regulations on learning to drive in Ireland, the Steer Clear Driving Skills Manual and Logbook is designed to help you as a learner driver to get the most from structured driving lessons and accompanied driving practice. This manual has two distinct parts; the first part contains ten structures driving lessons that will take you through the essential skills and techniques required for safe driving, the second part of the manual provides you with complementary practice sessions to help you to develop your competence. Handy log sheets are provided in the centre of the manual to help you, your driving instructor and your mentor to keep track of your progress throughout your entire learning to drive experience.

The lessons in the first part of the manual are numbered and marked with yellow page tabs. They range from simple to complex and cover everything from approaching the vehicle for the first time to assessing your readiness to take your driving test. The aim of each lesson is to teach you the correct procedures and techniques for driving your car in a safe and considerate manner.

The second part of the manual is marked with red tabs and contains structured practice sessions outlines that will help you to concentrate on putting into practice what you learn in the corresponding driving lessons. Structured practice sessions provide you with opportunities to practice and gain confidence with newly acquired driving skills in a relaxed way that is also purposeful and effective.

Practicing between lessons will help you to reinforce your learning. Practice session number one should follow driving lesson number one and take place before you take driving lesson number two and so on. Scheduling your learning and practice sessions in this way will enable you to gain competence at each level before you attempt to take on more complex skills in the following lessons. By using this book to structure your learning you will be able to progress more effectively from simple to complex skills. Each lesson builds on the skills learned in the previous one, practicing your new skills, in the interval between lessons enables you to gain maximum benefit from subsequent lessons. It is important to stay within the parameters of skills learned in the previous driving lessons and not to jump ahead of the driving instructor.

Although anyone can use this method to learn to drive, to get the maximum benefit, the lessons in part one are designed to be delivered by Approved Driving Instructors (ADI) using a dual control car. The driving practice sessions are designed to help committed experienced drivers to become effective mentors when they accompany you. Accompanying you, as you learn to drive, should be a rewarding experience for you and for your mentor, but be advised that accompanied driving can also be frustrating and at times stressful if you go about it in the wrong way, beginning on page 160 you will find some useful guidelines which you should take a few minutes to read to help you to make the process a lot more positive and rewarding. We strongly advise that you and your mentor read these guidelines before commencing the practice sessions.

In preparing for the practice sessions if you find that you are unclear about how a skill or a technique should be preformed, you can just flip open the corresponding lesson outline in the yellow tabbed section for more details. At the end of each practice session it will help if you take a few minutes to discuss the session's good and bad points and to discover solutions with your mentor. Use the check sheets located on the last page of each session to track your progress throughout the practice sessions, on completion of all of the skills in a session you can then complete the log sheets in the centre of the book to track and log your overall learning progress.

Instruction

Introduction

Effective driving instruction

The ten driving lessons contained in this manual are designed to be delivered by an approved driving instructor (ADI) and reinforced by structured driving practice sessions with an accompanying driver or mentor. When driving lessons take place after the learner has had the opportunity to study the steer clear driver education programme the outcome will be even more effective. Structure the delivery of the lessons with sufficient time between them for the learner to get plenty of mentored practice. The time spent practicing will help the learner to build competence in the new skills before they attempt to move to more advanced skills in the following lesson. The corresponding mentored practice sessions, in this book, are designed to reinforce and complement the procedures taught in these driving lessons. Mentored practice session one should take place after driving lesson one and before driving lesson two to be most beneficial. At the start of each lesson conduct a brief assessment to ascertain the level of competence reached after the previous practice session, correct any faults and provide assistance where necessary, don't forget to acknowledge progress and provide encouragement. Logging the learner's progress throughout the course of the lessons and the practice sessions helps to track progress, encourage learning and to identify problems that need attention.

Simple to complex
The lessons are designed for new drivers and follow a simple to complex structure. When you first meet a new driver it is important to find out how

much prior experience they have so that you can tailor the instruction to their learning gaps and needs. Everyone has some degree of past road user experience, whether as a pedestrian, a cyclist, motorcyclist or as a passenger, past experience needs to be built upon and transferred into the new learning role to develop good driving habits. Past experience can sometimes have a negative aspect, for example: as a passenger the learner will have gained a 'feel' for the speed generally used on approach to a corner and while this speed may be appropriate for an experienced driver it would be beyond the safe speed and ability of a new driver, therefore not an appropriate speed to adopt in the early stages of learning.

Effective learning

The most effective learning takes place when a learner is both physically and psychologically ready to learn, they must be motivated and relaxed. The learner needs to be comfortable and free from stress before beginning the lesson, you can create a stress free environment by setting out reasonable and attainable objectives and goals for each lesson and by recognising the learner's progress by acknowledging even small achievements with constant positive reinforcement. The learner driver will learn best when they can base new learning on information and skills that they already know for example; knowledge of the rules of the road and previous cycling experience will form a valuable foundation for learning to drive.

Overconfidence

Be mindful of building overconfidence in the new driver. Allowing the forgiving design of the road or the time of your lessons to create a false sense of security may reinforce poor or incorrect driving behaviour. If the lessons always take place in quiet neighbourhoods at weekends, for example, it can easily lead to complacency about scanning and making all the necessary checks, resulting in the learner being ill-prepared to deal with busy streets at rush hour or on wet school mornings.

Active learning

For new drivers to really benefit from the driving lessons it is vital to get them fully involved and active in the learning process. Just telling or showing a learner how to do something is much less effective than actually getting them to put the new skill or knowledge into practice. It is not good enough for the learner to be just physically present and going through motions, the learner needs to be mentally present and fully engaged in the process. For example; the beep of a mobile phone can seriously distract the learner, even though they are still physically going through the motions of a skill, the mind will be else where and the value of the lesson will be seriously diminished.

In the beginning there is a lot to take on board and the learner will tire easily, so keep the lessons short and interesting enough to maintain active learning. When the learner becomes a little more competent they may reach a learning 'plateau', the driving is no longer challenging the learner and they can easily get distracted as the mind wanders off to other matters. You may be able to reignite the interest by getting the learner to use 'what if' questions, for example, to check for potential hazards. When the learner reaches this stage it is time to push out the boundaries by transfer more of the responsibility and decision making to the learner. As competence grows so too should the difficulty of the task and of the driving environment to once again challenge and expand the level of competence.

Procedural training

The psychomotor or physical skill techniques necessary for driving are initially learned off by explanation, demonstration and repetition – until they become automatic, this is called procedural training and forms the subconscious basis on which we rely on when driving. Good procedural training and reinforcement through practice is essential to instil good driving habits, procedures are what drivers instinctively fall back on in emergency situations. Learning a skill or to recite information off by rote is the simplest form of procedural training and forms the foundation for more meaningful learning to follow. For example the learner needs to learn how to physically change gear to drive the vehicle and then practice how to do it smoothly, once this has been accomplished, knowledge can then be added to instil a better understanding of the value of the skill. When the learner understands how and why the gears are used their use of the gears becomes most effective. Learning with understanding is far more effective than learning off by rote, once the basic skills have been mastered the new driver should be encouraged to expand their knowledge and their understanding of how and why the skill is used to maximise its benefit and ensure retention.

Learning and understanding

When it comes to learning how to drive, there is a place for learning by rote and place for learning with understanding; procedural training for learning how to handle the vehicle and knowledge development to bring meaning and understanding. This kind of combined cognitive training enables the learner to apply newly acquired skills and knowledge to other more complex situations. Changing gears for example needs to be mastered in order to get the vehicle moving, but the same set of basic gear changing skills are required when manoeuvring, when slowing down, speeding up, in cornering and when climbing up or driving down a hill. Understanding how and when to change gears properly will ensure a smoother ride and a more economical and efficient use of engine parts and fuel. During driver training, combining both types of learning is most effective for long term skill retention and application.

Skills training teaches **how** and **what** to do, knowledge development enables the learner to choose; **why, where** and **when** to do it. In driving instruction we tend to teach the skill first then apply the meaning but in actual driving circumstances we use these abilities in the reverse order – first gathering the relevant information from the environment, then processing it, then making an informed decision and finally acting appropriately by using the correct vehicle control skills.

Progressive learning

Understanding a new skill or concept is easiest when it follows a natural progression, crawl – walk – run for example. In the driving context this means, using the learners past road use experience, as a pedestrian, cyclist or as a passenger as the foundation for good road use as a driver. Most learner drivers will already will have a whole range of skills and knowledge relative to their road use as a pedestrian, cyclist or passenger. Take hazard perception for example; while walking along a busy street a pedestrian has to constantly avoid colliding with buggies, umbrellas, lamp-posts, other pedestrians and traffic, a cyclist must avoid pot holes, road works and other such hazards.

Simple to complex

Introduce skills in logical order, simple to complex, initially breaking down skills into sub-skills, then putting all the parts together to achieve the required outcome. For example: Teaching how to gear up requires that you first teach the sub-skills within that skill before putting all the parts together as one skill:

- ease off the accelerator
- depress the clutch
- shift gear
- release the clutch while
- simultaneously depressing the accelerator

Once mastered these basic sub-skills combine together to become a single skill and in turn that skill becomes a sub-skill of a more complex skill and so on. As a seasoned driver breaking down the skills into component parts can be difficult after years of subconscious application. Skill analysis is essential to ensure that no critical step is overlooked. Teaching learner drivers who have some previous driving experience can be particularly challenging in this regard and while it may seem unnecessary to analysis each skill, this kind of procedural training is essential for building a solid foundation. When each of the critical parts of a skill can be identified, it makes it easier to find and deal with learning gaps when a problem arises.

Behaviour and attitude

Affective instruction has taken place when drivers understand the consequences of their actions – the cause and effect equation. Inappropriate or bad driving behaviour is by far the greatest killer on our roads. Having a good attitude to road safety is fundamental to good driving behaviour, conversely, a bad attitude to safety leads to bad driving behaviour. As an instructor you play a vital role in helping to develop a good attitude to driving safety and consequently to the good behaviour of the new driver. Attitudes are formed throughout life and are usually influenced by what we see around us, a new driver that has been constantly exposed to poor driving habits and a general disregard to the law is likely to have a bad attitude. Obviously a learner who has been influenced by negative attitudes will present more of a challenge than one who has been exposed to positive attitudes. It is more difficult to change a poor attitude than to build on a good one, but not impossible – it can be done. Bringing new understanding and helping to positively influence the beliefs and values of person with a negative outlook is the key to turning a negative attitude to a positive one. As an instructor when you demonstrate

- Change down through the gears to slow down.
- Decrease speed more rapidly by applying the brakes.
- When coming to a stop, depress the clutch as well as the brake to prevent stalling.

Changing gears

- Listen to the engine sounds, the different engine tones can help you to make smoother gear changes.
- Change gears by first easing off on the accelerator and depressing the clutch; then selecting the new gear; easing out the clutch; and gently increasing acceleration with the right foot. Being aware of the sound and feel of the vehicle helps to time gear changes correctly, giving a smoother drive.
- As the vehicle increases speed, change up through the gears to keep the engine running efficiently. Listening to the sound of the engine cues the driver when to change gears. When the clutch is depressed the gears are temporarily disengaged and this enables the driver to select another gear.
- Changing gears too soon or too late will cause the engine to labour.

- When changing down gears, reduce speed by decreasing acceleration before depressing the clutch and then gently matching the revs of the new gear as it is engaged.
- Don't force the gear lever, if you are having difficulty finding the correct position for the gear lever, ease it back to the neutral position and try again.
- Avoid coasting because it lessens the control you have over the vehicle. Coasting means moving along while still in gear by keeping the clutch depressed or remaining in neutral for any length of time.
- Normally gears are changed in sequence but this is not mandatory. To slow down more quickly, it's possible to 'block' change several gears at a time.
- To block change, keep the clutch depressed, move down two or more gears while simultaneously using the brake to modify speed to match the new gear selected.
- Smooth gear changes are more comfortable for you and your passengers; they cause less wear on the gear mechanism and also save on fuel consumption.

Staying on course

- Pay constant attention to road position and direction, making small corrections as needed.
- Always looking well ahead helps the driver to anticipate when a change in direction or position is likely to be required. This makes it easier to make smooth and controlled corrections in plenty of time.

Moving off uphill

- Remember MSM – mirrors and signals before manoeuvring.
- Allow more time and space – that is, a more generous safe gap – before attempting to move off uphill from a stopped position.
- The engine requires more power to prevent stalling when starting off uphill. Apply firm pressure to the accelerator and hold the clutch in a little longer after reaching the biting point. As the parking brake is released, a little extra acceleration will be required to get the vehicle moving forwards.
- To ensure that the vehicle does not roll backwards during hill starts, practise the co-ordination of easing out on the clutch, increasing accelerator pressure and parking brake off until it can be done simultaneously and with confidence.

Moving off downhill

- As before, remember MSM.
- To prevent the vehicle from moving forward prematurely, keep the right foot on the brake.
- At the biting point, release the brake gently and ease out on the clutch fully, as the vehicle rolls forward increase acceleration.
- When the hill is very steep, selecting second gear initially makes for a smoother start.

Moving off at an angle

- Go through the routine steps for moving off: putting the vehicle into gear, controlling the clutch, finding the biting point and applying acceleration. Remember to indicate and make sure that there is no oncoming traffic, pedestrians or cyclists (MSM) and then steer away from the kerb or around any obstacles, such as another parked car.
- Be particularly careful when pulling out of a line of parked vehicles.

Left and right turns

Steering control

- Keep both hands on the wheel in a balanced position on either side moving the hands in unison for small changes of direction.

- Holding the wheel in an 8 and 4 position provides a lower centre of gravity than the traditional 10 and 2 position. This reduces unintentional over-steering and it also lessens the chances of your hands hitting your face should the air bag be deployed.
- When larger turning movements are required, feed the wheel through the hands using the push-pull method. By feeding the wheel from one hand to the other, you can maintain grip and control with one hand at all times and prevent the wheel from spinning back as the turn is completed.
- Avoid over-steering by straightening up the steering wheel at the recovery point.

The recovery point is when the front wheels reach the desired direction of travel – this happens before the front of the vehicle appears to be aligned.

Steering methods

In most cases, the push-pull method of steering is best because it affords smoother control but in tight slow manoeuvres the hand-over-hand method is sometimes more effective.

- The push-pull method. Grip the bottom of the wheel firmly with one hand and hold it loosely at the top with the other hand. Push the wheel up from the bottom, feeding it through the top hand until the hands are nearly together. Then change the grip to the other hand and slide the first hand back down to its original position. Repeat the procedure in the opposite direction to straighten up after the turn.
- Hand-over-hand method. In tight and slow turning manoeuvres, such as when parking in a confined space, it may be necessary to use the hand-over-hand method of steering, particularly in vehicles without power steering. When turning sharply to the right, hold the

wheel as normal and use both hands to move the wheel to the right. When the right hand gets to the 6 o'clock position, release it and continue turning the wheel with the left hand. Cross the right hand over the left arm and grasp the wheel at the top. Continue turning with the right hand and return the left hand to the normal position. Do likewise for a sharp left turning manoeuvre – but to the left.

- To return to the normal steering grip use the same technique in reverse or allow the wheel to slide through your hands in a controlled manner.

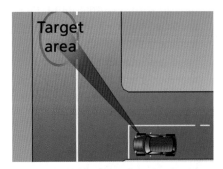

Observation

Prior to commencing any manoeuvre...

- Check that the target area is clear and that making the manoeuvre will not impede other traffic.
- Use the indicators to let other road users know of your intended manoeuvre.

- Adjust your speed to match the speed of the new position, the flow of traffic in a new lane or in preparation to make a turn.

Turning

- Turning the steering wheel when the wheels are not moving is not recommended because it causes excessive strain on the steering mechanism and wear on the tyres.
- Allow enough space for the length of the vehicle to follow through the turn. This is especially important in tight turns where the back wheels can clip the kerb if you don't leave enough room particularly in long wheel based vehicles.
- Vehicles with power-assisted steering are easy to turn and require less effort to execute a manoeuvre. Without power-assisted steering, the driver has to make a much bigger effort to turn the vehicle. You may need to adjust to a different type of steering when driving an unfamiliar vehicle.
- Looking towards the target area before commencing the manoeuvre, will help you to anticipate and make any adjustments necessary.

Safe changes of direction or position

The SIDE rule is a useful acronym for remembering all the steps for making safe changes in direction or position.

- Scan – all around, using the mirrors and an over-the-shoulder glance to check the blind spots.
- Identify – any potential hazards and be sure that the way is clear.
- Decide – the course of action and, when confident that the way is clear, use the indicators to communicate and warn other road users of your intended change of direction or position.
- Execute – the manoeuvre without delay while continuing to keep a good lookout all around.

Scan

Identify

Decide

Execute

Exiting the vehicle

Safe parking and exiting

- Select a suitable parking position and be sure that the parked vehicle will not hinder or endanger the movement of other road users.
- Never park in a disabled drivers parking bay, unless you have a legitimate requirement and permit to do so.
- Engage neutral and apply the parking brake.
- Remove both feet from the pedals.
- Turn off the ignition.
- Check that all lights and electrical devices are turned off.
- Remove the key.

- Put the vehicle into gear or into 'park' in an automatic.
- Remove your safety belt, and check that all windows and roof openings are closed.
- Check the rear-view mirror and over your door-side shoulder before opening the door.
- Get out of the vehicle, close and lock the doors.
- Walk to the footpath or away from the vehicle, facing the oncoming traffic.
- From outside the vehicle, check again to make sure that all the lights are off and that all of the windows and doors are closed.

Lesson 1 · Initiation to driving

Instruction assessment record

	Progressing	Mastered	ADI Signature	Date
Approaching and entering the vehicle				
Checking surrounding area	○	○	⬭	⬭
Exterior vehicle check	○	○	⬭	⬭
Entering the vehicle	○	○	⬭	⬭
Sitting comfortably				
Seating positions	○	○	⬭	⬭
Safety restraints	○	○	⬭	⬭
Controls and instruments				
Vehicle controls	○	○	⬭	⬭
Using the instruments	○	○	⬭	⬭
Mirrors	○	○	⬭	⬭
Cockpit drill	○	○	⬭	⬭
Using the controls				
Steering-wheel grip	○	○	⬭	⬭
Foot positions	○	○	⬭	⬭
Gear selection	○	○	⬭	⬭
Parking brake	○	○	⬭	⬭
Indicators and signalling	○	○	⬭	⬭

	Progressing	Mastered	ADI Signature	Date

Moving forward

Starting the engine	○	○		
Turning off the engine	○	○		
Moving off	○	○		
Stopping	○	○		
Foot controls	○	○		
Smooth speed and gear changes	○	○		
Changing gear	○	○		
Staying on course	○	○		
Moving off uphill	○	○		
Moving off downhill	○	○		
Moving off at an angle	○	○		

Left and right turns

Steering and control	○	○		
Steering methods	○	○		
Observation	○	○		
Turning	○	○		
Safe changes of direction or position	○	○		

Exiting the vehicle

Safe parking	○	○		
Safe exiting	○	○		

Note to ADI: When every skill has been mastered please note this by signing off lesson 1 in the training log in the centre of the book.

Lesson 1

Notes

2

Basic driving skills

In this lesson we will discuss...

- Reversing
- Turning around
- Maintaining proper speed
- Following distances
- Changing lanes on dual carriageways

Introduction

Having the ability to reverse competently is an essential skill required for vehicle manoeuvring and parking. Whether reversing in a straight line, reversing in a turn, reversing around an obstacle or reversing around a corner the basics are the same. Reversing is not difficult but it needs plenty of practice to reach competence.

Reversing

Moving the car slowly maximises steering control, makes it easier to stop if necessary and is the key to good reversing manoeuvres.

Setting up for a reversing manoeuvre

- Good all-round observation is essential before and during a reversing manoeuvre.
- Check the mirrors and then over the left shoulder. Loosening the lap section of the safety belt allows you to turn slightly in your seat so that you can see more clearly.
- While it is permissible by law to unfasten your safety belt when reversing, it is seldom necessary.

If you do unfasten your belt to reverse, you must remember to refasten it before moving off.

- Check the target area and to the left and right of the vehicle.
- Be especially vigilant if children are in the area because they might not be visible in the rear-view mirror. Check also for pedestrians, motorcyclists and obstacles. If in doubt, get out of the vehicle or get someone else to check behind before reversing.

Reversing in a straight line

- Turn around slightly to look over the left shoulder. Slide the right hand up to the top of the steering wheel and the left hand to the bottom. Alternatively, if this position is too difficult, hold the steering wheel with just the right hand and place the left arm on top of the seat back or on the passenger seat.

- Ease the clutch out to the biting point. As soon as the vehicle begins to move, hold the clutch. If the vehicle is moving too quickly, depress the clutch very slightly. If more drive is needed, ease the clutch out a little more. Small movements of the clutch help to control the car's speed.

- Keep the clutch at or near the biting point, gently increase acceleration or apply the brakes as needed to keep the vehicle under control.

- Use small movements of the steering wheel to keep the vehicle on a straight course. Anti-clockwise (left) pressure applied to the steering wheel will help you to guide the back of the vehicle towards the left, when you want to correct to the right apply clock-wise (right hand side) pressure to the steering wheel.

- Be aware that any turning of the back of the vehicle while reversing results in a corresponding and opposite swing to the front of the vehicle. This means that when the rear of the vehicle goes left the front will be moving to the right. The opposing front movement of the vehicle is even greater than the movement to the rear because the pivot point when reversing is located at the centre of the back axel. Leave plenty of room for this swinging action.

- Keep checking all around during the manoeuvre.

- Apply the foot brake gently to bring the car to a halt. Remember to depress the clutch before the car stops to prevent the engine from stalling.

When you have completed the manoeuvre, return to forward movement or select neutral and apply the parking brake if remaining stationary.

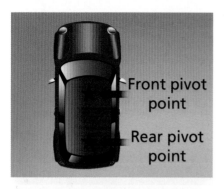

Front pivot point

Rear pivot point

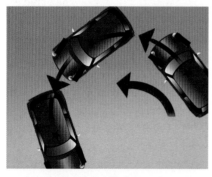

Reversing in a turn

- Remember that reversing slowly allows for more controlled steering.

- After easing out on the clutch and when the vehicle has just begun moving, turn the steering wheel in the desired direction.
- Leave plenty of room for the front of the vehicle to swing out, especially if it might impede oncoming traffic.
- Turning the steering wheel before the vehicle starts moving is not recommended as it causes excess wear on the steering mechanism and tyres.

Reversing around an obstruction

- Observe and check the area around and beyond the obstruction.
- Use the mirrors and glance over the shoulder to keep the obstruction in view for as long as possible. The further away from the obstruction, the easier it will be to keep it in sight.
- Start turning when the middle of the vehicle is abreast of the obstruction.
- Leave sufficient room for the front of the vehicle to swing out as the back comes in around the obstruction.
- Straighten up when you can see the obstruction through the front windscreen.

Reversing around a corner to the left

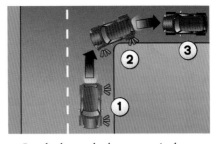

Before starting this manoeuvre for the first time, get out of the car and check the position of the back wheels in relation to an interior feature of the car. Usually, the back wheels are in line with the rear seat. Knowing where the back wheels are will help to determine the axis around which the vehicle will pivot and how much clearance you will need to leave to clear obstacles.

■ Slow down when passing the chosen junction or space to check that it is clear and safe to carry out the reverse turn.

■ Signal left when passing the junction and not beforehand (signalling too early will confuse drivers emerging from the junction).

■ It is illegal to reverse onto a main road from a minor one, so only choose to reverse around a corner in a safe and legal place.

■ Stop on the left-hand side about half a metre out from the kerb and about two car lengths beyond the junction.

■ Adopt the same sitting position that you use for reversing in a straight line.

■ Select reverse gear.

■ Make a full 360° observation starting over the right shoulder.

■ If it is safe, reverse slowly.

■ Look through the rear windows and look in the left side mirror occasionally to check the vehicle's position in relation to the kerb.

■ Try to stay parallel to and the same distance from the kerb during the manoeuvre.

■ When the back wheel is level with the junction, the kerb of the side road will have disappeared from sight in the rear window.

■ Stop or slow down and check over the right shoulder before continuing. If there is an approaching vehicle, stop and allow the vehicle to pass before continuing the manoeuvre. If a vehicle approaches along the side road, pull forward and commence the manoeuvre again.

■ You must also yield to pedestrians approaching on the pavement.

■ Turn the wheel to the left to bring the rear of the vehicle around the corner. The amount of turn will depend on the corner. Try to keep the back wheels parallel to the kerb. Use the left mirror occasionally to check the vehicle's position.

- Remember that in a reverse turn, the front of the car swings much wider than the back.
- Keep looking around during the manoeuvre, and keep the vehicle's speed constant and slow.
- The kerb should now be visible in the rear window and should appear to move across the window towards the centre.
- Just before the vehicle is straight, begin to turn the steering wheel to the right to straighten the wheels.

Again, small movements of the wheel will prevent over-steering.
- When the car is straight, continue to reverse for about two car lengths, keeping the speed down, maintaining a straight course and continuing to look all around for potential hazards.
- Bring the car to a halt with the foot brake. Remember to depress the clutch before the car stops to prevent the engine from stalling. Apply the parking brake and select neutral.

Turning around

When a right turn or junction is obscured by a hill or dip in the road, stopping in the middle of the road, to wait to make the turn, exposes you to the danger of being hit from behind. A safer option is to drive past the junction, find a safer place or junction at which to turn and then drive back and make the turn, much more safely, from the left.

There are several options available for turning a vehicle; a three-point turn, a turn about, a turn on a hill, a U-turn or a turn in a confined space, such as a car park, for example.

Where traffic is heavy it may be safer to drive on to a roundabout or find a safer location to turn around. Where possible drive into a side road to turn rather than attempting the manoeuvre on a main road.

Making a three-point turn on flat ground

- Look around to ensure that the way is clear. When it's safe, slow down close to the left-hand side of the road then turn the steering wheel fully to the right, move forward to the far side of the road and stop.
- Select reverse and turn the steering wheel fully to the left as you begin to move backwards, stop at the far side of the road.
- Select first gear and turn the steering wheel in the desired direction of travel.

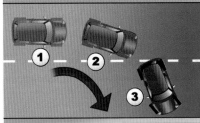

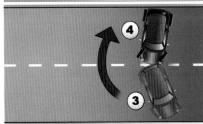

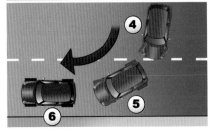

Making a turn-about

- Where possible, drive around the block or go to a side street to make a turn rather than attempting a turn-about on a main road.
- Use good observation all around before attempting the turn.
- Do not attempt to turn when your view is restricted, such as near a hill top or a bend in the road. You should be able to see for at least 100m in both directions.
- Use the SIDE rule.

Turning on a hill

- Leave a generous safe gap before starting.
- Use the same procedures for a turn on flat ground, but note that the parking brake and a little more acceleration will be needed to prevent the vehicle from slipping back during the turn.
- Avoid turning on a hill if there is an alternative.

Making a u-turn

- Check all around and be sure that the way is clear and the road wide enough before attempting a U-turn.
- Pull well over to the left and check again for oncoming traffic. Put on the right indicator and move forward while turning in a sharp arc to the right.
- Straighten up at the end of the turn and check again for oncoming traffic before moving out into the driving lane.

Making a tight turn in a confined space

- Use the SIDE rule and the three-point turn method to turn in a confined space such as a car park.
- Be vigilant for pedestrians in car parks.
- Make as many points or directional changes as is necessary; some turns need five or seven points!
- Remember to leave swing room for the front of the vehicle when reverse turning.

Maintaining proper speed

It is good to develop a feel for the vehicle's approximate speed so that you don't have to keep looking at the speedometer to know when you are doing the appropriate speed for the prevailing conditions.

Observing the rate at which you pass static objects and noting how the vehicle sounds and feels at different speeds helps you build a better awareness of your speed. Being able to drive at a consistent speed without having to constantly look at the dials is much safer because it enables you to spend more time looking at the road ahead.

Choosing the appropriate speed

Choose an appropriate speed by considering:

- Your own experience level,
- The traffic volume and speed,
- The vehicle size, loading and condition,
- The weather conditions,
- The type and condition of the road,
- The posted speed limit and other restrictions for example; when towing,
- Adequate progress to avoid impeding the progress of other road users.

Approaching speed-limit changes

- When approaching a reduced speed-limit sign or area, gear down and slow down so that the correct speed is reached as the vehicle arrives at the sign.
- When leaving a restricted speed area, accelerate and gear up gradually to increase speed as appropriate to the traffic and conditions.

- Avoid making harsh or erratic speed changes as this may be contrary to the expectations of other road users.
- Harsh speed changes lessen vehicle control and use more energy than smooth speed changes.

Following the general traffic speed

- Adjust speed smoothly to match the general flow of traffic and to achieve the correct distance from other vehicles.
- Matching speed to the general speed of the traffic flow (assuming it is within the posted speed limit) will help to maintain a comfortable position in the traffic.
- Vehicles driven at just 10km faster or slower than the general speed of other vehicles in heavy traffic cause a domino effect of braking and slowing that consequently leads to slowing down and delaying of all the following traffic.

Following distances

The two-second rule is a valuable tool for establishing a safe distance between vehicles. Choose a stationary object up ahead, such as a lamppost or building. Count the seconds between the instant the vehicle ahead passes the object and the instant you pass the same object. A minimum of two seconds should pass. Leave even more time when conditions are poor, such as in wet weather or in reduced visibility.

Maintaining enough space between vehicles travelling ahead and behind is essential for safe driving. It is up to you to create your own safety margins at all times and especially in adverse conditions or when following oversized vehicles.

Maintaining the appropriate following distance

- Drive at a safe distance with a minimum of two seconds behind the vehicle in front.
- Allow more than two seconds' space when conditions deteriorate. Slow down to create the extra space required.
- Maintain the proper position within the lane and establish a safe zone around the vehicle by slowing down if necessary so that you are not driving along side or too close to another vehicle.

- In very slow moving traffic, always leave sufficient space to move around the vehicle in front. This way you will be able to get around them if they stop or stall. Space left to the front will prevent you from crashing into the vehicle in front should you be hit from behind.
- In slow moving or stationary traffic you are too close if you cannot see the road beneath the back tyres of the vehicle in front.

Protecting the rear of your vehicle

In situations where a sudden stop might be needed – for example, in an area where wildlife or children might run onto the road, always leave a generous gap in front. When you leave a generous gap, if the car ahead has to stop suddenly, there is more time and space for you to brake. Leaving a generous gap also helps to reduce the risk of a pile-up, because drivers following you are able to brake more gradually and safely too.

Following oversized vehicles

- Leave a longer following distance when travelling behind trucks, overloaded vehicles, trailers or any other road users that might present a hazard.
- The drivers of large and oversized vehicles have restricted vision and can only see following vehicles in the side-view mirrors, so they cannot see you if you are too close.
- It's worth remembering that if you can't see the side mirrors of large vehicles then the driver of that vehicle cannot see you.
- Large and heavy vehicles tend to throw up a lot of road debris. Staying well back lessens the chances of getting hit by flying objects and also from driving in unnecessarily poor visibility created by heavy vehicles in wet conditions.

Changing lanes on dual carriageways

Your lane changes should never force other drivers to take evasive action. Remember to use good observations and to communicate your intentions in plenty of time, change lanes only when there is an ample safe gap.

Whether it's for merging, diverging or overtaking, smooth lane changes are the best option. Anticipating and accommodating the needs of other drivers who are changing lanes, entering or exiting from slip roads is equally important.

Use the SIDE rule when changing lanes
- Scan – all around. Use the mirrors and glance over your shoulder to check the blind spot.
- Identify – hazards and opportunities.
- Decide – on course of action.
- Execute – the manoeuvre without delay remembering to MSM.

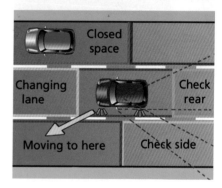

Indicating intentions in plenty of time
- Routinely check the mirrors before making a lane change.
- Indicate in plenty of time to allow other road users ample opportunity to accommodate your needs.
- Cancel the indicators once the manoeuvre is complete.

Smooth lane changes

- Do not make sudden or erratic lane changes. Only make a lane change when there is plenty of room to smoothly enter the new lane at a slight angle and without inconveniencing other drivers.
- Adjust acceleration to maintain the correct speed when moving across and into the new lane.

Maintaining position within a lane

- Keeping the proper lane position makes driving safer and less stressful.
- Drive in the centre of the left-hand lane whenever possible.
- Change position within the lane to allow for obstructions, and when passing parked cars, pedestrians, cyclists or animals.
- Move to the right-hand lane to overtake or to accommodate traffic entering from a slip or side road.
- Temporary use of the hard shoulder is allowed for passing a vehicle that is making a right turn or to avoid a hazard.

Adjusting speed

- Alter speed when necessary to match the general flow of traffic.
- Change speed when joining a new lane or a road with a different general speed.

- Change speed when necessary to establish a better safety margin.

Establishing a safe zone around the vehicle

- When driving in heavy traffic, select a position relative to the traffic ahead and to the side that affords the best safety margin.
- Slow up if necessary to establish more space around the vehicle, to lessen the potential hazards and to create more options should a problem arise.
- Avoid travelling directly beside another vehicle. Being slightly ahead or slightly behind is safer; by slowing a little you can eliminate an overlap and create a gap beside your vehicle.

Merging safely

- Adjust speed to match the traffic on the road being entered.
- Look for a gap to enter the traffic without disrupting the flow.
- Check mirrors, blind spots and signal.

- Merge into the traffic smoothly at a gentle angle.
- Maintain good observation throughout the manoeuvre by checking over the right shoulder and using the mirrors.

Passing slip roads

- Be prepared to accommodate traffic that is exiting or entering at slip roads.
- Road signs that indicate a turn-off or exit/entry point should alert drivers to traffic merging and diverging.
- Prepare to accommodate other traffic by adjusting speed, leaving a gap or moving over to the right hand lane.
- Exit slip roads are usually followed by entry slip roads and are indicated by hatched markings on the roadway or green cats eye reflectors at night to alert you that traffic may be entering from a side or slip road.

Diverging

- Being prepared helps you to diverge with ease.
- Route planning helps you identify upcoming exits in advance.
- Get into or stay in the left-hand lane once you observe the advanced warning signs that point out the upcoming slip road.
- Use countdown markers indicate as you pass 300, 200 and 100 metres from the commencement of the slip road or the exit.
- Check the mirrors and use your indicators to communicate intentions to other traffic.
- Maintain speed while still in the travelling lane. Gear down and lower speed only when on the slip road.
- Prepare to stop if there is a junction at the end of the slip road.
- Reduce speed to suit the new environment if continuing on a minor road.

Lesson 2 · Basic driving skills

Instruction assessment record

	Progressing	Mastered	ADI Signature	Date
Reversing				
Setting up for a reversing manoeuvre	O	O		
Reversing in a straight line	O	O		
Reversing in a turn left/right	O	O		
Reversing around an obstacle	O	O		
Turning				
Three-point turn on flat ground	O	O		
Turning on a hill	O	O		
Making a U-turn	O	O		
Tight turns in confined spaces	O	O		
Speed				
Choosing the appropriate speed	O	O		
Approaching speed-limit changes	O	O		
Following the general traffic speed	O	O		
Following distances				
Maintaining safe following distance	O	O		
Protecting the rear of your vehicle	O	O		
Following oversized vehicles	O	O		
Lane changing				
Using SIDE when changing lanes	O	O		
Indicating in plenty of time	O	O		
Making smooth lane changes	O	O		
Maintaining position within a lane	O	O		
Establishing a safe zone all around	O	O		
Merging/diverging safely	O	O		
Passing slip roads	O	O		

Note to ADI: When every skill has been mastered please note this by signing off lesson 2 in the training log in the centre of the book.

Notes

3

Intersections

In this lesson we will discuss...

- Identifying and interpreting road signs
- Intersection fundamentals
- More challenging intersections
- Roundabouts

Introduction

Road signs and markings provide essential information about the rules required for using the road safely. The signs and markings tell you what specific rules apply in a given situation, they provide useful information and they warn about hazards to watch out for. Common shape and colour designs for the different types of messages make the signs easier to identify from further away and help to alert drivers earlier.

Circular shaped regulatory signs give orders

- Red outlines indicate what you **must not** do
- Blue backgrounds indicate what you **must** do

Warning signs

- Yellow diamond or rectangular shaped signs with black borders and symbols

Information signs

- Rectangles and pointed rectangles
- Brown: tourist information
- Green, white or blue: directional

Road-work warning signs

- Orange diamonds or rectangles with black symbols and lettering

Motorway signs

- Rectangular in shape, white writing on blue background

Distinct shapes

- Used to emphasise certain messages

Identifying and interpreting road signs

Identifying road signs

- Look well ahead to where the vehicle will be in 15-18 seconds, this enables road signs to be identified from a distance.
- Stating the meaning of road signs out loud helps during initial driving; not only will it reinforce their significance to you but it also lets the instructor know that you have seen the signs and understand what they mean.
- Consider how signs in the vicinity pertain to the current driving situation. For example; on the main road a sign indicates a side road on the left, what should the driver be looking out for even if they are just passing the side road?

Adhering to regulatory road signs

- It is essential to comply with road signs that carry mandatory instructions, such as **Stop** or **Yield**.
- Advisory road signs, direction or tourist information signs give important information, help drivers to progress smoothly and support good traffic flow.
- It is up to each driver to drive responsibly and although most drivers obey the regulations most of the time, unfortunately not everyone does, so it is important to be vigilant and **expect the unexpected**.

Expecting the unexpected

- Good drivers take nothing for granted; therefore they encounter few unexpected situations. Experience teaches drivers to anticipate, to expect and to recognise hazards in driving situations that may, to the inexperienced, seem contrary to reasonable expectation.
- Gaining experience takes time and practice. During the learning period, you must compensate for your inexperience by driving more carefully and by leaving extra time and space. It takes considerable time and practice behind the wheel to be able to **read the road** effectively and likewise to develop a good **feel** for how the vehicle handles in different situations.
- By recognising the limitations of your inexperience you will be better prepared to **expect**, what may still be, **the unexpected**!

Cues and information from sources other than road signs

- Natural and environmental signs along the roadway, such as gaps in tree lines and disappearing curves, can give clues about what lies ahead.
- So too can man-made structures – for example, a gap in a line of houses can often let the driver know well in advance that an intersection or side road is coming up.
- Conditions on the road vary with the time of day. For example, more congestion at school closing times or slower-moving traffic at dawn and dusk when the quality of light is poor.
- Anticipate and leave plenty of room for hazards related to construction and agriculture, such as slow-moving and oversized vehicles, mud on the road or unusual vehicular movement.
- Be aware of how the weather can affect driving conditions not just for drivers but for other road users too. Motorcycles, for example, can stop very quickly in dry conditions but cannot stop as easily in wet conditions and pedestrians are often more mindful of the weather than of traffic movements around them.

Interpreting road markings

- Road markings are invaluable, they give a continuous message and emphasise the importance of the message by increasing the size or amount of markings.
- Studying the various road markings and their meanings, not just in books but also in each practical driving lesson, will help you to understand the implications and importance of the road markings and signs in practice.
- Use the Rules of the Road and the Official Driver Theory Book to clarify and elaborate on the functions of the markings observed when out driving.

Stop lines
Thick single white lines across the road indicate where you must stop at junctions.

Give way lines
Indicate where to stop when traffic on the main road has priority.

Written messages
Self explanatory e.g. Slow, stop, give way or bus lane.

Arrows/direction markings
Enable drivers to get into correct lane in advance.

Continuous longitudinal white line/lines
Divide the traffic and must not be straddled or crossed, except to pass a stationary or very slow (≤16 km/h) works vehicle or rider. A white line may be crossed to enter/leave a side road or entrance on the opposite of the road. Parking is prohibited in these areas.

Broken centre lines
Divide traffic travelling in opposite directions, drivers may only cross them or overtake when it is safe to do so.

A break in a continuous white line
Indicates a hazard such as a side road. Where a broken line and a continuous line run side by side, drivers should obey the line closest.

Lane dividers
Broken white lane dividing lines indicate where traffic should travel unless changing direction or overtaking.

Hatch markings
Indicate dangerous areas where traffic is safer separated. When bordered by a solid white line do not enter except in an emergency; where the border is broken vehicles may enter if safe to do so.

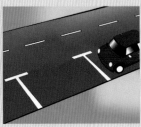

Bus lanes

With-flow bus lanes run in the same direction as other traffic and can be used by buses, taxis and cyclists. Contra-flow bus lanes run in the opposite direction and are restricted to bus use only. The solid white line bordering the bus lane prohibits entering or exiting the bus lane except where the line is broken at either end.

Cycle lanes

Cycle lanes bordered by solid lines are restricted to cyclists during posted times and vehicles are prohibited from driving or parking in them. When the border is a broken line vehicles may share the lane. Parking in a cycle lane puts cyclists using the lane in danger.

Parking

Park centrally within designated parking spaces; reversing in makes exiting safer and easier. Do not park on a road opposite a solid white line or where a solid white line divides the road approaching a junction.

Yellow box areas

Keep this area clear unless preparing to turn right and only when you will not hinder the flow of other traffic by waiting in the box junction.

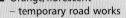

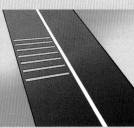

Reflective studs

Placed 6, 12, and 24m apart. The closer together the more danger indicated.

- White – road centre and lane division
- Yellow – left edge of road and left of centre medians
- Green – on approach to slip or side roads
- Red – left hand side of right-hand junction
- Orange/florescent – temporary road works

Speed reduction lines

Raised lines running across the road help to alert drivers that a speed reduction or junction is imminent. Often used at the end of motorways/dual carriageways ends as a warning.

Pedestrian crossings

Do not park, stop or overtake in the area 15m before or 5m after a pedestrian crossing area.

Shared road areas

- Identify and note the different types of markings that delineate shared areas of the road, such as bus and bicycle lanes.
- Practice the correct use of shared lanes.
- At stop signs, stop at the line on the near side of the red box that is reserved for cyclists. The red box gives cyclists priority and a safer means to make right turns at the junction.
- Discussing the implications of vehicles parking in or obstructing shared lanes will help to bring a better understanding of the dangers or problems of doing so.
- Vehicles may cross over into bus or cycle lanes that are bordered by broken white lines.

- Private vehicles cannot cross into bus or cycle lanes that are bordered by solid white lines – similarly vehicles permitted to use bus lanes must also obey the white line rules, they may only enter or leave the bus lane at the beginning or end of the lane where the line becomes a broken white line.

Intersection fundamentals

Recognising intersections in advance

Use advance road signs and other clues to recognise different types of intersections and their level of difficulty or potential hazards.

Look for:

- Warning signs – type of junction.
- Direction signs and road markings.
- The volume or amount of traffic and/or pedestrians.
- Traffic control systems, lights, stop or yield signs.
- Breaks in the line of buildings or trees.
- Texture changes in the road surface, high grip or rumble strips

Approaching an intersection always presents hazards for drivers.

- Pay attention to intersection or side-road advance warning signs, even when you do not intend to change direction at the intersection.

- You should be aware of upcoming junctions so that you can anticipate what other road users may do.

Your approach to an intersection depends on what you want to do when you get there:

- Travel straight through – stay on a major road or cross over from one minor road to another minor road or to roads of equal importance.
- Leave a major or minor road by turning left or right.
- Join another road of a different priority.

Road signage usually indicates which road has priority, where this is not clear take extra care.

There are 6 basic junction types that drivers need to be acquainted with:

- Crossroads.
- T junctions.
- Staggered junctions.
- A fork in the road or Y junction.
- Roundabouts.
- Side roads.

Each of these junctions can have plenty of variations, with or without signals.

Crossroads

T junctions

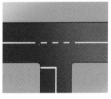

Staggered junctions

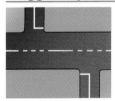

A fork in the road or Y junction

Roundabouts

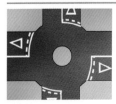

Side Road

Approaching an intersection

When approaching an intersection the continual use of the MSM and SIDE acronyms, will help new drivers to correctly remember all the essential steps.

M Check mirrors to assess other traffic speed and position.
S Signal in plenty of time.
M Manoeuvre when it is safe.

 Mirror

 Signal

 Manoeuvre

S Scan all around, in front beside and behind.
I Identify and hazards or potential problems.
D Decide what action to take; to wait, slow down or to go.
E Execute the manoeuvre – do what you are going to do decisively.

Scan

Identify

Decide

Execute

Use of these procedures at every intersection will quickly make them routine, well established habits enabling you to:

- Recognise when a intersection is imminent.
- Position your vehicle correctly in good time.
- Select the appropriate gear and speed when approaching the intersection.
- Read and understand the signs, signals and road markings at junctions.
- Be extra vigilant on the approach.
- Look out for and interpret the needs of pedestrians, cyclists and other traffic.
- Watch for changes in traffic signals and movements.

Travelling through intersections

- Take extra care when travelling through an intersection where others are turning out of or entering into the roadway.
- Slow down when approaching an intersection, but maintain a steady course and speed to enable others to predict likely manoeuvres.
- You should always be prepared to slow down even further, to alter course or to stop if necessary to avoid collisions.
- Look well ahead to anticipate what lane, road position or speed will be needed.
- Stay in lane throughout the intersection. If a vehicle ahead slows or changes lane, accommodate it; do not attempt to overtake in the junction.
- Be prepared for erratic or sudden movements / lane changes of other road users.
- Watch out for and be prepared to accommodate traffic emerging from side roads, their view may be obscured or they may take time to build up speed.

Interaction at intersections

- Traffic on the main road has priority.

- Traffic from minor roads should yield to traffic on main roads.
- Traffic entering a roundabout must yield to traffic already on the roundabout or traffic approaching from the right.
- Pedestrians and other vulnerable road users require extra time and space at intersections.
- Never assume priority over another vehicle or road when there are no road markings or signs, what seems obvious to you may not be so obvious from the viewpoint of the other road or road user.

Traffic leaving intersections

- Prepare to slow down or to stop to accommodate traffic that is turning into or exiting from an intersection.
- When there are no traffic signals, pay attention to the body language of other road users, such as the direction in which a driver is looking or facing and other telltale signs like indicators, brake lights or the direction of the front wheels of a vehicle, These signs give valuable hints as to what the other person intends to do.
- Be prepared for other road users to be indecisive or to change their mind at the last minute.

- Anticipate that traffic may try to enter or exit from a junction without prior warning, and evasive action may be required to compensate and avoid confrontation.
- Do not rely too much on other vehicles' indicators. Drivers sometimes use them incorrectly at roundabouts for example, or inadvertently leave them on in error after a manoeuvre.
- Remember to look for other signs, such as the direction in which a driver is looking, to anticipate what they're going to do.

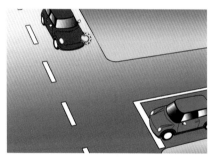

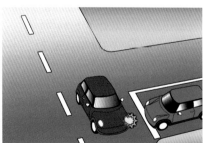

Lane positioning

- Use the MSM and SIDE routines and remember to indicate intentions clearly.
- Select the correct lane and position within the lane in plenty of time before attempting to turn at an intersection.
- Move to the left of the lane when turning left and to the right-hand side of the lane when turning right.
- At junctions, position yourself so that you have the best view of the road that you intend to turn into.
- Stay well clear of large vehicles at junctions to allow them plenty of room to turn. Large vehicles require more room to turn and may need to take up a position that seems incorrect to you. Trucks may need to swing right in order to make a left turn or to swing left to go right.

Stopping and giving way

- Yield or stop signs, stop lines and triangular yield markings on the road all indicate that you must give priority to traffic that's on the road you wish to enter.

- Yield regulations allow vehicles to enter the intersection without stopping when the way is clear to do so. Vehicles must slow or stop if there is traffic on the priority road.

- Stop signs and road markings indicate that you must stop before the sign or line whether or not there is any traffic on the main road.

- Where roads of equal importance meet, you must yield to traffic on the right.

- Signal-controlled junctions indicate which traffic has priority but they only allow the movement of vehicles when the way is clear.

- Red lights = must stop.

- Amber light or arrow = must stop; vehicles can continue only if the amber light comes on as the vehicle is passing or is so close to the stop line that it would be unsafe to stop.

- Green light = proceed if the way is clear.

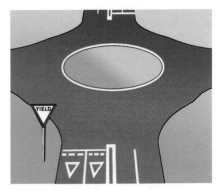

Respond appropriately to turn signals and traffic lights

- Look for and anticipate signal changes when approaching traffic lights.

- Be prepared to stop if the sequence changes from green or when other traffic or pedestrians are using the intersection incorrectly.

- When the signal changes back to green, check first before proceeding, because other road users may not comply with the signals.

- Flashing amber arrows are designed to keep the traffic flowing. They are similar to a yield sign; vehicles must give way to traffic on the main thoroughfare.

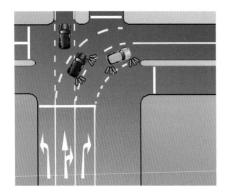

Exiting intersection to the left, right or straight ahead

- When making a right turn, vehicles must yield to traffic coming from the opposite direction.
- Allow oncoming traffic to make a left turn into a road before they proceed to make a right turn into the same road.
- Where two lanes are permitted to turn, vehicles must stay in the same lane throughout the turn. For example: Vehicles starting in the right-hand lane should only move over to the left when the turn is fully completed and when the way is clear.
- Do not cross from one lane to another when traversing an intersection.
- In preparation for a left turn, check mirrors, slow down and indicate intention to turn in plenty of time.
- When preparing to make a

left turn, check for cyclists, pedestrians and motorcyclists approaching on the left, particularly in slow-moving traffic.

- When crossing bus lanes, where it is permitted to make a left turn, be particularly vigilant for faster moving traffic approaching on your left.

Due care and attention for pedestrians and cyclists

- Motorists must always give way to more vulnerable road users such as pedestrians and cyclists.
- Motorists must yield to pedestrians on a crossing or to anyone waiting to use a zebra crossing.
- When starting off or turning left at a junction, check to the left for cyclists who may come up on the inside while the traffic was stopped or moving more slowly.

- In areas where pedestrian traffic is high, watch for pedestrians stepping off the path and onto the roadway.
- Take extra care at pedestrian lights because sometimes pedestrians cross without looking or they rush to catch a light just as it changes. Remember pedestrians do not always adhere to the rules.
- Children are even less predictable and require extra vigilance and care.

More challenging intersections

When waiting to turn right at an intersection adopt a position just left of the centre line to await a safe gap in oncoming traffic. Ensure that the front wheels are pointed straight ahead to reduce the risk of being shunted into the path of oncoming traffic, should the vehicle be hit from behind.

Peep and creep

- When attempting to enter a road from a junction or area with restricted sight lines, slow down to a crawl and inch forward slowly to a position that affords a better view. Approaching traffic must be able to see and be seen by the vehicle attempting to enter the road.
- Headlights switched on even in daylight hours help to make vehicles more visible.
- Check to the right and left and

then right again until you are sure there is plenty of time and space to pull out.

- Take extra care to check for cyclists and motorcyclists.
- When pulling out in a left turn avoid swinging out over the centre line.
- When making a right turn, drive straight out over the centre line and then make the turn. Do not 'cut' across the corner.
- When the turn is complete the driver should pick up the appropriate driving speed for the new road without delay and maintain good observation in the mirrors and for approaching traffic up ahead.

Crossing or joining a dual carriageway with a centre median

- Wait behind the stop line on the minor road until it is safe to turn onto the dual carriageway.
- When making a right turn onto a dual carriageway, the presence of a centre median provides a protected space in the middle of the road.
- If the median is deep enough to protect the full length of your vehicle it enables each side of the dual carriageway to be treated separately. In this case, when the way is clear on the near side,

cross it and then pause at the centre median to wait for a safe gap on the far side. Only proceed when the way is clear.

- Move into the left hand lane and remember not to cut the corner.
- If there is another vehicle already occupying the centre median, the second vehicle must wait until the first one has cleared it before commencing the manoeuvre.
- When driving a larger vehicle or when towing a trailer it is extremely hazardous to attempt to cross a dual carriageway, it is safer to drive on to another junction that allows the traffic to join or cross at a controlled junction or roundabout.
- If there is no alternative and a vehicle must cross a dual carriageway while towing a trailer, the driver must not start the crossing manoeuvre until there is a sufficient gap to allow the vehicle to cross both sides of the road at once, as the centre

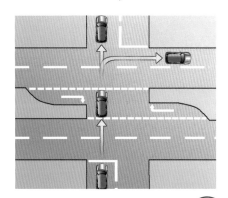

Lesson 3

medians are not large enough to accommodate longer vehicles making it unsafe to pause there.

Turning at a box junction

- Yellow boxes are designed to prevent traffic from blocking the flow at junctions. Vehicles must not enter a yellow box unless they can clear it without stopping.
- The exception is when waiting to make a right turn, vehicles are permitted to wait in the yellow box for a gap in oncoming traffic, provided the road they wish to turn into is clear.
- You should only enter the yellow box for the purpose of turning right, when your presence there will not impede other traffic that has the right of way.

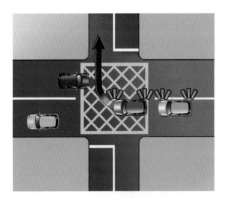

When the traffic lights are not functioning

- Take extra care and be prepared to stop at a junction when the lights are malfunctioning, especially when the roads are of equal importance.
- Where one road is obviously a major road and the other a minor one the normal give way rules apply but always exercise extra care in this situation. Never assume other drivers will yield right of way.
- Traffic on the minor road should yield to traffic on the major road but it is dangerous to assume that all drivers will yield right of way to traffic on the main road. Be prepared to stop.
- Where the roads are of equal importance, traffic travelling straight ahead will have priority over turning traffic, so you should give way to traffic coming from your right.

Slip lane use at junctions

- Road signs and road markings guide motorists when using a slip road to join or leave a road.
- The slip road provides a safe area to adjust the vehicles' speed to match the traffic flow on the new road.

- Use the MSM routine to check the mirrors and indicate in plenty of time to alert other traffic of your manoeuvring intentions.

- When the way is clear, use the SIDE and MSM routines to merge smoothly into the new lane or road.

Intersections with rail or tram lines

Check the rules of the road for information about the three types of level crossings: those guarded by gates or barriers with lights; those with gates or barriers only; and those with lights and no barriers.

- Never enter a crossing when the warning lights are flashing or if any of the gates or barriers are down.
- Do not enter if a train is within sight or if there is any obstruction on the other side (such as traffic) that would prevent you from exiting the crossing.
- In rural areas where unmanned gates need to be opened manually, stop well clear of the line. Check for trains in both directions, open both gates, check again and, if clear, proceed to the other side. Once clear of the crossing check for trains again and close both gates.
- On approach to the intersection look for information and instructions posted near the crossing.

Roundabouts

Roundabouts allow traffic at junctions to intersect more freely and without necessarily having to come to a stop. In most cases traffic on the roundabout has priority and traffic should keep moving when the way is clear. On larger roundabouts road markings or traffic signals control the traffic flow and may require traffic on the roundabout to stop or yield. Always look well ahead, note advance direction signs and anticipate required moves in plenty of time.

Roundabout fundamentals

- Look for road signs and markings that indicate a roundabout ahead.
- Note that the law states that a driver enters a roundabout by turning left. This means that vehicles travel around a roundabout in a clockwise direction.

- Note the directional signs posted before the roundabout. Knowing which exit is required will aid correct lane selection and a smoother transit through the roundabout.
- Treat the roundabout as a normal junction – vehicles must yield right of way to traffic already on the roundabout. Be prepared to stop!
- Get into the correct lane in good time to avoid making erratic or sudden lane changes at the last moment.
- Take extra care on the approach and be prepared to stop. Don't assume vehicles ahead will continue without stopping or changing direction suddenly even if the way ahead seems clear.
- Use the SIDE rule to help with decisive driving at roundabouts.
- Look ahead before making lane changes as vehicles ahead may stop.
- If in doubt always err on the side of caution and yield.
- Looking across the roundabout and being able to identify the required exit, where possible, will help you to anticipate and plan your course.
- Look out for pedestrian and

cyclist crossing areas at the approaches and at exits from roundabouts and be prepared to stop.

- Be especially aware of motorcycle movements at roundabouts.
- Make allowances for large vehicles which need more space to turn.
- Make allowances for vehicles changing lanes ahead.

Using the first exit

It helps to visualise and understand directions on a roundabout using the same layout as the face of a clock. You always enter as if you were at the 6 o'clock position; the first exit would therefore be at the 9 o'clock position.

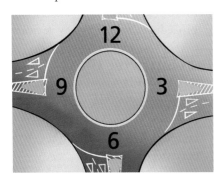

- Take up a position on the left-hand side of the lane (or in the left lane if there are two lanes).
- Check the rear view mirror and the left wing mirror and glance quickly over the left shoulder to check the blind spot.

- Signal left on the approach to the roundabout.
- Scan the roundabout on the approach. Pay special attention to traffic coming from the right. Decide if a stop is required or if it is safe to proceed without stopping. It may be most effective to slow to a speed that enables filtering into the traffic without having to stop.

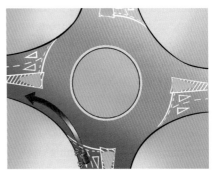

- Once on the roundabout, stay in the left-hand lane and ensure that the indicator remains on.
- Check the rear-view, left mirror and the blind spot before leaving the roundabout at the first exit.
- Switch off the indicator, check the mirrors again and proceed.

Using the second exit or travelling straight ahead

- When there is only one exit before the exit straight ahead, approach the roundabout in the left-hand lane and stay in it throughout.

- Take up a position on the left-hand side of the lane or in the left lane if there are two lanes.
- No indication is required as you approach or enter the roundabout when you intend to travel straight through (2nd exit or the 12 o'clock position).
- Where the left hand lane is marked left turn only or if it is blocked or closed it is permitted to use the right hand lane to travel straight through or to take the second exit from a roundabout.
- Remember to MSM to check the mirrors and the blind spot.
- Scan the roundabout on the approach, paying special attention to traffic coming from the right.

 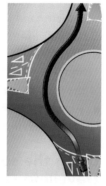

- Decide whether to stop or to slow to a speed which allows filtering into a gap in the traffic.
- Once on the roundabout, stay in the left-hand lane.

- Stay alert for other traffic cutting across your path to access exits.
- Once past the exit before the intended one, indicate left, check the mirrors and glance quickly over the left shoulder to re-check the blind spot as you proceed.
- On the new road, drivers should enter the same lane or side of the lane from which they exited the roundabout.
- Switch off the indicator and check the mirrors again.
- Vehicles that come off the roundabout from the inner (right hand) lane should stay in the right hand lane of the new road until they have fully established their position on the new road. Move over to the left hand lane following normal lane changing procedures when the way is clear.

Leaving after the second exit

- On approach to the roundabout check the directional signs and prepare to move into the correct position.
- Check the mirrors and the blind spot over the right shoulder.
- If it is safe, signal right and take up a position on the right-hand side of the lane, just to the left of the centre line, or in the right-hand lane if there are two lanes.
- Scan the roundabout on

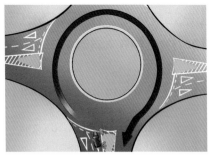

approach, paying special attention to traffic coming from the right.

- Decide whether to stop, slow down or to proceed.

- Once on the roundabout, stay in the right-hand (inner) lane, close to the roundabout's centre.

- As you pass the exit before the intended one, check the rear-view mirror and left wing mirror, glance quickly over the left shoulder to check the blind spot, indicate left and, if it is safe, exit the roundabout maintaining lane position.

- Look out for and be aware of traffic in the left hand lane.

- When clear of the roundabout, switch off the indicator and check the mirrors again.

- On larger roundabouts, the lane or road markings dictate which lane to take to reach the intended exit, plan ahead and stay alert.

- Leave a gap behind vehicles ahead to make it easier to observe lane changes and information marked on the road surface.

- When clear of the roundabout, check mirrors, signal left and move back to the inside lane when it's safe to do so.

Mini-roundabouts

- Approach a mini-roundabout in the same way as a conventional roundabout, pay careful attention while using mirrors and signals.

- Pay particular attention to traffic approaching from straight ahead and from the right and be prepared to stop.

- Allow vehicles approaching from straight ahead to turn to their right if they are signalling their intention to do so.

- Allow for the fact that there is less space to manoeuvre and time for signalling.

- Pass around the central markings unless your vehicle size prevents you from doing so.

- If there are double or multiple mini-roundabouts, treat each one as a separate hazard. Be especially vigilant in these situations.

Lesson 3 · Intersections

Instruction assessment record

	Progressing	Mastered	ADI Signature	Date
Identifying and interpreting road signs				
Identifying road signs	○	○		
Adhering to regulatory road signs	○	○		
Clues from other sources	○	○		
Interpreting road markings	○	○		
Shared road areas	○	○		
Intersection fundamentals				
Recognising intersections in advance	○	○		
Approaching an intersections	○	○		
Travelling through intersections	○	○		
Interaction at intersection	○	○		
Traffic leaving intersections	○	○		
Lane positioning	○	○		
Stopping and giving way	○	○		
Appropriate response to signals	○	○		
Exiting an intersection	○	○		
Due care for pedestrians & cyclists	○	○		

	Progressing	Mastered	ADI Signature	Date

More challenging intersections

	Progressing	Mastered	ADI Signature	Date
Peep and creep	O	O		
Crossing/joining dual carrigeways	O	O		
When traffic lights malfunction	O	O		
Slip lane use at junctions	O	O		
Intersections with rail & tram lines	O	O		

Roundabouts

	Progressing	Mastered	ADI Signature	Date
Roundabout fundamentals	O	O		
Using the first exit	O	O		
Second or straight through exit	O	O		
Leaving after the second exit	O	O		
Mini-roundabouts	O	O		

Note to ADI: When every skill has been mastered please note this by signing off lesson 3 in the training log in the centre of the book.

Instruction Lesson 3

Notes

4

Different driving environments

In this lesson we will discuss...

- Scanning ahead and using the SIDE rule
- Urban driving
- Accommodation pedestrians and cyclists
- Using one-way streets
- Driving on dual carriageways and negotiating road changes
- Rural driving

Introduction

Practice and experience will enable you to better judge the dangers associated with potential hazards but until you have the benefit of experience, you should give yourself a larger safety margin. Having a larger safety margin will create extra space and give you more time for decision making and responding when you encounter a hazard when driving.

Scanning ahead and using the SIDE rule

Practice and experience enables you to better judge the dangers associated with potential hazards. Until you have the benefit of experience, give yourself a larger safety margin. Extra space gives you more time for decision making and responding.

- Looking well ahead gains extra time to gather and interpret information and to act accordingly.
- Pay attention to the road signs, environmental factors and other cues, such as the time of day, traffic density and the weather, to get advance warnings of possible hazards ahead.
- Use the mirrors frequently to stay fully informed of everything that's going on around the vehicle.
- Use the SIDE rule to assist in making the right decision when changing speed or direction.

- S – Scan ahead, behind (mirrors) and to the sides (over shoulder) for possible hazards and/or open areas.
- I – Identify the possible problems and/or opportunities.
- D – Decide what course to take or to avoid.
- E – Execute the manoeuvre after indicating and checking the mirrors again.

 Scan

 Identify

 Decide

 Execute

Urban driving

- Adjust driving style and speed to meet the requirements of driving in built-up areas.
- The speed limit is the **maximum** speed permitted. It is not a target.
- Route-planning and having an alternative route may help to avoid congestion and stress.
- Allowing ample time to complete the journey helps to keep stress levels under control.
- The AA or the local city council can provide specific information for a particular area – for example, about parking, road signs, orbital routes and road closings, all of which will help avoid delays or stressful situations.
- In towns and cities, expect that delivery or heavy goods vehicles (HGV) and public transport vehicles will be stopping from time to time, often in unexpected places.
- Give HGVs room and remember that when behind a HGV, 'if you cannot see the side mirrors, then the HGV driver won't be able to see you'.

- Stay alert for bus lane traffic that may approach or pass on the left. Take extra care when making a left turn that crosses a bus lane. Switch on the indicator in good time to alert traffic in the bus lane but don't assume that other drivers will accommodate you. Check the mirrors frequently.
- Although vehicles travel more slowly in urban areas, always keep a good lookout and manage your safety margin when the traffic is heavy. This gives more options and it should mean there will be fewer surprises to deal with.

Accommodating pedestrians and cyclists

- There are usually more pedestrians and traffic moving around in urban areas. People are often distracted and may not be paying full attention to what's happening on the road – for example, a pedestrian attempting to cross the road while using a mobile phone.

- Expect pedestrians to attempt to cross anywhere, not just at the designated pedestrian crossings. When pedestrian traffic is particularly heavy, expect people to follow the crowd without thinking or checking to see if the traffic lights have changed.

- Even when the traffic light is green at a pedestrian crossing, check that it is clear before proceeding. Hitting a pedestrian even at a slow speed will cause serious injury.

- In bad weather, pedestrians can be even more unpredictable as they run to avoid getting wet. Everyone's ability to see and be seen is diminished in poor weather. Take extra care and keep the headlights on.

- Give cyclists plenty of room in case they wobble or need to

Speed Kills 9 out of 10 pedestrians are killed when hit at speeds over 60 Km/hr

60 km/hr

50 km/hr

30 km/hr

If hit by a car travelling at 30 Km/hr, 9 out of 10 pedestrians will survive. If hit at 60 Km/hr only 1 in 10 will survive.

swerve out to avoid obstructions. Remember that cyclists usually have to go around drains, potholes and debris on the road so look ahead to anticipate their needs and leave room accordingly.

- In heavy traffic, keep a good lookout for cyclists and motorcyclists filtering along the inside or between the lanes of traffic.

- Drivers planning to make an imminent left turn should not overtake a cyclist close to the turn, instead slow down to allow the cyclist to move through the junction and then make the turn behind the bicycle.

- Check the left side mirror for cyclists before beginning a left turn. This is especially important when stopped in traffic because cyclists often move up the inside of slow moving traffic unnoticed.

Using one-way streets

One-way streets are common in cities. If you are not familiar with an area, check a map before setting out to help you to get around more efficiently and avoid frustration. One-way streets with multiple lanes may have traffic passing on both sides. Always check before changing lanes and get into the correct lane in plenty of time before attempting to turn from a one-way street.

- When entering a one-way street from a two-way street, stay in the near-side lane initially. Once a good driving position has been established on the new road then you can change lanes if necessary – for example, to make a turn.

- When exiting from a one-way street onto a two-way street, check in advance to identify the correct lane for making the turn. Do not cut across the opposing lane and be alert for other vehicles that cut across lanes.

- Occasionally, a contra-flow bus lane runs along a one-way street. This allows buses to travel in the opposite direction of the general traffic flow. Watch for warning signs and take extra care when entering a junction with a contra-flow system.

- Parking is often allowed on both sides of a one-way street. Drivers should anticipate and leave room for doors being opened and also for vehicles to enter and leave parking spaces.

Driving on dual carriageways and negotiating road changes

Travel in the left-hand lane, unless overtaking or where directed otherwise by arrows on the road or overhead signs.

Dual carriageways allow traffic to move more freely and safely because they have a centre median that separates the traffic travelling in different directions. However, unlike motorways, dual carriageway junctions and intersections are at the same level as the road. There may also be private entrances and exits on the dual carriageway.

All types of vehicle are allowed on dual carriageways, there are a wide variety of potential hazards to deal with from cyclists to oversized commercial vehicles.

Driving decisively on dual carriageways

Remember: courtesy breeds courtesy and aggression fuels aggression – the more you give, the more you receive.

- Maintain a safe gap and speed appropriate to the conditions and the posted speed limit. Keep control of the speed; don't be antagonised or tempted into driving faster just because others are doing so.
- Traffic moves more quickly on dual carriageways. It is important to anticipate the need for lane

changes by looking well ahead for signs or other indications that might require a lane change.

■ Move into the correct lane in plenty of time.

■ Keep a good lookout for motorcycles passing between lanes or overtaking on the left as well as on the right, this is particularly important before a lane change or when preparing to overtake.

■ When traffic is entering or exiting the dual carriageway, be courteous and adjust driving speed or lane position to accommodate.

Protecting the lateral space on dual carriageways

When other drivers compromise your safety margins, use compensating techniques to regain control by re-establishing the safety margin.

■ Driving in the middle of the lane creates the most space on either side of the vehicle. This also leaves more room when passing an obstruction.

■ Avoid unnecessary overtaking.

■ When overtaking, plan the manoeuvre in plenty of time. Use the SIDE rule and MSM before moving out at a narrow angle. Overtake and move back into the left lane only when a two-second gap has been established in front of the vehicle that you have passed. You should be able to see the other vehicle fully in the rearview mirror before pulling back into the left lane.

■ Do not attempt to overtake if the traffic volume will prevent you from completing the manoeuvre.

■ Avoid prolonged travel alongside a vehicle that you are overtaking, as this eliminates the lateral safety margin and prevents you from making a sideways safety movement should a problem arise.

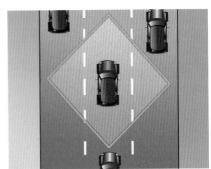

- When overtaking or being over taken by a HGV leave plenty of lateral space to avoid being sucked into the slipstream created alongside large fast moving vehicles.
- In heavy traffic, adopt a staggered position in relation to the vehicles travelling in parallel lanes.
- Slowing down and allowing another vehicle to move ahead is the quickest way to re-establish a lateral safety margin that has been compromised by another vehicle driving alongside.

Protecting your safety margin

- If another driver cuts into your safety margin as they complete an overtaking manoeuvre, re-establish the safety margin by pulling back.
- When another vehicle is tailgating or driving too close to you, allow it to pass if it's safe to do so.

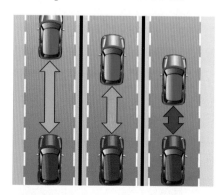

- Slowing down gradually will create more space in front and reduce the likelihood of having to stop or change direction quickly.
- Try not to get distracted by the close proximity of a tailgating vehicle as this only adds to the problem and may cause you to make a driving error.
- Stay well back from trucks and other large vehicles to avoid being hit by debris thrown up from their wheels.
- Staying well back from HGVs makes you more visible to the driver. Remember you must be able to see a truck's side mirrors for the driver of the truck to be able to see you.

Negotiating road changes

- When changing from a main road to a minor one, slow down and adjust speed to suit the conditions and traffic volume on the new road.
- Look for speed-limit signs on the approach to the intersection – these will indicate the appropriate speed for the new road.
- Come to a complete stop at the junction of a minor and a major road.
- Enter a major road only when the gap in the traffic will allow you to adequately accelerate in the

merging lane to match the general speed of the traffic on the major road before beginning to merge.

- In the merge or slip lane, get up to speed without delay. Check the mirrors and over your shoulder, if the way is clear indicate and move over smoothly to the new lane. Remember to switch off the indicator if it doesn't cancel automatically.

Tunnels

- Get into the correct lane in good time before you enter the tunnel, stay in this lane throughout the tunnel.
- Switch on your dipped headlights if they are not already on.
- Remove sunglasses if you are wearing them.
- Adjust your speed to suit the appropriate tunnel speed and leave plenty of room between vehicles.
- Look for advance warning or advisory signs.
- When you know you are going to be using a tunnel check in advance which radio frequency is used for advisory notices and preset your radio frequency so that you can tune in easily as you approach the tunnel.
- In heavy traffic if you have to stop, leave at least five metres from the vehicle in front. Turn

on your hazard lights if you are joining the end of a line of stationary traffic.

- Be vigilant for visual and audio messages from the tunnel authority.

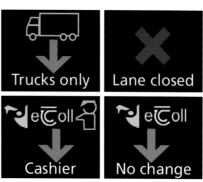

Rural driving

On rural roads driving slowly is generally the best option, however if your progress is holding up other traffic, it is common courtesy to pull over in a safe place and allow the traffic to pass.

Hazards on country roads

Being mindful of the rural environment will enable you to drive with more care.

- Rural and country roads seldom have footpaths so you may expect to share the road with pedestrians, cyclists and horses amongst other things; be prepared to slow or stop to accommodate them.

- When driving on country roads, looking ahead and observing the surroundings gives clues to hidden hazards. Look for changes and breaks in the tree line, electric cables or hedgerows

to give advance warning of side roads, hills, dips, bends and entrances ahead.

- Always pay attention to warning signs even if they are not directly related to your specific journey needs. A sign indicating an upcoming side road may not seem important when you intend to continue straight on, however it warns that other traffic may be using the junction to enter or exit the road.

- Homemade signs advertising farm produce for sale may not be regulation or legal but they are important to heed because they indicate that there may be activity up ahead, and should alert you to the possibility of having to slow or stop to accommodate.

- When you see or smell fresh grass cuttings or fresh manure on the road, slow down and expect a hazard further ahead.
- Look out for differences in the road surface. Areas in shade take longer to dry out in wet or icy conditions and will have less traction as a result.
- Watch for areas where gravel, leaves, mud, standing water and other debris gather.
- Be aware of the time of day and the seasonal activity of the countryside. At harvest time, for example, it is not unusual to find large agricultural machines on the roads; at milking time in the morning or evening, there may be cows on the move.
- Roads in rural areas may not be well maintained so watch out for potholes and leave room for cyclists and pedestrians who are sharing the road and who also need to avoid the uneven terrain.

Accommodating agricultural vehicles

Be patient when you encounter tractors and other slow-moving agricultural vehicles. Tractors, for example, generally only use the main road for short periods to access another work area.

- Be prepared to wait behind agricultural vehicles until it is safe to pass.
- Give agricultural vehicles plenty of room to manoeuvre. The driver may not be aware of the presence of other vehicles due to the noise of the vehicle. Also, the vehicle may not have mirrors.
- Staying well back makes it easier to see the road beyond the obstructing vehicle and affords more protection to the rear from following vehicles.
- Mud on the road or between the tyre treads reduces traction dramatically and will affect vehicle control. Take extra care after exposure to soiled surfaces.
- Remember that farm and field entrances may be concealed behind a bend in the road or hedgerow. Agricultural vehicles can take between 10 and 15 seconds to enter or cross a road; your speed must allow you to stop in time should you encounter one.

Dangerous rural junctions, blind bends and community areas

- It may be safer to pass a dangerous right-hand junction, drive on to a safer place further up the road, turn there and then return to approach the original junction from the safety of the opposite direction.

- Driving past and returning is the best approach if stopping in the middle of the road exposes you to unacceptable danger. For example, where the junction is in a dip in the road or is located shortly after a blind bend in the road.

- When you can't see around a bend, you need to anticipate that there may be hidden hazards obscured from your view, therefore you need to slow down to a speed that will allow you to stop where you can see clearly. Slowing down allows more time to stop if an obstruction appears suddenly.

- When your view is completely obscured and you have doubts about whether other road users are aware of your presence, use your lights or the horn as a warning.

- Slow down when approaching towns, villages and community areas – especially where traffic calming zones are not marked or if schools and play areas are located close to the road.

Lesson 4 · Different driving environments

Instruction assessment record

	Progressing	Mastered	ADI Signature	Date
Scanning				
Scanning	O	O		
Identifying	O	O		
Decision making	O	O		
Executing the manoeuvre	O	O		
Urban driving				
Driving in urban areas	O	O		
Accommodating pedestrians & cyclists	O	O		
Using one-way streets	O	O		
Dual carriageways driving				
Driving decisively on dual carriageway	O	O		
Protecting lateral space	O	O		
Protecing your safety margin	O	O		
Negotiating road changes	O	O		
Tunnels	O	O		
Rural driving				
Anticipating country road hazards	O	O		
Accommodating agricultural vehicles	O	O		
Handling dangerous junctions	O	O		
Control through blind bends	O	O		
Consideration in community areas	O	O		

Note to ADI: When every skill has been mastered please note this by signing off lesson 4 in the training log in the centre of the book.

Instruction Lesson 4

Notes

5

Parking

In this lesson we will discuss...

- Parking
- Perpendicular or bay parking
- Angle parking
- Parking on a hill

Introduction

Parking is an essential skill to master as you will be using it every time you drive. While the vehicle manoeuvring skills of parking can be easily mastered through good instruction and plenty of practice, good parking comes from decisions you make to conscientiously choose to park in a place or position that shows consideration to those with whom you share the road. Always use common sense and courtesy to park in such a way that your vehicle does not impede or endanger other road users.

Parking

Start out with a large space, as your parking skills improve, try parking in smaller spaces.

- Reverse into a parking bay or space whenever possible, steering and control are easier when reversing into tight spaces.
- Driving forward when leaving a parking space gives you a better view of the road and of any hazards or obstructions.
- Parking in the same direction as the traffic flow is a lot safer. When it's time to leave the space, you will have an earlier and better view of the roadway.
- At night vehicles parked in the same direction as the traffic won't dazzle or be dazzled by on coming headlights and the rear reflectors will warn passing traffic of the presence of the parked vehicle
- Take extra care in busy car parks, particularly in shopping areas, because pedestrians, especially children, are often distracted and are not paying attention to manoeuvring vehicles.
- In car parks, when reversing, be alert for other vehicles manoeuvring at the same time.
- When parked in built-up areas, be vigilant for cyclists travelling alongside. If necessary, open the window and look out to make sure the way is clear before attempting to pull out.

In Northern Ireland and in the UK it is an offence to park facing oncoming traffic after the hours of darkness.

Parallel parking

- 'Mirror, signal and manoeuvre' (MSM) before stopping slightly ahead of and about 1 metre out from the vehicle parked in front of the chosen space.
- The left wing mirror should be almost in line with the front bumper of the vehicle in front of the empty space.
- Look all around. If the way is clear, reverse slowly until the back of the car is slightly beyond the other vehicle – i.e., your rear seats should be in line with the back bumper of the other vehicle.
- If the way is clear, turn the steering wheel one full turn to the left.
- Aim to position the car at a 45° angle to the kerb.
- Look out the back window and watch the kerb move across the window. When it disappears from view, the car should be at a 45° angle to the space and kerb.
- Continue to move back slowly until your left wing mirror is in line with the rear of the other vehicle.
- While still moving slowly, turn the steering wheel two full turns to the right (away from the kerb).
- When the front of the car is clear of the rear of the other vehicle,

lock hard to the right.
- Continue to reverse until the car is fully within the parking space.
- Straighten up and centre the vehicle within the space. This will help when moving off later and also facilitate the movement of the vehicles parked in front and behind.
- The vehicle should now be parallel to and about 15cm out from the kerb.
- Select neutral, apply the parking brake and turn off the ignition.
- Secure the vehicle by selecting first gear.
- Before opening any doors, look in the mirrors and all around (including over the shoulder) to che ck for passing cyclists, motorcyclists or other traffic.
- Once outside, lock the doors and walk to the path, facing the oncoming traffic, without delay.

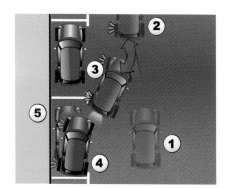

Perpendicular or bay parking

Parking in a bay to the left

- To get a good starting point to begin the manoeuvre, remember to MSM before pulling up alongside the chosen parking bay.
- Allow a 1-metre gap between the side of the vehicle and the end of the space.
- Align the left wing mirror with the parking-space line that is now closest to you, the line that was furthest away on approach.
- Look over both shoulders to check that it is safe to continue the manoeuvre. Watch out for pedestrians, cyclists, children and other vehicles.
- Select first gear and move slowly away from the space, turning the steering wheel fully to the right - full right lock.
- Aim to stop at a 45° angle to the parking bay.
- Just before you stop moving, turn the steering wheel to the left to straighten the wheels.
- Check all around again.
- Reverse slowly while turning the steering wheel to the left.
- Aim to get the left-hand side of the vehicle inside the white line. Continue to look all around.

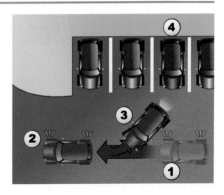

- When the vehicle is almost straight, turn the steering wheel back to the right to straighten the wheels.
- Once the vehicle is straight, continue to reverse slowly, again looking all around.
- When the vehicle is safely inside the bay, stop and apply the parking brake.

Parking in a bay to the right

- MSM before pulling up alongside the chosen parking bay.
- Allow a 1-metre gap between the side of the vehicle and the end of the space.
- Align the right wing mirror with the parking-space line that was farthest from you as the space was approached. This is a good starting position.

- Look over both shoulders to check that it is safe to continue the manoeuvre. Watch out for pedestrians, cyclists, children and other vehicles.
- Select first gear and move slowly away from the space, turning the steering wheel fully to the left. A full left lock is required.
- Aim to stop at a 45° angle to the parking bay.
- Just before stopping, turn the steering wheel to the right to straighten the wheels.
- Check all around again.
- Reverse slowly, turning the steering wheel to the right. Aim to get the right-hand side of the vehicle inside the parking bay line.

- Continue to look all around.
- When the vehicle is almost straight, turn the steering wheel back to the left to straighten the wheels.
- Once straight, continue to reverse slowly, again looking all around.
- When safely inside the bay, stop and apply the parking brake.
- Check that the vehicle is centred between the lines of the bay.
- Do not straddle the lines. If necessary move out and in again to reposition.
- When you are happy with your position, turn off the ignition, apply the parking brake and first gear to secure the vehicle.

Angle parking

- Be alert for vehicles reversing when you are passing angled parking spaces.
- Watch for reversing lights and observe the activity of drivers inside the vehicles.
- Look ahead to find a free space.
- Check mirrors and signal before slowing down.
- Stop about 1 to 1.5 metres before and out from the free space.
- Angled spaces are usually designed for front-in parking

– that is, the vehicle drives in rather than reverses into them.
- When driving into an angled space, the vehicle usually moves into the space in the same direction as the traffic flow.
- Usually and unless parking on a one way street, approach the space from the left.
- In first gear, move forwards slowly until the parking space line furthest away is aligned with the centre of the bonnet.

- Look to the centre of the parking space and turn sharp left while advancing slowly into it.

- Continue moving into the space until the recovery point is reached. Then straighten up to centre the vehicle in the space.

- Stop when the front bumper is 15-20 cm from the end line or kerb.

- Be careful not to scrape the leading edge of the front bumper when the kerb is raised or when the road dips sharply.

- Occasionally, an angled parking space may be on the right hand side of the road (e.g., on a one-way street). In this instance align the steering wheel with the line that's nearest to the driver's side before beginning to turn sharply into the space.

- Take extra care when preparing to exit a parking space that's at an angle.

- Scan the intended course and select reverse gear but do not move. Allow time for your vehicle's reversing lights to alert other road users that a reversing manoeuvre is imminent.

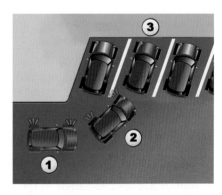

- Wait for a suitable gap in traffic before attempting to reverse straight back slowly and carefully.

- When your seat is in line with the rear bumper of the vehicle next you, start moving the steering wheel in the direction required while continuing to reverse.

- Check the clearance of the front bumper. Remember that the far side swings wide around the outside arc of the turn.

- When the vehicle is all the way out of the parking space, stop, check all around, signal and shift gears in preparation for moving off.

Parking on a hill

- When parking on a hill, always engage the parking brake and leave the car in gear.
- Leaving the front wheels turned at an angle will help to prevent the car from crashing into other traffic should it accidentally roll down the hill when unattended.
- When facing downhill, turning the wheels towards the kerb will steer the vehicle into the kerb and stop it if necessary.
- When parked facing uphill, turning the front wheels away from the kerb will help guide the front wheels towards the kerb should the vehicle slip backwards.
- When there is no kerb, turning the wheels towards the edge of the road will help to steer the vehicle off the road in the event of slippage, whether the vehicle is facing up- or downhill.
- When moving off from a hill parking space, it is important to leave extra time for manoeuvring and getting up to speed.
- Check ahead, to the sides and to the rear. Signal, check again and prepare to move off.

- With the parking brake still engaged, select first gear and begin to ease out on the clutch and increase acceleration. When the biting point is felt, ease out on the clutch completely while simultaneously disengaging the parking brake.

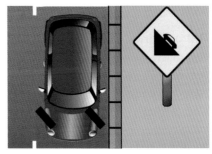

Lesson 5 · Parking

Instruction assessment record

	Progressing	Mastered	ADI Signature	Date
Parallel parking				
Approach	O	O		
Set up	O	O		
Manoeuvering	O	O		
Completion	O	O		
Bay parking				
Approach	O	O		
Set up	O	O		
Manoeuvering	O	O		
Completion	O	O		
Angle parking				
Approach	O	O		
Set up	O	O		
Manoeuvering	O	O		
Completion	O	O		
Hill parking				
Approach	O	O		
Set up	O	O		
Manoeuvering	O	O		
Completion	O	O		
Moving off				
Approach	O	O		
Set up	O	O		
Manoeuvering	O	O		
Completion	O	O		

Note to ADI: When every skill has been mastered please note this by signing off lesson 5 in the training log in the centre of the book.

(6)

Avoiding skids

In this lesson we will discuss...

- Emergency braking
- Brake-and-avoid techniques
- Skid avoidance and control
- Dealing with minor incidents

Introduction

The quickest and safest way to stop in an emergency is to brake to a point just before the wheels lock up. If the wheels lock, steering is seriously compromised and can quickly lead to loss of control. In this event you must decide rapidly whether to continue braking to a harsh standstill, (which may be possible when the vehicle is on a straight dry course) or to relax the brake sufficiently to enable you to maintain control and steer out of trouble. ABS or cadence braking can greatly assist in maintaining vehicle control.

Emergency braking

Look well ahead, pay attention and leave a safe gap to avoid late or harsh braking. Always try to anticipate what is likely to happen given the traffic, pedestrians, road conditions, weather, environment and time of day.

Braking systems: Antilock (ABS) / conventional

- In general, avoid harsh and late braking. Braking should be smooth and gradual.

- Antilock Brake Systems (ABS) use electronics to prevent the wheels from locking up when the brakes are applied with force.

- When the ABS senses that the wheels are at the point of locking, the system automatically releases the brakes momentarily and then re-engages them to avoid lock up and prevent skidding.

- To brake quickly with ABS, press fully and firmly on the brake pedal, keeping the pressure on until the vehicle comes to a stop. A shuddering or pulsating feeling may be detected through the pedal as the brakes are engaging and releasing; pressure must be kept on the pedal to allow the ABS to function correctly.

- ABS enable safe manoeuvring of the vehicle while braking and therefore reduce the risk of collision.

- When performing an emergency stop with conventional brakes, it is important to prevent the wheels from locking and causing the vehicle to skid out of control.

- Use a pump action applying, momentarily releasing and then re-applying the pressure on the brake pedal to prevent wheel lock with conventional brakes.

Control to a gentle stop

Pressure on brake pedal

When driving in adverse weather conditions, you will need to take extra care, increase your safety margins and reduce your potential for error.

Stopping in adverse conditions

- When driving in wet or bad weather, slow down and brake gradually, always leave a larger following distance than usual because traction and the ability to stop are significantly compromised by the condition of the roads.
- Increase the two-second safety margin to at least a four-second gap in wet or adverse conditions.
- To maintain a rear safety margin allow drivers behind to pass if they get too close.
- If vehicles compromise your forward safety margin by pulling in too soon after overtaking or changing lane, ease back as soon as possible to re-establish the gap.
- Allow at least twice the stopping distance when stopping in wet conditions.
- Braking early gives you more time to slow down.

Stopping distance

50 Km/h DRY 25 Metres

50 Km/h WET   30 Metres

100 Km/h DRY   70 Metres

100 Km/h WET   125 Metres

Braking in a turn

- Braking in a straight line is more effective than braking in a turn. When the wheels are in line the tyres have better grip on the road surface, enabling the vehicle to stop effectively.
- Braking in a turn is less effective because centrifugal force created in a turn tends to throw the weight of the vehicle onto the wheels on the outside of the curve and to the outer edges of the tyres. This lifts the inner tyres, and the inside edges of the outer ones, seriously compromising traction.

- Added to the compromised traction is the inertia (momentum) of the vehicle which continues to push the vehicle in the original direction that the vehicle was travelling before the turn.

Hazard lights

- Use the hazard lights to warn other traffic when slowing down or stopping unexpectedly on a dual carriageway or on a motorway.
- Use the hazard warning lights if the vehicle is causing a temporary obstruction, especially if stopping on or near a bend, or at the scene of a collision – or to warn others of a breakdown.
- The hazard lights are not to be used as an excuse to park illegally.
- Using the hazard lights to say 'thank you' to another driver is incorrect and can be dangerous. In a situation where a driver has just used the lights to say 'thank you' and then soon after needs to warn of a hazard, this may cause following drivers to misinterpret the hazard warning signal, which could then result in a collision.

Brake-and-avoid techniques

Constantly look well ahead to ensure sufficient time to slow down and stop. Even with the best observation there will be times when it is necessary to take evasive action; it will then be essential to assess the options quickly and respond correctly to avoid a collision.

Braking and avoiding an obstruction

- In emergency braking situations where there is doubt about being able to stop before coming into contact with an obstruction, look for ways to steer around the obstacle.
- Look for and choose alternative paths as soon as you begin the braking process to afford you more options.

- Do not leave the decision to steer around an obstacle to the last second because it is more difficult to maintain control in a swerve due to shifting weight and loss of traction.

Selecting the best option

- To avoid collisions, always drive at a speed that allows you maximum control of the vehicle. Choosing the correct speed for the conditions and maintaining a safe gap will allow you to stop in the distance that you can see to be clear.
- If a safe gap has not been maintained and a collision is imminent, running off the road onto the hard shoulder or into a soft barrier such as a hedge may be the best option.
- Hitting a yielding object such as a bush that 'gives' is less hazardous than hitting a hard object, such as a wall.
- Impacting with a non-yielding obstacle causes lots of damage and should be avoided where possible because the full force of the impact will be dissipated through the vehicle and the occupants.
- Vehicles travelling in the same direction have less potential to cause harm than those travelling in opposite directions because

the momentum of both vehicles will dissipate more evenly in a collision.
- The most damage occurs when two vehicles meet head on.

Common dashboard warning lights

Brake fluid level	Coolant temperature is too high
Brake pads or parking brake on	Oil level warning
Alternator is not charging battery	Diesel glow plug
Faulty anti lock braking	Diesel fuel filter warning
Fuel is low	Airbags are not functioning

Dealing with brake failure

Brake failure is least likely to happen in well-maintained vehicles.

- Keeping a safe distance from vehicles in front gives more time to select an alternative should the brakes fail.
- The correct response will depend on where and at what speed the failure occurs.
- Possible options:
  - remove pressure from the accelerator and gear down
  - gradually apply the handbrake
  - steer to avoid obstacles
  - hold the steering wheel firmly but do not over steer
  - remain composed, don't panic
  - use a soft run off: hedge, grass verge, hard shoulder etc.

Skid avoidance and control

Paying attention to the road conditions, driving well and maintaining your tyres all help to prevent getting into a skid, however you need to be able to regain control should a skid occur.

Recognising when skids are more likely

- Road surfaces that are:
  - wet,
  - icy,
  - muddy,
  - oily,

  and surfaces that are badly worn, all decrease road-holding and vehicle traction and increase the risk of skidding.
- Trying to stop or to take a bend too quickly can easily lead to a skid.
- Avoid harsh braking, slow down and make turns gradually.

Observe and discuss the road condition and surfaces you encounter during this lesson. Think about how the road surface might affect vehicle control.

Regaining control after a skid or loss of traction

- Remove your foot from the accelerator and brake pedals.
- Steer in the direction of the skid to help regain control of the vehicle.
- As the vehicle slows and traction is regained look for spaces and clear areas to steer the vehicle towards.
- Try not to concentrate on obstacles in the vehicle's path or you may end up colliding with them.
- Regain full control before attempting to resume the original direction.

Avoiding skids by monitoring your tyre tread

- Get into the habit of checking the tyres regularly for wear and tear and for correct inflation. Make a quick glance every time you approach to enter the vehicle and do a more thorough check when refuelling.
- Correctly inflated tyres have up to three times more contact and grip with the road than over or under-inflated tyres.
- Correctly inflated tyres save money on fuel consumption and prolong the life of the tyre.
- The law requires a minimum of 1.6mm of tread – that's approximately the thickness of a €2 coin. Remember that this is the minimum. Far better to have a tread of 5-6mm.
- Minimum wear bands are placed between the treads of the tyre. When any part of the tyre tread wears down, to within 1.6mm of the wear band, it is time to replace the tyre.
- Balancing and rotating the tyres diagonally front to back will extend their life.

 The first line of defence in skid avoidance is correctly inflated tyres with good tread; this gives the vehicle the best possible traction. Take a minute to check the tyre condition and pressures before you start this lesson; tyre checks are a necessary part of everyday safe driving.

Dealing with minor incidents

When pulling off the road to deal with minor problems, be aware of the risk presented by other traffic, act carefully to avoid further problems.

- Remember: Control the vehicle, choose the best course of action and then communicate your intentions to other road users.
- Grip the steering wheel firmly, look for an appropriate place to pull over, indicate or use hazard lights to warn other road users.
- Get as far away from the traffic stream as possible.
- Switch on the hazard lights if you have not already done so.
- Get out of the vehicle on the side farthest from the road.
- If appropriate, put out a warning triangle.

- Do not stand behind the vehicle because this may block the view of your lights from approaching vehicles and if your vehicle were rear-ended, you would be crushed between the two vehicles.
- Keep a hi-viz vest in the glove box for emergencies, this will allow you to put it on more quickly and safely than if it is stored in the boot.

Lesson 6 · Avoiding skids
Instruction assessment record

	Progressing	Mastered	ADI Signature	Date
Emergency braking				
Using ABS	○	○		
Cadence braking	○	○		
Stopping in adverse conditions	○	○		
Braking in a turn	○	○		
Using hazard lights	○	○		
Brake-and-avoid techniques				
Braking and avoiding an obstruction	○	○		
Selecting the best option	○	○		
Dealing with brake failure	○	○		
Skid avoidance and control				
Recognising when skids are likely	○	○		
Regaining control after a skid	○	○		
Monitoring tyre tread	○	○		
Dealing with minor incidents				
Pulling off the road	○	○		
Stopping safely	○	○		
Protecting yourself and passengers	○	○		
Re-entering traffic	○	○		

Note to ADI: When every skill has been mastered please note this by signing off lesson 6 in the training log in the centre of the book.

Notes

7

Advanced procedures

In this lesson we will discuss...

- Driving at night
- Driving in wind and rain
- Driving in ice, snow, fog or bright sunshine conditions
- Emergency vehicles and collision scenes
- Mobile phones

Introduction

Driving at night presents additional challenges; it is more difficult to see at night, depth and colour perception are affected by the lack of light which can result in objects being overlooked or appearing further away than they really are. Headlight glare or moving between well and poorly lit areas further diminish your ability to see as well as you can during daylight. Driving at night often coincides with normal periods of fatigue or rest, so extra care is needed to account for your own shortcomings and the limitations of others.

Driving at night

Adjust speed and safety margins to allow for the challenges of night driving.

At night:

- Look for tell tale signs such as illuminated trees and buildings ahead to help you gather information in advance.
- You must be able to come to a stop within the distance that you can see to be clear, at night this means within the area that is illuminated by your headlights.
- Avoid looking into the lights of oncoming traffic as this will affect your night vision, look down or to the near side of the road and following the road edge or markings.
- Adjust the rear view mirror to avoid being dazzled by following traffic.

- Get familiar with reflective road markings (cat's eyes, delineators) and other useful night-driving aids.
- Being able to recognise and understand the meaning of a road sign by their shape and colour gives you an added advantage and extra time for hazard perception.
- Dip the headlights when vehicles approach and when approaching other vehicles from behind. Dazzling other road users is not just discourteous it is dangerous; when you 'blind' the other person you temporarily disable them and create a hazard for both of you.

- Keep the windows clean inside and out to lessen the effect of glare being defused on smears and grime. Windscreens that are clean on the inside do not mist up as quickly as dirty ones, which is particularly important on cold wet nights.

- Dim the dashboard lights to reduce internal glare.
- If you feel drowsy, pull over in a safe place and take a break. It is important to be able to recognise the signs and dangers of fatigue while driving.

Driving in wind and rain

Wind and rain affect traction and road-holding. Compensate for the loss of control by adjusting your driving style and speed.

Wind

- The faster the vehicle is moving the greater the 'lift' generated. Speed lift coupled with the de-stabilizing effect of strong winds can seriously affect the traction and control of the vehicle.
- Slowing down will help to regain traction and make it easier to keep the vehicle under control in high winds.
- Remember that other vehicles will also be affected by the wind.
- Take particular care around high-sided vehicles; wind and air flow will be affected by the larger vehicle and can cause down drafts and other wind related problems that can push or pull lighter vehicles around quite violently.

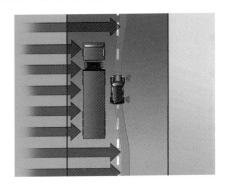

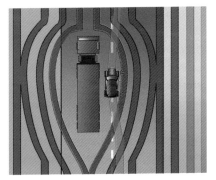

- Leave extra space around motorbikes, bicycles and other light vehicles to allow for erratic movement should they be blown off course by a strong gust.

- In windy conditions be extra vigilant for flying debris especially near construction sites or residential areas.
- The most effective way to counteract the effect wind has on a vehicle is to slow down.

Rain

Maximise your ability to see and be seen when it's raining:

- Clean the windows inside and out.
- Make sure the wiper blades are in good working order.
- Keep the window washing fluid topped up.
- Clean all the mirrors.
- Clean the glass of the lights front and rear.
- Make sure all lights are functioning correctly, replace worn indicator bulbs.

Dirty interior windows mist up more quickly than clean ones. Dirty exterior glass on windows and mirrors retain rain drops for longer, while rain drops add to vision problems by creating distortion and prism like effects when bright light deflects off them.

Practicing wet-weather braking and skid avoidance/recovery in an-off road area will help you to recognise the feel of traction loss. You can simulate traction loss by placing two cones about a car length apart and then driving around them in a figure of eight. Start slowly and gradually build up speed until the vehicle starts to lose traction; regain control by easing up on the accelerator and steering into the skid.

- Good tread and correct pressure give the best possible traction in wet conditions so check them regularly
- To lessen the effect of inhibited visibility caused by spray from tyres, stay well back when following other vehicles in the rain.
- Staying well back, when following other vehicles, affords a better view of the road beyond the vehicle ahead, giving you advanced warning of upcoming hazards and more time to deal with them.
- Avoid overtaking in rainy conditions. If overtaking is necessary, allow plenty of extra room. Start the manoeuvre from

well behind the 'spray zone', overtake without delay and put the wipers on high speed. Allow plenty of room before pulling back in front of the other vehicle to avoid affecting the other driver's view with spray.

- Excessive rain and standing water can lead to aquaplaning as the tyres rise up over the water and lose traction. Driving at speed and having poorly inflated tyres add to this problem. Avoid aquaplaning by slowing down in the rain and keeping the tyres properly maintained.
- Motorcycles lose traction and can skid more easily than cars or trucks in wet conditions. Motorcyclists must slow right down even in light rain conditions especially on bends and on roundabouts to avoid losing traction.
- Leave extra room for motorcyclists in wet conditions and be prepared to slow down to accommodate their needs.
- Pedestrians and cyclists need extra consideration and space to avoid standing water, be prepared to accommodate.

Flooding

Choosing an alternative route is an important element of safe driving in adverse conditions.

- To cross a shallow flooded area or a large puddle, select the highest part of the road and proceed slowly.
- Watch how other similar vehicles have successfully crossed the water and follow their track.
- Keeping the engine revs up should help to keep water out of the exhaust pipe.
- Once through the flooded area, check the brakes before resuming normal driving.
- When unsure of the depth, where water is running rapidly or if you are worried that it will reach more than halfway up the wheels, do not attempt to cross. It takes relatively little water to float a vehicle and wash it away or to do serious damage to the engine.
- Falling leaves and clogged drains from heavy wind and rain in Autumn should alert you to the possibility of flooding.

Driving in ice, snow, fog or bright sunshine conditions

Ice

Driving in icy conditions.

- Watch for the signs of freezing conditions: frost on windows, glistening pavements, frosty grass verges. Frost is more likely on cold cloudless winter nights where the moon appears to have very sharp edges.

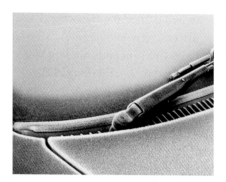

- Be alert for changes in the sound of road noise on very cold days, when the normal driving sound changes to smooth and silent it may be an indication that the road is covered in ice.

- Keep a clear view by cleaning all windows, lights and mirrors before starting to drive in freezing weather.

- Use the de-misters and heaters to keep windows and side mirrors clear and be sure to adequately warm the engine before setting out when the weather is cold.

- Add anti-freeze to window washing fluids at the beginning of winter to prevent freezing and burst reservoirs.

- Elevated stretches of road such as bridges and fly-overs tend to freeze before other roads because of the cold air that circulates beneath them. Pay extra attention to these areas in freezing conditions, even if the rest of the road seems free of ice.

- Sheltered areas under trees or in dips in the road can stay frozen long after the rest of the road has thawed; take extra care in freezing temperatures in these areas.

- Avoid harsh braking, slow down by using deceleration and gear selection to maintain better control in ice, snow or sleet.

- In a skid, steer in the direction of the skid. Then look for a space and steer in that direction. Take care not to over steer.

Fog

Staying safe in fog.

- Use the front and rear fog lights when visibility is less than 100 metres. Full beams inhibit the ability to see because the light reflects off the fog droplets and bounces back creating glare.

- Drivers must be able to come to a stop within the distance that can be seen clearly. In fog, this usually means driving very much more slowly.

- Don't be fooled into driving at a higher speed because the tail lights of the vehicle ahead are visible. As it moves, the vehicle ahead pushes the fog aside, making the visibility seem better than it really is. This can lull drivers into using a shorter following distance than is necessary in the foggy conditions. Allow plenty of room in case the vehicle ahead comes to a sudden stop.

- In thick fog or heavy mist, if you can see the lights of the vehicle in front you are probably too close to be able to stop safely should the other vehicle come to a sudden stop: pull back to increase safety.

- Fog may clear in patches – in dips and hollows or beneath trees along the road; don't be tempted to speed up in the clear areas. The clearing may be short lived and speeding into the next fog bank could result in hitting a vehicle or another obstacle hidden within it.

- Driving in fog requires a high level of concentration and attention, and can be very tiring; take a break if necessary.

- In the event that the fog makes driving too dangerous, choose a safe place to stop – well off the road – and wait until the fog clears.

Snow

- Due to the mild climate in Ireland, most vehicles and road maintenance providers are not equipped for driving in anything more than a light dusting of snow, so when conditions are bad it's best, if possible, to avoid driving completely.
- If driving is a must, slow down and allow a much greater safety margin to compensate for the lack of vision, traction and other vehicle control difficulties.
- Leave plenty of room for other drivers, remember they are unlikely to be familiar with driving in snow or have snow tyres fitted.
- Prepare well especially when travelling in a rural area. Bring a mobile phone, rug, shovel, scraper, brush and some emergency food and drink. Keep a jacket and boots in the vehicle in winter.

- To improve traction, drive in the ruts left by other vehicles.
- Avoid any distractions. Turn off the radio and mobile phones.
- If a snow storm starts, pull over as soon as possible. Put on the hazard lights. Leave the car only if it is possible to walk to safety, otherwise, stay put and wait for the snow storm to pass.

Sunshine and glare
In bright sunlight...

- Position the sunshade to block out sun glare.
- Sit up straight and adjust the seat to give yourself a better vantage point for looking down at the road.
- Adjust the mirrors to help eliminate glare when there is a low sun behind the vehicle. Glare can easily hide a motorcycle or other vehicles approaching from the rear.
- Use dipped headlights to improve the ability to be seen by others when the sun is coming from behind. It is easier to see vehicles

with headlights on when looking towards low sunlight.

- Signal early and use hand signals if there is a danger that the glare is preventing other road users from seeing the indicators and brake lights.

- Remember that pedestrians are usually unaware that they are difficult, or even impossible, to see when bright sunlight is coming from behind them.

Emergency vehicles and collision scenes

Slow down, remain calm and manoeuvre carefully when passing the scene of a collision or when encountering emergency vehicles.

Yielding for emergency vehicles

- Being constantly aware of your surroundings helps you to hear and to detect other signs that an emergency vehicle is approaching.
- When an emergency vehicle approaches, check your surroundings and select a safe place to pull over.
- Indicate and pull over to the side of the road, away from the approaching emergency vehicle.
- It may be necessary to move onto the hard shoulder, between two lanes or onto the centre median to make way for an emergency vehicle.

- Pay attention to how other drivers respond, for example, when other drivers pull to the right, do the same, so that the emergency vehicle can pass on the left.
- When the emergency vehicle has passed, look out for other vehicles behind it; for example, an ambulance may be following a fire engine. There may be several vehicles, so remain vigilant.
- Extra loud music reduces your ability to hear emergency vehicles.

Moving off after an emergency vehicle has passed

- When the way is clear, MSM and continue. Leave at least 150m behind the emergency vehicle in case it needs to stop suddenly.
- Take particular care when pulling back out after yielding for emergency vehicles because some drivers may get back on course more quickly than others. Thoughts about the emergency can easily distract drivers so pay attention.

Passing the scene of a collision

- Slow down and pass the scene of a collision with due care.
- Give emergency personnel ample room to work; do not put them in danger by passing too close or too quickly.
- Watch for instructions from the emergency service personnel and look out for temporary signs.
- When approaching an emergency scene or line of traffic tailing back from one, slow down, put on the hazard lights and leave a gap of at least two car lengths in front until several vehicles have safely slowed or stopped behind you. Leaving a gap gives the option to

move to the side to avoid being rear ended.
- Stop if you are the first on the scene or if you can offer valuable assistance, otherwise continue with caution unless directed to stop.
- If stopping is necessary, do so only in a place that will not cause further disruption or danger.
- It may be necessary to drive onto the hard shoulder, between two lanes or onto the centre median to avoid a collision scene. Watch how other drivers are responding. Be prepared to wait and/or give way.
- It is dangerous to focus attention on the scene of a collision when passing. If the driver's attention is diverted from the task of driving, in a situation where others may also be distracted, it can easily lead to another crash.

Mobile phones

Using any form of mobile phone while driving is a major distraction, even hands free devices detract from your ability to fully concentrate on the primary task of driving. Using a mobile is not the same as conversing with a passenger or listening to the radio because it entails interaction with someone who is not party to the prevailing conditions.

The safe option: ignoring calls

- The safest option is not to have the mobile phone turned on in the vehicle, even a ring tone or a missed call can be distracting.
- If the phone is switched on, it is safest to ignore an incoming call until you are stopped and it is safe to answer it.
- Safety is paramount. Phone calls are a low priority while driving. Far better to attend to an ignored call or text at a later time when it is safe to do so.
- It is illegal to make a call or to take a call while driving unless it is 'hands free', but even 'hands free' calls are very distracting and dangerous when driving.
- Never attempt to read or write texts while driving.

No call is as important as your safety or the safety of those around you.

When a call must be made

- If an important call must be made or taken, pull well off the road to a safe place.
- The hard shoulder is not a safe place to use a mobile phone. UK Collision records show that on average, vehicles stopped on the hard shoulder get hit by other vehicles within 15 minutes.
- Finish the call and return your complete attention to the task of driving before attempting to move off.
- If a call or text has been emotional or distressing, take a break or find a way to calm down before continuing to drive.
- No matter what the content of the call, it must be put aside to allow full concentration on the driving task. Your life and the lives of others depend on it.

- When receiving a call on a 'hands free' set you must remain vigilant to the surroundings and the traffic at all times.
- Letting the other party know that you are driving is a good idea as they will be more likely keep the conversation short or allow you to call them back at a more suitable time.
- When you call someone that is driving remember to give them the opportunity to call you back at a better time or to pull over safely before continuing the conversation.

Lesson 7 · Advanced procedures

Instruction assessment record

	Progressing	Mastered	ADI Signature	Date

Driving at night

	Progressing	Mastered	ADI Signature	Date
Preparing & optimising night vision	○	○		
Speed adjustment	○	○		
Avoiding oncoming glare	○	○		
Dealing with rearview mirror glare	○	○		
Recognising & using night time cues	○	○		

Driving in wind and rain

	Progressing	Mastered	ADI Signature	Date
Wind	○	○		
Rain	○	○		
Flooding	○	○		

Driving in adverse conditions

	Progressing	Mastered	ADI Signature	Date
Ice	○	○		
Fog	○	○		
Snow	○	○		
Sunshine and glare	○	○		

Emergency vehicles and collision scenes

	Progressing	Mastered	ADI Signature	Date
Yielding for emergency vehicles	○	○		
Continuing after emergency vehicles	○	○		
Passing the scene of a collision	○	○		

Mobile phones

	Progressing	Mastered	ADI Signature	Date
The safe option: ignoring calls	○	○		
Stopping to take/make a call safely	○	○		

Note to ADI: When every skill has been mastered please note this by signing off lesson 7 in the training log in the centre of the book.

Notes

8

Motorway driving

In this lesson we will discuss...

- Motorways
- Changing lanes and passing on motorways
- Leaving the motorway

Introduction

Although driving on motorways is not permitted for learner drivers, motorway driving skills are essential for new drivers to acquire. Most motorway driving techniques can be practised on high grade national routes and dual carriageways, which have motorway-like conditions.
In addition a lot can be learned about good driving practice by travelling as a passenger and observing good motorway driving techniques being demonstrated by your driving instructor. For maximum benefit take another motorway driving lesson with your instructor as soon as possible after you have obtained your full driving licence.

Motorways

A fast-paced environment
Because traffic moves much faster on a motorway, conditions change and incidents occur more abruptly than on other roads. Drivers must remain alert at all times.
Being aware of the positions and movements of other vehicles is vital to safe motorway travel. So too, is lane discipline. Drive in the left-hand lane except when overtaking.

Joining the motorway

- While still on the entry slip road, accelerate and begin to adjust speed to match the speed of the vehicles already on the motorway.
- Look for a safe gap in the traffic, check the blind spot over the right shoulder and continue increasing speed.
- Put on the indicator and check ahead, to the side and over the shoulder again.
- Check for traffic approaching from behind and for vehicles changing lane.
- When it is safe to do so, merge seamlessly onto the motorway.
- Stay in the left lane, do not attempt to cross into another lane until fully settled into the general traffic flow.

Travelling on the motorway

- Maintain adequate progress to match the other traffic on the motorway but do not exceed the maximum speed limit for the vehicle or for the prevailing conditions e.g., the weather, traffic volume or restricted speed limits.

- In good weather conditions, use the two-second rule to maintain an adequate safety margin. Increase the safety margin if conditions deteriorate.
- Following other vehicles too closely is the primary cause of crashes on the motorway. Don't be a tailgater. Leave plenty of space.
- Travel in the left lane unless overtaking or moving over to accommodate traffic entering the motorway.
- When the motorway is congested, the queue of traffic in the left lane is permitted to move faster than traffic in the overtaking lane.
- Be particularly careful when changing lanes on motorways that have three or more lanes, vehicles from other lanes may be heading simultaneously for the same gap as you.
- When travelling for long distances or when using the same route regularly, it is particularly important to scan constantly. Switching the focus of attention helps in staying alert and avoiding motorway monotony.
- To combat monotony and boredom, try adjusting the seat position, listening to lively music, getting some fresh air or getting off the motorway for a while to take a break.

- Do not pull over or stop at the side of a motorway unless there is a genuine emergency.
- When stopped in an emergency, get out of the vehicle, without delay, from the side that is furthest from the road and then move well away from the vehicle.

Passing merging and diverging slip lanes

- Road signs, overpasses and green cat's eyes signal upcoming slip lanes for getting on and off the motorway.
- When approaching or passing motorway entries and exits, keep a lookout and adjust lane position to allow for other vehicles that are leaving or entering.
- The road markings are designed to alert drivers that vehicles will be diverging and merging. Advanced warnings enable drivers to anticipate and adjust position and speed to accommodate the needs of other motorists.

Toll Booths

Many motorways operate on a toll system:

- When availing of a toll road, plan the route prior to starting out and prepare by having sufficient money ready, preferably in the right coinage, to cover the charges.
- If the money is not to hand in advance, do not attempt to find it in the congested run up area before the toll booths.
- Look for the correct change well in advance or when you have stopped at the booth. Don't feel pressured by the drivers behind you.
- Get into the correct lane early when approaching the booths. Refrain from jumping from one lane to another.
- Just as in general road use, it is an offence and dangerous to cross a solid white dividing line between lanes in a toll booth area.
- Keep a lookout for other drivers who may be 'lane hopping'.

- When the toll has been paid, move off without delay.
- Take care when leaving the toll area as many lanes will be merging.
- Frequent users of toll roads, should invest in prepaid tags to save time, money and ease congestion.
- Many toll roads are changing to electronic tolling systems and will no longer accept cash at the toll booths, you will require a prepaid electronic tag or you will be subject to a higher payment later. Electronic tags can be purchased online and mailed to you. Web links are listed in the back of this book.

Changing lanes and passing on motorways

- Check all around before indicating your intention to overtake or change lanes on a motorway.
- Remember that traffic is travelling faster on the motorway, vehicles behind you that are travelling faster catch up very quickly.
- Use MSM and the SIDE rule to guide observation and communicate when changing lanes or when overtaking on a motorway.
- Start the overtaking manoeuvre from well back. Leave plenty of lateral space around vehicles being overtaken. Return to the left lane only when a two-second gap can be left in front of the vehicle that has been overtaken.
- You should be able to see the vehicle that has been passed in the rear view mirror before moving back in front of it.

- Driving alongside another vehicle for any length of time is dangerous because it severely limits the options.
- Before beginning an overtaking manoeuvre, ensure that you will be able to get out of the side-to-side position without delay.
- Fast moving high sided trucks and other large vehicles create unusual wind disturbances that can easily affect the vehicle handling characteristics of smaller vehicles travelling in close proximity. Use caution especially in high wind or wet conditions.

Leaving the motorway

Preparing to leave the motorway

- Plan well ahead so that you can anticipate when you will arrive at your chosen exit.
- Check the number of the exit or road you wish to take in advance.
- Junction signs with road numbers are posted approximately one kilometre before each exit.
- Signs with destinations and place names are posted half a kilometre before the exit.
- Make appropriate observations and signal in plenty of time to allow other motorists to facilitate you.
- You should be in the left lane at least half a kilometre before your exit.

Safely diverging from the travel lane

- Maintain speed while in the travel lane. Slow down only when fully in the slip lane.
- Blue 'countdown' signs with white bars are posted at 300m, 200m and 100m prior to the beginning of an exit slip lane. Use these to prepare for the lane change. Check your mirrors and the movements of other vehicles, and put on the left indicator while maintaining the appropriate speed and safety margin.
- As the slip lane opens up, diverge into it smoothly and adjust your speed to match the reduced speed-limit signs. You may need to slow down further or come to a full stop to suit the traffic conditions (e.g., if there is a queue on the exit ramp).
- If the slip road has a curve or sharp bend, reduce speed in plenty of time to remain in control.
- On larger exits that have two or more slip lanes, do not cross the lanes unnecessarily, use due care at all times.

- If you miss the exit, continue on to the next one. Never attempt to cut into a slip lane at the last second or to reverse along the hard shoulder back to the exit.

Adjusting to the new environment

- While still on the slip road, anticipate and prepare for the new conditions that will be encountered on leaving the motorway.
- Speed-limit signs will usually guide you to slow down in plenty of time, allowing for a smooth change to the new road.
- Watch your speed when leaving the motorway. When you've been driving at a high speed, it can be difficult to judge your speed on the new road – travelling at 60 km/h feels like 40km/h or less after 120km/h.
- When you leave the motorway, look out for pedestrians and cyclists who may also be using the minor road.

- On the motorway, intersections consist of slip lanes and usually an overpass; off the motorway, junctions and intersections are at road-level and need to be handled differently. Keep this in mind as you leave the motorway.
- Occasionally a motorway ends and the road continues as dual carriageway or another road type; apart from the colour of the road signs the road may look very similar. On motorways the road marker and sign background colour is blue, when the background colour of the road signs changes from blue to green or black, it means that you are no longer on the motorway and the motorway rules no longer apply. Therefore the speed limit will be lower and there will be intersections and other such hazards to take into account.

Lesson 8 · Simulated motorway driving
Instruction assessment record

	Progressing	Mastered	ADI Signature	Date

Entering and driving on a motorway

	Progressing	Mastered	ADI Signature	Date
Joining the motorway	○	○		
Travelling on the motorway	○	○		
Passing merging lanes	○	○		
Passing diverging lanes	○	○		
Toll booths	○	○		

Changing lanes and passing

Observation	○	○		
Communication	○	○		
Leaving safe gaps	○	○		

Exiting

Preparing to leave the motorway	○	○		
Safely diverging from the travel lane	○	○		
Adjusting to the new environment	○	○		

Note to ADI: When every skill has been mastered please note this by signing off lesson 8 in the training log in the centre of the book.

9

Maintenance and navigation

In this lesson we will discuss...

- Basic vehicle checks and routine maintenance
- Navigation

Introduction

Keeping the vehicle roadworthy and running smoothly is an integral part of safe motoring. Responsible road use means always driving vehicles that are fit for the purpose, while maintaining the vehicle is essential if you expect it to respond properly when driving. Aside from the roadworthiness and safety reasons, a well maintained vehicle looks better, holds it's resale value and is a lot kinder to the environment. Maintaining your vehicle doesn't mean you have to be mechanically inclined or skilled, it just requires that you look after it between regular professional servicing.

Basic vehicle checks and routine maintenance

Daily

- Check all around the car as you approach to make sure nothing is damaged.
- Check the tyre pressure and condition.
- Ensure that all windows and mirrors are clean and clear.
- Check the petrol level and start up electrics before moving off.
- Check brakes at slow speed shortly after moving off.

Weekly

- Top up fuel if below the half way mark.
- Check oil, maintain level at half way, look for leaks.
- When the engine is cold check that coolant is within correct range.
- Check brake and clutch fluids for leaks.
- Check windscreen washer fluid levels, top up if necessary.
- Check battery connections are sound.
- Check all lights especially the brakes.

Monthly

- On cold tyres, check pressures and tread on all tyres including spare.
- Check the wiper blades for wear.
- Check the fan belt for wear and tightness.
- Clean the car inside and out at least once a month.

Annually

- Book your car in for an annual service.
- Check the owner's handbook for advice on what should be changed at each service.
- Make sure the technician completes the service log so that you can keep track of changes made or needed in future services.

Use the acronym **POWER** to help you to remember all the essential checks.

P **Petrol** – Check the level of petrol before every trip to ensure you have sufficient for the intended journey.

O **Oil** – The oil level needs to be kept within the required min/max level. Make a habit of checking it weekly to ensure the correct level is maintained.

W **Water** – Check the levels of the windscreen washer, coolant and brake fluids.

E **Electrics** – Check all the lights, indicators, and warning devices to ensure they work correctly and are free from dirt or obstruction.

R **Rubber** – Check the tyres for correct inflation and tread. Include a brake and steering check.

The frequency of routine checks depends on how much driving you do; the easiest way to remember to do the checks regularly is to make them routine. Linking the checks to some other routine activity makes them easier to remember, for example, every time you refuel, at a defined distance on your odometer or on a set day of the month.

Checking the lights
Driving with defective lights is dangerous and illegal.

- Check the light bulbs by walking around the vehicle with the lights switched on.
- Enlist the help of another person to check the brake lights.

- Look for the reflection of the vehicle's lights against a wall or shop window, or in the rear of the vehicle in front when stopped in traffic.
- A quick flashing dashboard indicator light will alert you to a malfunctioning indicator.
- Check the indicator light bulbs for faded or missing orange colour; replace the bulbs when they are no longer bright orange.

Changing light bulbs

Practice replacing each light bulb so that you will be able to do it when needed.

- Carry a spare for each type of light bulb in the vehicle.
- Turn off the lights before attempting to replace a blown bulb.
- Check the owner's handbook for specific instructions about changing the bulbs.
- Check all the lights to make sure they're working properly after changing a bulb.

Most headlight bulbs are accessed from behind the light, under the bonnet but some are accessed by removing the glass or the full housing from the front of the vehicle. The headlight bulb is usually in the largest socket, which has three wires connected to it.

- Remove the holder from the back of the bulb. If necessary, release the clip or spring to access the bulb itself.
- When removing the old bulb, note how it fits into the socket. Don't touch the glass of the new bulb – hold it through its wrapper or a cloth. Grease left on the bulb from your fingers can create uneven heating which can cause a new bulb to blow prematurely.

- Once the bulb is in place, reposition the spring/clip and insert the bulb in its holder back into position. Then lock the whole lot back into the lamp socket.

Side lights, indicator bulbs and rear light bulb.

- The side lights are normally found in the same area as the headlights. There are usually two wires coming out of the plug. Use a twist and pull action to release the bulb and socket together. Remove the bulb from the socket and replace it with a new one.

- Indicator bulbs vary from one vehicle to another but most are the bayonet type that require a slight push inward as you twist, similar to installing a household bulb.
- To change the rear bulbs, you usually need to remove an access panel. Once the panel is off, remove the bulbs from the front of the mounting by using a gentle press-in-and-twist method.

Oil level maintenance

- Park on level ground and turn off the engine before checking lubricant levels.
- Before checking the oil level, allow adequate time for the oil to drain into the oil pan.
- Check the oil level with the dipstick. Remove the dipstick and wipe the end clean, reinsert it, remove it again and check that the oil level is within the normal range.

- If the level is low, add the appropriate grade of oil for the vehicle and for the time of year.
- Over-filling can cause serious damage to an engine, add a small amount of oil and then re-check the level before repeating the process if necessary.

Refuelling

Filling the fuel tank is potentially a hazardous procedure and requires your full attention to prevent mishap.

- Pull up close to the desired pump and switch off the engine.
- Do not smoke or use a mobile phone when filling petrol or diesel.
- Petrol and diesel fumes are carcinogenic. Stand upwind to avoid inhaling fumes.
- Begin filling by squeezing the pump handle, it should click off automatically when full.
- Allow the nozzle to drip into the tank before putting it back into the pump holder.
- If you spill or splash petrol, wipe it up without delay.
- Remove petrol-soaked clothes before coming close to naked flames or cigarettes.

- Keep the fuel level above the halfway mark to save loss of fuel through evaporation and to avoid running short of fuel unexpectedly.
- Always fill up the tank before embarking on a long journey, especially before using a motorway or if travelling through unfamiliar areas.

NEVER attempt to open the coolant reservoir, or the radiator, when the engine is hot, extremely hot liquid can quickly escape under pressure and cause severe burns.

Window-washer fluid and engine coolant

- Check the water level in the window-washer reservoir by looking at the level from outside the reservoir, top it up where necessary.
- Washer fluid is best for cleaning and is less prone to freezing in cold weather; however tap water can be used if no washer fluid is available.
- Some vehicles have a separate rear window washer reservoir.
- Check the coolant level by looking at the reservoir. The minimum and maximum

indicator lines are marked on the outside of the container. Check the manufacturer's guidelines on the coolant level. Insufficient coolant can cause the engine to overheat; in older vehicles it may be necessary to top up the coolant more frequently.

Tyre pressure and tread

Under inflated tyres use up to two full tanks of extra fuel per year! Think of the money and carbon emissions you can save by just keeping your tyres properly inflated.

Regular tyre pressure checks help to ensure maximum fuel efficiency and tyre life. Incorrectly inflated tyres have far less traction and stopping ability than correctly inflated tyres.

- Check the owner's manual or the tyre pressure chart, located on the back of the fuel door or on the frame of the driver's door, for the correct pressure required for the vehicle and its load.
- Remove the cap from the valve and push the air pump onto the valve. This releases some air and displays the pressure on the gauge. Add or release air to obtain the correct pressure.
- Check the tyre walls and the tread for wear.
- Check the tread depth manually with a gauge, a rough assessment can be made by looking at the wear indicator knobs within the grooves of the tread. The minimum legal tyre tread is 1.6mm – less than the thickness of a two-euro coin. This is an absolute minimum and is not very safe.

TYRE INFLATION

Correct Inflation   Over Inflation   Under Inflation

Check your tyres regularly

- Tyres with minimum tread can take up to five times the distance to stop than tyres with new tread.
- Under - and over - inflated tyres or tyres that are not correctly balanced wear out unevenly and much more quickly than tyres that are properly inflated. This means they'll need to be replaced more frequently which adds to your running costs and your carbon footprint.
- Check all the tyres, including the spare, on a regular basis. Get into the habit of checking your tyres when refuelling.
- Get the tyres checked at a tyre-service centre at least once a year. Many tyre centres offer

free balancing services and will rotate the tyres front to back and diagonally for a small fee. This will prolong the tyres' life.

Changing a wheel

Practising changing a wheel in preparation for managing a flat tyre.

- Park the vehicle in a safe location. Turn off the engine and apply the parking brake. Shift into first gear or into the park position in an automatic.
- If attempting to change the wheel at the side of a road, put on a reflective jacket and place a safety triangle at least 50m back from the vehicle.
- Take out the spare wheel, brace, jack, gloves and wheel chocks, if available or use some suitable stones instead.
- Place the spare wheel under the vehicle, close to where you will be working, to provide a buffer if the jack slips.
- To stop the vehicle from moving while you work, place the chocks on either side of the wheel that's on the furthest corner from the flat tyre.
- For comfort you can use one of the vehicle's floor mats to kneel on.
- If there is a hub cap on the damaged wheel, take it off. You may need to use a special tool or cut a plastic cable tie.
- Use the wheel brace to loosen the nuts on the wheel. Do this before lifting the vehicle with the jack; if attempted afterwards, the wheel will spin, making it impossible to loosen the nuts. It may be necessary to use an extension bar or foot pressure on the wheel brace if it won't move with hand strength.
- Some vehicles have a special locking nut to prevent theft – a key or unique device is supplied to open the lock. It should be with the jack and brace or in the glove box.
- Open the jack and place it under the vehicle at the jacking point nearest to the damaged wheel. Ensure that the jack is level and on firm ground.
- Open the jack by turning or pumping it until the vehicle and the wheel are raised above the ground. Give yourself enough room to work. Remember that the spare will be slightly larger than the flat tyre because it is fully inflated.
- DO NOT PUT ANY PART OF YOUR BODY UNDER THE VEHICLE WHILE IT IS RAISED ON THE JACK.
- Now remove the nuts completely and place them to one side. Remove the flat and mount

the spare without delay. Hand-tighten the nuts back in place.

- Lower the Jack and allow the vehicle to sit back down on all four wheels, tighten all the wheel nuts with the brace.
- Replace the hub cap and put the wheel chocks, jack, brace, warning triangle and damaged wheel back into the vehicle.
- Wipe your hands, put the floor mat back into the vehicle and prepare to resume the journey.
- If the spare is a compact temporary wheel, do not exceed 80km/h or the specified maximum speed. Go to a garage as soon as possible to have the regular tyre repaired or replaced.

- If carrying a spare wheel is not practical, such as on a motorcycle, chemical tyre inflation aerosols are available to enable a temporary repair. These chemicals are convenient in an emergency when it would not be safe or practical to change a flat tyre.

The safe way to change a tyre.

Stop in a safe place, in gear and brake applied.

Place a warning triangle 50m behind.

Wear a high visibility safety vest.

Check the diagonally opposite wheel.

Wear gloves and use a mat to kneel on.

Lift out spare and place it near to hand.

Fit wheel brace and use key security adapter.

Loosen nuts a half turn.

Open the jack so it just fits under the car.

Locate jack head in the correct jacking point.

Carefully begin to jack up the car.

Push the spare under the car beside the jack.

Raise the wheel to give a clearance of 50mm.

Remove each nut with the wheel brace.

Carefully place each nut on the mat.

Lift off the punctured wheel.

Lift the spare into place and locate on studs.

Screw on all the nuts by hand.

Hand tighten the nuts with the wheel brace.

Lower the car with the jack.

Remove the punctured wheel from under the car.

Place the punctured wheel in the boot.

With wheel on the ground, tighten nuts.

Work diagonally around the wheel tightening each nut.

135

Window wipers

Wiper blades that do not clear the windscreen properly or wipers that are split or cracked need to be replaced. The driver's view can be badly obscured if the wipers aren't working correctly.

- Check for damaged wipers by lifting the wiper off the windscreen and inspecting it. If a wiper is leaving streaks on the windscreen, it's time to replace it.

- Remove damaged wipers by lifting the wiper arm away from the glass to an upright position and then releasing the locking clip. Depending on the type of wiper this may be a squeeze mechanism or achieved by turning the blade to a 90° angle to release it from the arm.

- Replace the blade with a compatible new one. Wiper blades are available in larger garages, from car dealers and from motor accessory shops. New wiper blades usually have

installation instructions printed on the box.

- Check that the arm spring is pressing the blade against the glass. The arm may need to be replaced. This is something to watch out for in older vehicles. Most car supply shops are helpful with this type of minor repair, if you have difficulty following the instructions, ask for help.

Mirrors

Clean mirrors are vital for safety. Before setting off ensure that the vehicle's mirrors are clean and adjusted correctly as part of the cockpit drill.

- Mist and rain stays on dirty wing mirrors longer than on clean mirrors. Even the smallest spots on the mirrors tend to distort images and create glare, especially when the sun or lights are reflected in the mirrors.

- During the cockpit drill, quickly check that all the mirrors are adjusted to give the best view to the rear and to the sides of the vehicle. This is especially important after parking in a confined space or public car park where you may have adjusted your side mirrors for parking. The mirrors sometimes get knocked out of position by passing pedestrians.
- As part of routine vehicle checks, move the mirrors to check that they are securely mounted.
- Cracked or broken mirrors distort images and could mask or obscure a hazard. Replace damaged mirrors without delay.

Safety belts and other safety restraints

Check the integrity of the vehicle's safety restraints regularly:

- Check that all of the safety belts can run freely in and out.
- Be sure that there are no twists or areas that are worn or frayed.

- To check the inertia tension mechanism, pull on the belt sharply. It should lock if it is working properly.
- The driver is responsible for ensuring that all seat belts and safety restraints in the vehicle are in good working order and that they are suitable for each passenger.
- Be sure that you know how to adjust all restraints correctly, especially when there are children on board.
- Head restraints should be in line with the back of the occupant's head. The middle of the restraint should be roughly at the same level as the occupant's ears.
- The steering wheel must be positioned at least 25cm from the driver's chest. If there is an airbag in the steering wheel, the wheel should be tilted so that the bag is aimed at the driver's chest and not at the face.

Seats

- Check that the driver's seat is properly anchored and locked into position by shifting your weight in the seat, do this every time before beginning to drive as part of your pre-driving routine.
- Ensure that the all seats are correctly secured in position, especially after the seats have

been reconfigured or moved.

- Make sure that nothing is placed or stored directly behind the front seats in vehicles fitted with WIPS safety systems. Anything obstructing the back of the seat will render the WIPS ineffective. WIPS safety systems are designed to prevent whiplash when a vehicle is hit from behind – the back of the seat immediately reclines and helps to dissipate energy away from the occupant's spine.

- In vehicles with drop-down seat backs, be sure that the seat backs are properly secured and that the belts are not snagged or obstructed after the seats have been dropped down or fully opened.

Navigation

Plan a safer journey or trip to an unfamiliar area.

- Get a map or road atlas of the local area and examine the legend to learn what the various colours and symbols mean.
- Identify the present location on the map and then use the map to find an efficient route to another location, for example, the best route to the nearest hospital or airport.
- Plan a journey and write down the names of large towns and road identification numbers en route.
- Sometimes it's easier to find a destination by identifying a larger town or city further along the same route. For example, when travelling from Cork to Clane in Co. Kildare, it would be prudent to follow the Dublin route signs most of the way until reaching Naas in Co. Kildare, then switch to the local road information closer to the destination.

- Identify primary, secondary, rural and urban roads on a map.
- Use the information on the map to estimate the distance and time required to get from one location to another.
- Consider the road classes and the maximum speed limits permitted or likely on these roads. Think about how the various roads might affect your journey, fuel consumption, rest stops etc.

- On a city map, identify one-way streets.
- Use a map to find other useful information such as rest stops or places for refuelling or getting something to eat.
- Call AA Road Watch and check for traffic updates for a planned journey.
- Look in the newspaper for traffic advisories and then check on the web for traffic information for an unfamiliar area.

And when on the road...
- If using GPS and RDS navigation systems, read the owner's manual to learn how to use them before setting out on a journey.
- Do not allow the GPS to distract you from the driving task.
- Remember to allow extra time for taking rest stops and breaks when travelling long distance or when using an unfamiliar route.

Lesson 9 · Maintenance and navigation

Instruction assessment record

	Progressing	Mastered	ADI Signature	Date
Basic vehicle checks and routine maintenance				
Checking the lights	O	O		
Changing light bulbs	O	O		
Oil level	O	O		
Filling up with fuel	O	O		
Window washer fluid and coolant	O	O		
Tyre pressure and tread	O	O		
Changing a wheel	O	O		
Window wipers check/replacement	O	O		
Mirrors	O	O		
Safety belts and other safety restraints	O	O		
Seats	O	O		
Navigation				
Map use - rural	O	O		
Map use - urban	O	O		
Route planning	O	O		
Distance calculation	O	O		
Travel time estimation	O	O		
Fuel consumption estimation	O	O		

Note to ADI: When every skill has been mastered please note this by signing off lesson 9 in the training log in the centre of the book.

10

Loading, towing and driving test readiness

In this lesson we will discuss...

- Vehicle loading
- Towing a trailer
- Large or hazardous vehicles
- Independent driving and test readiness

Introduction

Freedom of mobility and the ability to transport items big and small is a wonderful asset and just like all other aspects of driving there is potential risk involved if it is not managed properly. Everything you carry inside, on top of or tow behind your vehicle must be properly secured to prevent it becoming a lethal projectile in the event of a sudden stop. Whether its passengers, pets or parcels take the time to make sure they are secure and will not create a dangerous blind spot that could obscure your view.

Vehicle loading

Internal loading

As the driver it is your responsibility to ensure that the vehicle is not overloaded and that all passengers and items carried in the vehicle are properly secured.

- Stow and secure loose items properly to protect the vehicle's occupants.
- Never place items on the dashboard or over airbags.
- Ensure that luggage or cargo storage does not obstruct the drivers view by creating extra blind spots that hinder the driver's observations.
- When carrying articles in the main seating area, stow them as low down as possible or secure them with a seatbelt or another tie-down mechanism.
- Where possible, secure articles in the vehicle's boot.
- Most car boots have tie down rings or other mechanisms to make transporting items or cargo more secure.

- Hatch backs and estate cars usually have a cargo net to prevent cargo and/or pets from shifting dangerously forward in the event of a sudden stop.
- Cargo nets are very good for securing items but they must be properly positioned and attached to be effective.
- For larger loads, consider using a roof box or trailer.
- Overloading can seriously affect vehicle balance, how the vehicle handles and how safe it is on the road.

A few minutes leaning how to use the cargo securing mechanisms in your vehicle is time well spent.

Loading a roof rack or roof box

When transporting large loads one alternative is to use a roof rack. Items carried on a roof rack or in a roof box must be properly secured.

- Before using the roof rack, make sure it is securely attached to the vehicle.
- Use straps or good rope with well-tied knots to secure items onto the rack.
- After travelling a short distance, stop and check the security of the load, because loads often settle or move in transit. Secure the load again if necessary.
- Loads on roof racks are exposed to intense wind pressure, so any waterproof covering must be securely fastened down.
- Larger items that overhang the front or rear of the vehicle should, in addition to being secured to the roof rack, also be secured to the tie-down points under the front/rear bumpers to prevent wind lift.
- Mark extra long or overhanging items with a red flag to warn other road users.

- As the driver you are responsible for any damage caused by items that fall from your roof rack, be sure to secure all items well.
- Only stop to retrieve lost items from the road if it is safe to do so, otherwise phone the Gardaí to report any items lost from roof racks or trailers. The Gardaí can then remove it safely and prevent the item from becoming a hazard to other motorists.
- Never stop on a motorway to retrieve lost cargo. Get off the motorway at the next exit and call the Gardaí.
- Loaded vehicles use more fuel than regular driving, remember to factor this in when planning longer trips.

Adjusting tyre pressure, lights and driving style

When transporting extra heavy loads of people or cargo:

- Increase the tyre pressure to ensure correct traction and control. Check the owner's manual or pressure chart located in the vehicle for the correct pressure.
- Adjust the vehicle's headlights with the headlight levelling switch to suit the load.

- Take extra care when driving a laden vehicle. It takes longer to stop and longer to build up speed.
- Slow down and corner more gently.

Carrying heavier loads, whether passengers or cargo, affects how the vehicle handles. An adjustment in driving speed and style is required to accommodate for the change in vehicle control and balance that the extra weight creates.

Responsibility for passengers

The driver is responsible for the security of everyone in the vehicle. Unrestrained passengers have the potential to do massive damage in the event of a sudden stop or impact.

- Adults can be independently penalised for not wearing safety belts in your vehicle, insist that all of your passengers wear the proper restraint correctly to protect yourself and your passengers.

- As a driver you are directly responsible for ensuring that all passengers under 17 are securely restrained in child safety seats or with the appropriate safety belts.

144

- Take time to study the correct procedure for fitting and securing child safety restraints before using them.
- Rear-facing infant seats must not be used in the front seat of vehicles with active front air bags. It is safest to install all child seats in the rear.
- Installing an extra mirror will allow you to keep an eye on children in the back.

Securing pets

It is dangerous to travel with unrestrained pets in the vehicle.

- Unsecured pets are an unnecessary distraction for the driver.
- Unrestrained pets can become deadly missiles in the event of a sudden stop or impact.

- Most vehicles have luggage tie-down points in the boot or rear. Use these to attach a dog's lead or to secure a cat's box.
- If a pet is secured inside the vehicle, it won't be able to dash out onto the road when you open the door at the end of the journey. This is safer for the pet and for other drivers.

Towing a trailer

Attaching a trailer

Fully licensed drivers are legally entitled to use and tow small trailers behind their vehicle but before doing so it is important to be capable of using the trailer safely. Having the ability to tow a trailer can be a wonderful asset. Use this opportunity to discuss the correct procedure for attaching and towing a trailer, even if it is not possible to demonstrate how to use a trailer at

this time, you should at least know the following for future reference.

- Before hitching up a trailer, make sure that it is correctly balanced. The weight should be evenly placed over the axle.
- The laden weight of the trailer must not exceed the vehicle's towing capacity. The towing capacity can be found in the owner's manual.

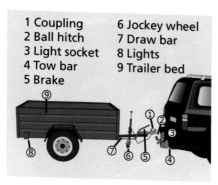

1 Coupling
2 Ball hitch
3 Light socket
4 Tow bar
5 Brake
6 Jockey wheel
7 Draw bar
8 Lights
9 Trailer bed

- In general the weight of the trailer should not exceed 85% of the weight of the vehicle.
- Depending on the driver's licence, the combined weight of the vehicle and trailer may not exceed certain specified weight. Details found in the rules of the road for example: EB licence ≤750kg; EC1 ≤12,000kg.
- Ensure even weight distribution so that when coupled to the vehicle the trailer is in line with the tow hitch.
- The trailer must not pull up or push down the back of the vehicle.
- Hitch the trailer to the vehicle by releasing and then securing the locking mechanism once the hitch is in place. Make sure it is secure.
- Retract the jockey wheel and secure it in the up position.
- Secure a breakaway cable to both the vehicle and the trailer.

- Attach the lights and registration plate and make sure the indicators and lights are working correctly.
- Adjust the headlight level of the towing vehicle as necessary to account for the extra weight.
- Check the trailer's braking system where one is fitted.
- Check the trailer's tyre pressure and treads.
- On long journeys, carry a spare wheel or a chemical inflator.
- When the trailer is used infrequently, check the wheel bearings for adequate grease.

Tips for loading a trailer safely

- Check that the load on the trailer is securely tied down in more than one place. It should not move to the sides, forwards or backwards.
- Boats and other tapered or irregularly-shaped loads should be secured at the narrowest point or secured in such a way that the ties will not slip to the narrowest point and come loose. Securing two tie-down straps together across the wider part of the load can help prevent slippage from the wide part to the narrower part.

- Once the load and the trailer are secured, travel a short distance and then pull over in a safe place to check all tie downs again for settling and loosening.
- When towing a caravan, ensure that all windows, doors and vents are closed. Check that all fuel supplies (e.g., gas bottles) are turned off and well secured.

Adjusting driving style when towing

Towing a trailer affects the towing vehicle's stability and control. When towing be sure to allow for a larger turning circle, a greater stopping distance and more time to build up speed.

- Take extra care when towing and manoeuvring a trailer.
- Practice in a quiet area until you feel comfortable.
- Check mirrors and blind spots. If necessary, attach a mirror extension. When driving, use the mirrors frequently to check the trailer and other traffic.
- Before beginning a manoeuvre, remember that trailers and loads can affect your ability to see clearly.
- Be aware of the extra weight, length and width. You will require a larger turning area and a greater stopping distance. Brake earlier than usual.

- Allow three times more time/distance for overtaking.
- Travel in the left lane at all times unless the way is blocked.
- The maximum speed limit for towing trailers is 80 km/h or less on minor roads.
- Take extra care and/or avoid towing a trailer in high winds.
- Be considerate and allow other traffic to pass if you are causing a tailback.
- If the trailer begins to 'snake', slow down by easing off the accelerator. Allow the steering wheel to 'twitch' a little. Do not use the brakes to slow down. Do not try to correct the movement by zigzagging or by making sharp steering corrections.
- Never try to accelerate out of a shaking motion.
- Towing uses more fuel than regular driving, remember to factor this in when planning longer trips.
- Towing a trailer for a long distance requires heightened concentration and usually extends the length of journey time, plan extra rest stops accordingly.

Large or hazardous vehicles

Restricted vision

- When driving near an oversized vehicle, choose a position that will enable the driver to see you. This usually means keeping well back.
- In general, if you can't see the bus or truck's mirrors, the driver won't be able to see you.

- Drivers of buses, trucks and other large vehicles may not be able to see what is directly in front of them; close beside them; or for a considerable distance behind them. Stay out of these areas when possible or clear them quickly if you must enter.
- When reversing, large vehicles are required to make a sound signal as a warning. However, it is not safe to rely on sound alone. Observe the vehicle's movements and tail lights.

- Never enter the area inside of a larger vehicle's turning circle when they are preparing to make a turn, stay out of the area on the left hand side of a truck indicating left.

Following large vehicles

- Stay well back to get a better view of the road ahead
- Avoid getting hit by dirt or spray from a large vehicle by staying well back.
- Adjust driving to allow a greater safe gap when following large vehicles. Trucks and buses require a greater stopping distance than cars.
- Leave as much space as possible when passing or being passed by a large vehicle. Be prepared to be buffeted by wind after passing.
- Fast moving large vehicles create an inward suction of air flow as they move, lighter vehicles can

get sucked towards the larger vehicle if they pass too close in either direction; avoid loss of control by leaving plenty of lateral space.

Loading and unloading

Be considerate of the needs of larger and commercial vehicles:

- Anticipate when commercial carriers may need to stop or unload their cargo.

- Don't park too close to a commercial vehicle that may need room to unload goods or passengers.
- When passing a large vehicle that has stopped, leave room to allow for doors that swing outwards or for personnel to walk around the vehicle.
- Being considerate and allowing buses to re-enter the traffic flow helps the traffic move better for everyone.

- Park well back from vehicles that require extra room for disabled persons to embark and disembark.

Large vehicles and corners

- Leave enough room for large vehicles to get around corners.
- Large vehicles may need to pull over to the right to make a left turn or to the left to make a right turn.
- Never pass a large vehicle on the inside when it is attempting to manoeuvre.
- Large vehicles turning into minor roads or commercial areas may need to approach the turn from the other side of the road. Be prepared to stop to accommodate their needs.
- Move over if necessary to accommodate a large vehicle if it is having difficulty in attempting to join a minor road that you are on.

- Do not attempt to pull out of a junction in the shadow of a large vehicle as it is turning in, other vehicles may be overtaking the large vehicle as it negotiates the turn and fail to see you.

- Leave extra room when pulling out from a junction when a large vehicle is approaching, heavy vehicles take longer to slow and to stop than cars.

Independent driving and test readiness

During a relaxed drive discuss driving competence, driving test readiness and general preparedness for independent driving. When you feel ready and adequately prepared for a driving test use the test sheet in the training record section of the book to make a critical assessment. At the end of the assessment have a frank discussion with your instructor, identify weak areas and discuss ways of eliminating them. Do another assessment after remedial work if necessary.

To obtain a full driving licence, drivers are expected to be able to demonstrate that they have the requisite knowledge, skills and appropriate behaviour to use the roads in a safe and courteous manner. During the driving test, the applicant's driving competence and ability will be tested in the following areas:

1 Knowledge of rules of the road and vehicle checks.
2 Position of the vehicle when driving.
3 Taking proper observation.
4 Reacting properly and promptly to hazards.
5 Proper use of mirrors in good time and before signalling.
6 Allowing sufficient clearance when passing and when overtaking.
7 Giving correct signals in good time.
8 Motorcycles.*
9 Courtesy when driving.
10 Alighting with care.
11 Making reasonable progress and avoiding undue hesitancy.
12 Making proper use of vehicle controls.
13 Speed adjustments.
14 Compliance with traffic controls.
15 Yielding right of way as required.
16 Competent reversing.
17 Competent turnabouts.
18 Competent parking.

* These numbers correspond to item numbers on the driver test report form, note that number 8 only applies to motorcycle tests. A copy of a driving test report form can be found in the appendix of this book and this is how the tester uses it:

1(a) Knowledge of rules of the road.
You will be asked 18 questions on regulations regarding; road signs, road marking, right of way, headlights, traffic lights and pedestrian crossings.

1(b) Vehicle checks.
The tester will check that the vehicle is fully legal, road worthy and compliant, that it has all relevant tax, NCT, insurance discs and 'L' plates displayed correctly. You must be able to check and identify the functions of all the instruments and controls in the vehicle. The tester will ask you to verbally explain how to perform technical checks on any 3 of the following: the tyres, the lights, the indicators, the engine oil, the coolant, the windscreen washer, the steering, the brakes and the horn. You must be able to open and secure the bonnet correctly if asked to do so.

2 Position of the vehicle when driving.
During the test you are expected to drive reasonably close to the left-hand side of the road, mid-way between the central dividing line and the left-hand kerb or mid-lane between the lines on a multi lane road. When following other vehicles, always drive at a safe distance from the vehicle in front.

3 Taking proper observation.
Remember to take proper observation before moving off, overtaking, changing lane, at junctions, roundabouts and when turning.

4 Reacting properly and promptly to hazards.
You must demonstrate awareness and be able to read the road ahead, to anticipate and react in an appropriate manner to potential hazards.

5 Proper use of mirrors in good time and before signalling.
The tester will be looking for proper use of mirrors before moving off, overtaking, changing lanes, at roundabouts, and when turning, slowing and stopping.

6   Allowing sufficient clearance when passing and when overtaking.
Throughout the test, the tester will be checking to ensure that you have allowed sufficient clearance from pedestrians, cyclists, stationary vehicles, traffic and other objects.

7   Giving correct signals in good time.
Be sure to signal in good time before; moving off, overtaking, changing lanes, roundabouts, turning and stopping. During the test you may be asked to demonstrate proper use of hand signals.

8   See note above re motorcycles.

9   Courtesy when driving.
The tester will be looking for signs of courteous driving, for example: in slow moving traffic allowing oncoming vehicles to turn right or where appropriate allowing vehicles to emerge from private property.

10   Alighting with care.
Before getting out of the vehicle be sure to check that the hand brake is engaged, that the ignition is switched off and that correct observations are taken before you open the doors to alight.

11   Making reasonable progress and avoiding undue hesitancy.
Throughout the driving test the tester will expect you to make reasonable progress when; moving off, on the straight, overtaking, at junctions, at roundabouts, turning, changing lanes and at traffic lights.

12   Making proper use of vehicle controls.
The tester will be making continual assessments for the proper use of the: accelerator, clutch, gears, footbrake, steering and the secondary controls.

13   Speed adjustments.
Appropriate speed adjustments will need to be made to suit; the road and traffic conditions, roundabouts, junctions, turning and traffic controls.

14   Compliance with traffic controls.
The tester will be checking for compliance with: traffic lights, road signs, road markings, pedestrian crossings, school wardens, Gardaí, bus lanes, tram lanes and cycle lanes.

15 **Yielding right of way as required.**
Remember to yield the right of way as required; while moving off, overtaking, changing lane, at junctions, at roundabouts and when turning.

16 **Competent reversing.**
An assessment of your ability to reverse in a competent manner while making the best possible observations and allowing the right of way as required will be made.

17 **Competent turnabouts.**
Your competence, observations and ability to turn the vehicle around on the road, while allowing the right of way as required, will be assessed during the test.

18 **Competent parking.**
During or at the end of the driving test you will be asked to park the vehicle, this should be done competently, legally and with good observations.

When you can demonstrate competence in all areas you are ready to book your driving test. Once you have booked your test, use the time leading up to your test date to get as much practice as possible. Practice will help to build driving confidence and experience, the better prepared you are for the driving test the more confident and less anxious you will feel on the test day.

Lesson 10 · Loading, towing & driving test readiness

Instruction assessment record

	Progressing	Mastered	ADI Signature	Date
Vehicle loading				
Internal loading	○	○		
Loading a roof rack or roof box	○	○		
Adjusting tyre pressure, lights, driving	○	○		
Responsibility for passengers	○	○		
Securing pets	○	○		
Towing a trailer				
Attaching a trailer	○	○		
Loading a trailer	○	○		
Adjusting driving style when towing	○	○		
Large or hazardous vehicles				
Allowing for restricted vision of HGV	○	○		
Following large vehicles	○	○		
Consideration for loading / unloading	○	○		
Large vehicles and corners	○	○		

Note:

Use the test readiness check sheet in the training record section

	Progressing	Mastered	ADI Signature	Date
Driver readiness				
For driving test	○	○		
For independent driving	○	○		
For carrying passengers	○	○		

Note to ADI: When every skill has been mastered please note this by signing off lesson 10 in the training log in the centre of the book.

Training record

1 When you have sufficient ability in all of the skills in a lesson, your ADI should complete the instruction assessment record and the appropriate boxes in the instruction log. This will allow you to track your progress and to proceed to the corresponding practice session with your mentor.

2 When you and your mentor feel that you have mastered the skills listed on the practice session check-list, use the corresponding practice log boxes to record and track your progress. This will let the ADI know you have completed the practice session and that you are ready to progress to the next driving lesson.

3 When all of the driving lessons and practice sessions have been completed and you can routinely demonstrate competence in all of the essential skills, your ADI can use the independent driving and test readiness sheet to record and validate your progress.

Instruction log

Learners name			
Lesson number	**Date completed**	**Location**	**ADI signature**
LESSON 1			
LESSON 2			
LESSON 3			
LESSON 4			
LESSON 5			
LESSON 6			
LESSON 7			
LESSON 8			
LESSON 9			
LESSON 10			

Practice log

Learners name			
Session number	**Date completed**	**Location**	**ADI signature**
SESSION **1**			
SESSION **2**			
SESSION **3**			
SESSION **4**			
SESSION **5**			
SESSION **6**			
SESSION **7**			
SESSION **8**			
SESSION **9**			
SESSION **10**			

Independent driving and test readiness

ADI must initial each skill to verify competence	ADI Initials	Date
Rules of the road		
Vehicle checks: fluids; oil; water; coolant; tyres; lights/signals; controls; steering; brakes; horn		
Vehicle positioning when: on the straight; on bends; in traffic lanes; at roundabouts; when turning left/right; stopping; following traffic		
Observation when: moving off; overtaking; changing lanes; at intersections/roundabouts; turning		
Hazard perception and reaction		
Use of mirrors when: moving off; on the straight; turning; at all types of junctions; slowing and stopping		
Clearance when overtaking: pedestrians and cyclists; other vehicles stationary/moving		
Signals when: moving off; driving; turning; stopping		
Driving courtesy		
Making reasonable progress		
Proper use of vehicle controls		
Appropriate speed adjustments		
Traffic controls compliance		
Giving way as required		
Reversing competently		
Turning around/turnabouts		
Parking competently: parallel, angle, perpendicular		
Alighting safely		

_____   **is competent and ready to apply**
learners name   **for the driving test**

_____   _____
ADI signature   ADI full name

_____   _____
ADI registration number   date

Practice

Introduction

Being an effective mentor

Learning to drive is one of the most important milestones on the journey to maturity but it can be a dangerous one. It is essential for new drivers to seek professional help to prepare for the complexities of modern roads. Along with professional driving instruction, parents and guardians can provide supervised driving sessions that encourage the new driver to practice the techniques and skills learned in formal lessons. Planned practice sessions with a mentor give the inexperienced driver a low stress opportunity to gain confidence – free from any passenger or journey related pressures.

Teaming up for success

Mentored practice sessions are essential in helping new drivers gain valuable driving experience. Although driving skills and techniques are initially taught by the driving instructor, it's your job, as a mentor, to conduct good driving practice sessions that reinforce learning, build competence and foster good driving behaviour.

As parent or mentor you are the one who cares most about how safe and capable your new driver is. That's why we've designed this mentor's guide and practice log-book – to give you the skills necessary to be an effective and caring mentor. You'll get an insight into the complex nature of the learning process and you'll also find plenty of tips and guidance that driving professionals have accumulated from years of experience. Our aim is to help you to avoid the pitfalls that non-professional instructors often encounter in the early stages of accompanying a learner driver.

The practice sessions you conduct with your new driver will serve them well into the future. Your commitment and participation may also have the added benefit of helping to sharpen and improve *your own* driving skills and behaviour.

It is important that your practice sessions complement and reinforce the learning that has taken place with the professional driving instructor. Should you find that your way of driving seems to be at odds with something that the new driver has learned during a formal lesson, check the instructor's section of this book or contact the driving instructor for clarification.

Forming good habits

Given the volume and speed of traffic on today's roads, it's not enough to rely merely on trial and error or chance experience to prepare new drivers for a lifetime of safe driving. Drivers need knowledge, skill and practice to form good driving habits. Leaving new drivers to learn from the environment or from their peers is a mistake. The first eighteen months of driving and the six months after gaining a full driving licence are statistically the most dangerous periods of a driver's life. Many young people mistakenly equate the skill of controlling the car with the skill of good driving. Left to their own devices, the new driver will typically fall foul of an array of bad habits in the first couple of years of driving. Our road system is a harsh teacher, often giving the test before the lesson, and a new driver will not get away with bad habits as easily as an experienced driver might. As a mentor, your task is to provide guidance and encouragement during this vulnerable period, to help shape the good driving habits that will stand to the new driver not just in the immediate future but for years to come.

Gaining a full driving licence versus driving for life

The driving test is designed to allow new drivers to demonstrate that they know the rules of the road, have adequate control over the vehicle and can carry out basic manoeuvring skills – such as turning, negotiating traffic and parking. The tester doesn't expect perfect performance and will make allowances for the nervousness of the new driver. The tester expects the driver to be able to understand road signs, signals and road markings, and to be able to relate to other road users and traffic situations.

However, the road test only covers basic driving, and passing the test does not necessarily make a new driver completely safe or capable of coping with the many and varied situations that they'll encounter in a lifetime of driving. Many tragic road crashes have occurred because of overconfidence on the part of newly qualified drivers and their mentors, who assume that once the full licence is obtained all the learning is done.

The inexperienced driver may appear confident and in control but the reality is that he or she knows just enough to get by. As long as nothing unusual happens or nothing distracts them, they will probably be fine. But what happens when a problem arises? By working together as a team, you can guide the new driver through this dangerous period. You can share timely tips and reminders. Your presence, patience and guidance will reassure the new driver and relieve them of the pressures that result from task-oriented driving and from the peer pressures stemming from the desire to impress friends.

Principles of good driving

Attitude

Attitude is the single most important element in determining whether a driver will use their knowledge and skills to be a co-operative or a competitive road user. Having a good attitude will help shape good driving behaviour. By taking the time to mentor your new driver, you are demonstrating a positive attitude to driver education and road safety. Remember that you are the role model: demonstrate and encourage good behaviour every time you drive and the new driver will follow suit.

Time and space

What does it take to be a good driver? It's not just a matter of being cautious or experienced. The defining characteristic of a good driver is how he or she manages time and space to mitigate the risk involved in driving. (In fact, time and space awareness starts in the passenger seat, even before learning how to drive.) New drivers should practice scanning ahead to a distance 12 seconds – a lead time that allows you to adjust your speed and position well before an observation becomes a hazard.

The two-second following distance rule is especially helpful. It defines the minimum distance you should leave between your vehicle and those ahead of you when the roads are dry. Practice maintaining this two-second gap by counting the seconds between the instant the vehicle ahead passes a fixed point, such as a lamppost, and the instant you pass the same point. Extend the gap as conditions deteriorate. It takes approximately four seconds to come to a full stop at speeds in excess of 60km/h. Again, you can practice estimating this distance by counting to four seconds from the instant you pass a fixed point. Realising how far it takes to come to a stop is vital to grasping the concept of the 'safe gap'.

Getting the most out of your practice sessions

Planning and practicing

- Good driving doesn't come about naturally, it is a product of good training and practice. To make the most of your driving practice sessions, plan ahead, review the practice session and think about what you wish to achieve.
- Select a suitable location before you begin.
- Don't make any assumptions about what the learner knows. Go through the steps set out in this manual in a logical sequence.
- Emphasise the co-ordination of the manoeuvre. New drivers tend to concentrate on one aspect of a skill while neglecting others – for example, forgetting to check the mirrors because they're concentrating on the clutch and acceleration pedals.
- Start off in a quiet area free of traffic pressures with plenty of open space to manoeuvre and make mistakes – an empty car park, for example. Once the driver is comfortable with the basic stopping, starting, turning and control skills, then you can move onto a quiet road to begin the process of learning street sense.
- Encourage good lane and road positioning to make it easier for other road users to anticipate what the learner driver is going to do.
- It is important to help new drivers understand how their vehicle movements and road positions are interpreted by other road users. Your feedback is essential in getting the new driver to understand this – and, in turn, to learn how to interpret the signals communicated by other road users.

Procedural training and practice

The Steer Clear system of driver education and driving instruction uses procedural training to teach new drivers the correct techniques when learning to drive. During practice sessions it is very important that these procedures are reinforced so that they become the natural habits of the new driver. Instilling good driving procedures from the beginning enables the driver to store these procedures deep in the memory so that they can automatically be retrieved and used when called upon to do so both now and in the future. Procedural training is particularly important in emergency situations because it enables the driver to automatically respond appropriately.

Choosing the right location

When you commence the road practice sessions, start on quiet roads or streets with little traffic, if possible, choose an area with easy curves or turns. Heavy traffic or pedestrian movement will overwhelm a new driver because they are distracting and may lead to unpredictable situations and dangers. Taking a random route through an unfamiliar area can also spoil a practice session if the new driver faces a sudden or unexpected problem for which they were completely unprepared – a school at going home time for example. The added stress of not knowing what to expect can cause undue anxiety and even lead to the new driver freezing up and losing their ability to respond to the situation.

Communication

Give directions clearly and well in advance. Too much talk is a distraction and can be very confusing to the learner. Use consistent terminology – for example, if you use 'hand brake', don't say 'parking brake' next time; if you normally say 'accelerator', don't switch to 'gas'.

Avoid using the word 'right' to confirm a command – for example, 'At the next turn take a left, right?' Refrain from using hand gestures because they can distract the driver.

Encourage the early use of signals to let other road users know your intentions in plenty of time. Finally, discussing and deciding what you are going to do and where you are going to do it *before* you begin each practice session will reduce stress and help avoid uncomfortable situations.

Simple to complex

Don't give the learner too many tasks at once. Remember that even a basic left turn involves a lot of concentration and steps for the new driver: checking mirrors, checking blind spots, signalling, braking, changing gear, wheel turning and recovery. It's asking a lot of the new driver to master all these at once; better to introduce braking and steering first and then work in the other elements progressively. Start in low-stress environments and build to more complex situations. Keep track of the driving situations that the new driver experiences and gradually work in more of the different types of situations that are typical of regular driving.

Risk management

Think and look ahead to anticipate possible problems so that you can cue the new driver to slow or brake in plenty of time. Last-second warnings can make the learner panic and choose an inappropriate response. While it's important to remind the driver of checks and signals it's important that *you* don't become a distraction. Good pre-planning and choice of practice location will help keep the risk down. No matter what, try not to get anxious or too excited while you are mentoring because this will be readily apparent to the new driver and will make it difficult to concentrate.

New drivers typically overestimate their own capabilities and underestimate the risk of driving situations. The risk is highest when the gap between the drivers capabilities and the driving task demand is widest. For example: driving in dry weather with very little traffic around (small gap) versus driving in bad weather with lots of traffic and pedestrian activity (big gap). The new driver has the same capabilities but the task demand has significantly increased, the gap has widened therefore risk has increased. Use your knowledge and experience to help the new driver to identify the hazards and risks more realistically and to adjust their driving and safety margins accordingly.

Positive reinforcement

Complementing the driver when he or she does something well will build confidence and be reassuring. Short comments like 'good positioning' or 'good turn' may be all it takes. Negative comments are very easy to make but they seriously undermine confidence and performance. When a new driver makes a mistake, they may not realise what the problem was. It's better not to get into a discussion about it while driving, highlight the error but keep the discussion for the end of the session review. Discuss the problems and the solutions rationally. Remember to keep your composure – even if the mistakes were bad, making a fuss, you will just undermine the learner's confidence which will have a knock-on effect in the next practice session.

Try not to come across as the expert on everything. We all have room for improvement, especially in the complex task of driving. By having a willingness to learn you will be demonstrating a good attitude and you'll be an excellent example to the new driver.

Sloppy habits to look out for

We all have them: the naughty little habits that begin to creep in once we get comfortable with driving. However, left unchecked these bad habits build up and if we allow them to accumulate, they can become a time bomb – especially in newly-certified drivers. The result, sooner or later, will be a crash. Here are some typical bad habits:

- Lack of courtesy for other road users and their needs.
- Not bothering or forgetting to signal in adequate time.
- Cutting the corner and making sloppy right turns.
- Forgetting or omitting to check the blind spot over the shoulder before changing lanes.
- Not leaving sufficient space when following traffic – ignoring the two-second rule.
- Failing or forgetting to reduce speed when approaching a potential hazard.
- Erratic or sudden changes of speed or direction that catch other road users off guard.
- Reversing before properly checking behind the vehicle.
- Failing to come to a complete stop behind a stop line.
- Encroaching into red-box areas reserved for cyclists.
- Coasting around a corner – where you should have stopped.
- Continuing or accelerating through amber lights when it would have been safer to stop.
- Increasing disregard for or laxity towards speed limits, road signs and markings.
- Letting your attention get diverted from the task of driving by distractions such as mobile phones.

- Neglecting to pay heed to or adapting sloppy pre-driving checks and preparations.
- Parking for your own convenience without regard to the needs of others.

Our collective responsibility

With the freedom of being able to drive comes a great responsibility.

Most of this responsibility rests with the driver but all of those around a new driver also have responsibilities: we must support them and not tempt them to take chances or bend the rules. Using a new driver as a chauffeur just to ferry you home from a night on the town or allowing them to take groups of friends out to drive in the early hours of the morning is a recipe for disaster. As one of the primary stakeholders, you have a duty to care for your loved one. When it comes to driving, setting down reasonable rules and instilling discipline may be the best gift you can give. The time that you spend and the interest you take in the wellbeing of your learner driver during these first vulnerable months and early years of driving will benefit them for a lifetime. There is plenty of evidence to show that young and inexperienced drivers accompanied by their peers are far more likely to be involved serious road traffic incidents then those that are accompanied by mature mentors. By taking the time to accompany your new driver you are also providing valuable protection.

Finally we wish you every success and trust that your efforts and interest in helping your new driver to become a good driver will be well rewarded and enjoyable and will stand to you both for years to come!

Go n'eiri an bothair libh!

1

Preparing to drive

In this session we will practise...

1A ■ Approaching the vehicle, preparing to drive, starting and stopping
1B ■ Moving off, stopping, steering and using reference points

Introduction

This and all subsequent practice sessions follow the same simple-to-complex progress route, don't skip too quickly over the easy bits because learning the correct procedures at every level is well worth while and will stand to you later. Learning the correct techniques from the beginning builds a solid foundation. Anticipating and preventing problems before they begin is one of the key elements to safe driving and good pre-driving procedures are essential. Make a conscious effort to practice these skills every time you begin a practice session and they will soon become habit, serving you well for years to come.

1A Approaching the vehicle, preparing to drive, starting and stopping

Skills

- Approaching the vehicle.
- Preparing to drive – the cockpit drill.
- Spatial awareness and blind spots.
- Starting and stopping the engine.
- Leaving the vehicle.

Ideal location

- Conduct this session in a quiet place (e.g. an empty car park) free from distractions and with no other passengers. If you can arrange it, setting up cones or other markers will help you to get a better feel for the blind spots around the vehicle.

Recommended practice time

- Two 40-minute practice sessions. Remember that this is a guideline. You may find that you need more or less time, depending on how you progress.

Additional reading
Instruction Guide
Lesson 1

Approaching the vehicle

- When approaching the car, check all around for obstructions, debris or other potential hazards.

- Quickly check the car to make sure that the tyres and general bodywork are sound, and that the lights and windows are clean and clear.
- When getting into a car from the roadside, wait for a safe gap in traffic, face and observe traffic at all times, get in and close the door without delay.
- Once inside, put the key into the ignition but don't turn it on until you have completed the full cockpit drill.

The cockpit drill

- Adjust the seat position to a comfortable height and distance so that your feet can easily reach the pedals and fully depress them.
- Select a sitting height that gives you the best view out the windscreen, to the rear and to either side of the vehicle.

- The seat back should support all along the length of the spine. Adjust the head restraint so that the centre of it lines up with the middle of the back of your head. These simple adjustments will help to protect the spine from injury in the event of a crash and are vital for safe driving.
- Adjust the safety belt to fit snugly over your shoulder and across your chest and lap. Where possible, adjust the height for comfort and for maximum energy dissipation during braking and in the event of an impact.
- Discuss and demonstrate how to use the vehicle's other safety restraints for protecting passengers and cargo.
- Check and adjust the driving position relative to the steering wheel. The arms should be slightly bent and the wrists at a comfortable angle. Where air bags are fitted, leave at least 10 inches between the wheel and the chest; angle the steering wheel so that if the air bag is deployed, it will hit the chest rather than the face. Leave enough room for your knees, both during driving and when getting in and out of the vehicle.
- Check that the gear lever is in neutral position and that it's within comfortable reach.

- With the right foot on the brake pedal, check the locking mechanism and ratchet on the parking brake. Re-engage the parking brake and then release the foot brake.
- Ensure that all doors are fully closed and that there are no loose objects that could become projectiles in the event of a sudden stop.

Spatial awareness

- Before beginning to drive, it is essential to have a good sense of the size of the vehicle and of the areas around it that the driver cannot see during normal driving.
- Sit in the driving seat while your mentor remains outside. Starting from the front bumper, ask the mentor to walk away from the car until you can see their shoes on the ground. Place a marker at that point. Repeat this process all around the car. When you have completed a full circle, get out and look at the very large and uneven area between the vehicle and the markers. This is the area that you can't see from the driving position. It is important to be aware of this 'blind' area when driving.

- Now get back into the driving position, look into the mirrors, and then adjust your seating position to eliminate as many of these blind spots as possible.
- When sitting comfortably in the driving position, the rear-view mirror should frame the entire rear window and serve as the primary mirror for seeing what's behind the vehicle.
- Adjust the right-hand side mirror by leaning towards it. You should be able to see a small part of the vehicle's side reflected in the mirror. Set the left mirror by leaning towards the centre console; again, adjust the mirror until you can just see the side of the vehicle. To reduce glare from the lights of vehicles behind you, adjust the mirrors so that they reflect equal amounts of road and sky. These settings reduce the overlap between the rear-view and side-view mirrors and give better coverage of the adjacent lanes and of bikes travelling between lanes.

- **Note:** In vehicles with restricted rear-view mirror visibility, such as in a van or when towing, re-adjust the side mirrors so that you can just about see the sides of the vehicle from the normal driving position.
- Ask you mentor to stand close to the vehicle in a position just behind the drivers seat to demonstrate how easy it is to miss a vehicle or person in your blind spots. Spend time identifying all the blind spots from your vehicle. Check the mirrors and over the shoulder so that you realise the benefit of the 'lifesaver' check.
- Check that all the instruments and driving lights function properly before you start driving.

Starting and stopping the engine

- Check that the gear position is in neutral. Place the key into the ignition in the (O) off position. Rotating clockwise one position (I) disengages the steering lock. The next position (II) activates the ignition and turns on the warning lights as a start-up check automatically commences. The fourth and final position (III) activates the starter motor. When the motor starts, release the key and allow it to spring

back to the (II) position to keep the engine running.
- **Note:** Diesel engines require a pause at position (II) during the ignition sequence to allow the glow-plugs to warm up sufficiently to create the ignition. The glow plug indicator light will go out when they are ready, then you may proceed to the next position.
- Modern fuel injection vehicles do not require any acceleration during the starting sequence, but you should give the engine time to settle and allow all the warning lights to go out before you move off.
- Check all around the vehicle and prepare to move off, indicating if necessary. Apply the brake with your right foot, depress the clutch pedal to the floor with your left foot, and then select first gear. Keeping the left foot on the clutch, switch the right foot from the brake to the accelerator

and apply light pressure. Gently increase acceleration pressure while easing the clutch out. As you feel the biting point, release the parking brake with your right hand and you will feel the vehicle move forward.

- Repeat this process from the beginning until you can do it reasonably smoothly. Too much acceleration or releasing the clutch too quickly will cause a stall.
- Practice driving slowly straight ahead with both hands evenly gripping the steering wheel.
- Bring the vehicle to a gentle stop by easing back on the accelerator and then applying the brake gently. Just before coming to a complete stop, depress the clutch to prevent the engine from stalling.
- Practice changing gears as the speed increases. As the engine pitch changes, depress the clutch and select the next gear. When changing up to a higher gear, increase acceleration gently so that the engine power matches the new gear.
- Practice changing down gears as speed decreases.
- Applying the brake will stop the vehicle more rapidly but remember that you'll need to

depress the clutch to prevent a stall when coming to a complete stop.
- Along with concentrating on gear changes and speed, pay attention to where you are going and make small steering corrections as needed in a smooth and controlled way.

Leaving the vehicle

- Bring the vehicle to a complete stop in a safe place. Engage neutral gear and apply the parking brake.
- Remove your feet from all the pedals, turn off the engine, remove the key from the ignition and lock the steering wheel.
- Remove your safety belt and check that all windows and roof openings are closed.
- Check in the mirror and over your shoulder before opening the door.
- Get out and close and lock the doors. When exiting into a busy road, don't linger around the door area; walk to the footpath as soon as possible and keep looking out for approaching traffic.
- Check that all lights are off and that the position of the parked vehicle will not impede other road users.

1A Approaching the vehicle, preparing to drive, and starting and stopping

Check-list and log-sheet

Practice 1
Date

Practice 2
Date

Practice 3
Date

Before moving on to the next session, you should be able to demonstrate 'green light' mastery in each skill.
Use this sheet to track progress by **ticking the circles** as shown.

✓ Skill preformed with competence, consistently showing mastery
○ Skill performed correctly but driver sometimes needs prompting
○ Skill accomplished but driver sometimes forgets a check or step
○ Skill completed with some help or a prompt from the mentor
○ Skill cannot be completed or requires substantial help from mentor

○○○○○	Approaches vehicle with due care and awareness
○○○○○	Gets into car and completes cockpit drill
○○○○○	Checks and adjusts mirrors correctly
○○○○○	Checks and adjusts restraints correctly
○○○○○	Identifies and can operate all controls
○○○○○	Adopts correct seating position
○○○○○	Holds steering wheel correctly
○○○○○	Checks gear in neutral, with foot on brake, in preparation to start
○○○○○	Turns ignition key, pausing and releasing as necessary
○○○○○	Allows engine to settle before preparing to move off
○○○○○	Depresses clutch, releases brake and applies accelerator smoothly

Practice Session 1

○○○○○ Accelerates smoothly, keeping heel on floor

○○○○○ Releases clutch simultaneously and recognises biting point

○○○○○ Holds steering wheel in a balanced and controlled manner

○○○○○ Looks well ahead of vehicle

○○○○○ Can drive slowly in a reasonably straight line

○○○○○ Maintains good lane position and stays on course

○○○○○ Recognises when gear needs to be changed

○○○○○ Shifts up and down gears without stalling

○○○○○ Shifts gears and changes speed smoothly

○○○○○ Slows to a stop using deceleration and gear control

○○○○○ Applies brakes and uses clutch to come to a stop
more quickly

○○○○○ Stops and parks vehicle in preparation to exit

○○○○○ Applies parking brake, removes feet from pedals, removes
key from ignition and removes safety belt in preparation
to exit

○○○○○ Checks all windows and openings are closed and lights
are off

○○○○○ Checks mirrors and over shoulder before opening doors

○○○○○ Keeps a good look out when exiting, securing and
leaving vehicle

We have spent adequate time practising the skills from session 1A and feel competent enough to move on to the next skill-development session.

Student driver's signature

Mentor's signature

Date

1B Moving off, stopping, steering and using reference points

Skills
- Moving off.
- Handling gentle turns.
- Stopping smoothly at low and slightly higher speeds.
- Steering.
- Using reference points to judge the vehicle's position relative to the kerb and other obstacles.

Ideal location
- A wide open space, free of obstacles (such as an empty car park). If you can, place cones or other markers to define an oval 'track' for driving around.

Recommended practice time
- Three 30-minute sessions. Remember that this is a guideline. You may find that you need more or less time, depending on how you progress.

Preparing
Review what you learned in the previous practice sessions.
Refer to Lesson 1 in the Instructor's Guide.

Beginning to drive
- Drive around the outside of the practice area very slowly (about 20km/h).
- When competent, try going a little faster (30 km/h).
- Use the push-pull method of steering.
- Decrease acceleration and applying a little brake to slow down as the turn approaches.

- Gently accelerate out of the turn to overcome the effects of inertia and to bring the vehicle out of the turn with control.
- Avoid over-use of the brake and under-use of the accelerator when turning corners.
- Pass to the left and right of obstacles in different areas of the open space.
- Focus on smooth acceleration, stops, gear changes and good speed control.
- Practice smooth stops at slow speeds.
- Gently release on the brake pedal just before stopping by arching the foot and curling the toes to give a smoother stop.
- Practice smooth stopping at slightly faster speeds.

Reference points

- Practice using reference points to establish and recognise exactly where the car is positioned with respect to nearby obstacles at all times.
- Use left, right and centre reference points for determining the vehicle's location.
- Practice use of the reference points 10 or 15 times in each session.
- For each skill (e.g. for turning corners or driving straight), get out and check the position of the car relative to the kerb (or whatever boundary markers you're using). If the car is not parallel to and within a reasonable distance of the kerb, practice the skill again until your positioning improves.
- To establish the driver's-side reference point, look at the kerb over the bonnet. The kerb line should intersect the bonnet about 30cms (12") from the right-hand side of the bonnet.

Parking parallel to kerb

- To find the front reference point, drive slowly up to the kerb and look to the left and to the right. When the kerb line appears at the front edge of the side windows,

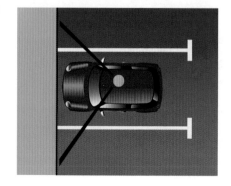

come to a stop. The vehicle should now be positioned with the front bumper approximately 10 to 16 cm back from and parallel to the kerb.

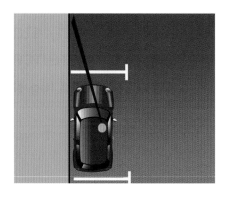

- To achieve proper passenger-side alignment, manoeuvre so that the kerb line intersects with the centre of the bonnet. When you see the kerb at this angle, the car should be positioned about 15cm from the kerb on the passenger side.

- It is worth taking the time to get out and check the position of the vehicle in relation to the road markings or to the pavement, then getting back into the car and adjusting the position as necessary until you are satisfied that the vehicle is positioned correctly. When happy with the position you should note the various reference points from the driving position for future use.

1B Moving off, stopping, steering and using reference points

Check-list and log-sheet

1B Practice 1	1B Practice 2	1B Practice 3
Date	Date	Date

Before moving on to the next session, you should be able to demonstrate 'green light' mastery in each skill.
Use this sheet to track progress by **ticking the circles** as shown.

✓ Skill preformed with competence, consistently showing mastery
○ Skill performed correctly but driver sometimes needs prompting
○ Skill accomplished but driver sometimes forgets a check or step
○ Skill completed with some help or a prompt from the mentor
○ Skill cannot be completed or requires substantial help from mentor

○○○○○ Approaches vehicle with due care and awareness
○○○○○ Gets into car and completes the cockpit drill
○○○○○ Identifies and can operate all controls in preparation for driving
○○○○○ Performs steps for moving off in correct sequence

○○○○○ Starts engine, observes all around the vehicle and signals correctly
○○○○○ Accelerates smoothly, keeping heel on floor
○○○○○ Holds steering wheel in a balanced and controlled manner
○○○○○ Looks well ahead of vehicle
○○○○○ Maintains good lane position and stays on course
○○○○○ Correctly uses push-pull method of steering

◐◑○○○   Controls vehicle through easy turns and directional changes

◑○○○○   Looks to the target area when approaching and during turns

◐◑○○○   Maintains required speed

◐◑○○○   Checks mirrors frequently and prior to braking

○◑○○○   Stops smoothly at 20km/h without locking wheels

◐◑○○○   Stops smoothly at 30km/h without locking wheels

◐◑○○○   Pulls up parallel and close to kerb on driver's side

◐◑○○○   Pulls up parallel and close to kerb on passenger side

◑◑○○○   Aligns the front bumper of the car about 15cm from the kerb

◐◑○○○   Parks and secures the vehicle before leaving it

We have spent adequate time practising the skills from Session 1B and feel competent enough to progress to the next skill-development session.

Student driver's signature

Mentor's signature

Date

When practice sessions 1A and 1B are complete be sure to record this in the training log in the blue section in the middle of the book so that the driving instructor will know that you are ready to progress to driving lesson 2.

Notes

2

Reversing

In this session we will practise...

2A ■ Reversing
2B ■ Turning around
2C ■ Maintaining proper speed and spacing

Introduction

Devoting plenty of time to practice the skills learned in lesson 2 is essential in order to become competent and fluid at reversing. You will need reversing skills when it comes to parking and tight turning manoeuvres. Good reversing is an integral part of good driving. Understanding how the vehicle pivots around a point located between the two back wheels helps you to judge how the vehicle responds to steering while reversing. Remember to take it slow, keep a good lookout and to allow ample room for the front of the vehicle to swing out further than the back.

2A Reversing

Skills
Reversing
- In a straight line.
- In a turn.

Ideal location
- An open space, a car park, or a quiet road, such as a cul-de-sac.

Recommended practice time
- Two 40-minute practice sessions. Remember that this is a guideline. You may find that you need more or less time, depending on how you progress.

Additional reading
Instruction Guide
Lesson 2

Steer Clear Driver Education Manual
Acceleration and speed control (p.215)
Steering (p.226)

RSA Rules of the Road
Reversing (p.46)

Reversing

- Choose a safe area in which to practice reversing. It may be helpful if the mentor demonstrates the correct procedure first.
- Practice controlling the steering, speed and turning rate in reverse gear.
- It is more difficult to see and to control a vehicle in reverse, so emphasise the need to manoeuvre slowly with careful use of the accelerator.
- Attempt sharp turns very slowly because reversing compromises vehicle balance.
- To avoid any difficulties with depth perception in the mirrors, start by turning around and looking in the direction in which you intend to travel.
- Shift around in the seat, hold the steering wheel at the top with the right hand and, if necessary, put the left arm behind you or over the top of your seat to improve vantage point and balance.
- Move your right hand and the steering wheel in the direction in which you wish to travel.
- Use both hands for tight manoeuvring such as reverse parking.

Reversing in a straight line

- Check that the area in which you want to reverse into is clear both prior to and during the manoeuvre.
- Put the right foot on the brake pedal, left foot on the clutch, and shift into reverse gear.
- While stationary, grip the top of the steering wheel in the centre with your right hand.
- Look over the left shoulder, shift around or swivel your hips if necessary to get a better view through the back window.
- Ease out on the clutch and brake pedals and give a small touch of acceleration to move backwards while maintaining steady control.
- Continually check all around the car throughout the manoeuvre.
- Bring the vehicle to a controlled stop at a designated place.

Turning in reverse

- Hold the steering wheel at the top with the right hand when turning to the left or with the left hand if turning to the right.

- Turn and look in the direction you intend to turn. Look through the rear window on that side of the vehicle.
- Reverse as before and once moving turn the steering wheel in the direction you want to go.
- Control the speed by careful use of the accelerator, clutch and brake pedals.
- Continually check all around throughout the manoeuvre.
- Be sure to allow room for the front of the vehicle to swing in the opposite direction to that of the turn.
- When reversing around a corner to the left, look over your left shoulder and keep the kerb visible through the top of the rear side window. This will keep the vehicle about one metre away from the kerb.

- Maintaining a one-metre margin when reversing around a corner to the right requires looking over the right shoulder and aligning the corner with the rear right wheel.

Stopping location

To stop perpendicular to and 15cm from a kerb or parking-space line, stop the vehicle when you see the kerb/line appearing in the middle of the rear left-hand side window as you look over your left shoulder. Check your position relative to the kerb by getting out to take a look. Continue practising until you achieve mastery.

Parking parallel to kerb

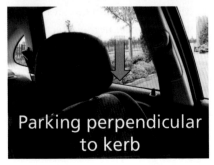

Parking perpendicular to kerb

2A Reversing

Check-list and log-sheet

2A Practice 1	2A Practice 2	2A Practice 3
Date	Date	Date

Before moving on to the next session, you should be able to demonstrate 'green light' mastery in each skill.
Use this sheet to track progress by **ticking the circles** as shown.

✓ Skill preformed with competence, consistently showing mastery
◯ Skill performed correctly but driver sometimes needs prompting
◯ Skill accomplished but driver sometimes forgets a check or step
◯ Skill completed with some help or a prompt from the mentor
◯ Skill cannot be completed or requires substantial help from mentor

Reversing in a straight line

◯◯◯◯◯ Checks all around vehicle before beginning reversing manoeuvre

◯◯◯◯◯ Correctly positions feet on brake and clutch

◯◯◯◯◯ Positions and grips right hand at top of steering wheel

◯◯◯◯◯ Turns and looks through back window to identify clear destination

◯◯◯◯◯ Selects reverse gear, eases out on clutch, pivots foot from brake to accelerator and moves off in control

◯◯◯◯◯ Maintains effective steering control

◯◯◯◯◯ Checks frequently to the front and all around

◯◯◯◯◯ Stops vehicle smoothly

◯◯◯◯◯ Brings vehicle to a stop within 10-15cm from kerb

◯◯◯◯◯ Completes the stopping manoeuvre fully before turning around

○○○○○ Uses sight line reference points to pull up parallel and close to kerb on passenger side

○○○○○ Uses correct sight line references to park perpendicular to kerb

Turning in reverse

○○○○○ Checks destination area in preparation for turn

○○○○○ Controls steering wheel with right hand in left turn

○○○○○ Controls steering wheel with left hand in right turn

○○○○○ Looks over correct shoulder through rear and side windows

○○○○○ Maintains a slow controlled speed throughout manoeuvre

○○○○○ Reverses straight back and stops at rear pivot point before commencing turn

○○○○○ Frequently checks all around during turn

○○○○○ Maintains adequate space (1m) from kerb throughout turn

○○○○○ Constantly checks direction and makes corrections

○○○○○ Brings vehicle to a complete and secure stop at a designated place

We have spent adequate time practising the skills from session 2A and feel competent enough to move on to the next skill-development session.

Student driver's signature

Mentor's signature

Date

2B Turning around

Skills
- Two-point turns.
- Three-point turns.
- U-turns.

Ideal location
- To begin with, find an open space, such as a car park; then move on to a wide road for turnabouts. Find a narrow, quiet road (such as a cul-de-sac) for practising three-point turns.

Recommended practice time
- Two 40-minute practice sessions. Remember that this is a guideline. You may find that you need more or less time, depending on how you progress.

Turnabouts

Often it is safest – and easier – to drive around the block or to a nearby roundabout or other form of intersection to turn around. But when this isn't possible, you'll need to be able to do an efficient turnabout. On a wide road a two-point turn is the most straightforward, but when space is tight a turn involving three or more points may be required.

Begin by practicing two and three – point turns in a large open area. Practice the turns at least 10–15 times until you feel competent. Draw on the skills learned previously to help in mastering these new skills. Remember to check for oncoming traffic and pedestrians and to indicate your intentions in plenty of time before commencing any manoeuvre.

Two-point turns

- Two-point turns require a wide area or a driveway to reverse into.
- Check mirrors and indicate before slowing down to make a turnabout.
- Slow down and stop just beyond the opening. Check the mirrors again and select reverse gear.
- Reverse back until you are in line with the near side of the area you're backing into.
- Turn the steering wheel in the direction of the target area and reverse into it, straightening up towards the end of the turn.
- Once in the target area, switch to first gear, check if the way is clear, indicate, and move forward slowly until you are in line with the centre line of the road. Now steer in the new direction.
- When the recovery point is reached straighten up and resume normal driving.

U-turns

- Some dual carriageways facilitate U-turns by providing a turning lane and/or a signal light. This is the safest place in which to attempt this dangerous manoeuvre.
- U-turns require a wide turning arch, so you should only attempt them in a wide road.
- Check in front and to the rear to ensure that you have plenty of time to complete the turn.
- Slow down or stop to the left of the centre median or on the left-hand side of the road.
- Indicate right and when you are sure that there's adequate time to complete the turn, move forward while sharply turning to the right.
- Turn right around 180° to face in the opposite direction.
- Check for traffic and resume normal driving.

Three-point turns

- Use the three-point turn when the turning area is narrow. You may need more than three points in a very tight space or until you've achieved proficiency.
- Pull over to the left and when it's safe to begin the manoeuvre, indicate and move forward and turn the wheel sharply to the right.
- Stop about half a metre from the opposite kerb or other obstacles.
- Change to reverse gear, make a safety check all around, and turn the steering wheel in the opposite direction (left) as you reverse backwards.

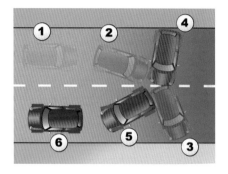

- Straighten up as the front bumper reaches the centre of the road.
- Stop and shift to first gear. When you start moving forward, turn sharply to the right.
- If it is possible to complete the turn, do so; if not, repeat the last two steps until the turn is complete.

2B Turning around
Check-list and log-sheet

2B Practice 1
Date

2B Practice 2
Date

2B Practice 3
Date

Before moving on to the next session, the learner should be able to demonstrate 'green light' level mastery in each skill. Use this sheet to track progress by **ticking the circles** as shown.

✓ Skill preformed with competence, consistently showing mastery

○ Skill performed correctly but driver sometimes needs prompting

○ Skill accomplished but driver sometimes forgets a check or step

◑ Skill completed with some help or a prompt from the mentor

● Skill cannot be completed or requires substantial help from mentor

Two-point turns

○○○○○	Checks mirrors, communicates and slows down correctly in preparation for the turn
○○○○○	Looks to target area before and during turn
○○○○○	Completes a two-point turn with good control of speed, gears and brakes
○○○○○	Steering is controlled and used smoothly only while moving
○○○○○	Observes all around before, during and on completion of the turn

U-turns

○○○○○ Selects an appropriate place to execute a U-turn

○○○○○ Checks blind spots and maintains good observation throughout manoeuvre

○○○○○ Masters a U-turn around a centre median

○○○○○ Masters U-turns in a wide road without a centre median

Three-point turns

○○○○○ Checks mirrors, communicates and slows down correctly in preparation for turn

○○○○○ Looks to target area before and during turn

○○○○○ Controls movement, direction and clearance throughout turn

○○○○○ Completes a full turnabout in three or more turning movements

○○○○○ Maintains full observation throughout turn

○○○○○ Only turns steering wheel when wheels are turning

We have spent adequate time practising the skills from session 2B and feel competent enough to move on to the next skill-development session.

Student driver's signature

Mentor's signature

Date

2C Maintaining proper speed & spacing

Skills
- Using the SIDE rule.
- Using the two-second rule to determine the following distance.
- Overtaking in built-up areas.

Ideal location
- Busy or moderately busy areas with a variety of intersections; faster-moving roadways such as dual carriageways.

Recommended practice time
- Two 40-minute practice sessions. Remember that this is a guideline. You may find that you need more or less time, depending on how you progress.

Using the SIDE rule
- Use the acronym SIDE to manage space and minimise the risk.
- **Scan** well ahead to identify open, closed or changing areas or paths of travel.
  - An open area is one where there are no obstructions or hazards.
  - A closed area is one that is occupied by another vehicle or object.
  - A changing area is one a vehicle or person is moving in or to.
- **Identify** potential risks, hazards, open areas and opportunities.
- **Decide** the best course of action and whether it is safe to progress or manoeuvre.

- **Execute** the manoeuvre, braking action, or speed/direction change.

Time and space management
- Maintaining a safe gap allows you more time and space to avoid problems.
- Space or gap adjustments become necessary when speed or conditions change.
- Space and time allow you to steer around a hazard to a safer area
- It takes less time to steer around a hazard than it does to break and stop safely.
- A constant awareness of open areas or escape routes gives

you more options should the
need arise.

- We tend to steer in the direction
  that we're looking, so if you
  spot a hazard, look towards
  the open area rather than at the
  hazard itself.

- To calculate the time gap between
  you and the vehicle ahead, count
  the seconds between the instant
  the vehicle passes a stationary
  object (such as a building) and
  the instant you pass the same
  object. Practice doing this at
  different speeds until you develop
  a feel for the appropriate gap size.
- A two-second gap allows time to
  steer out of trouble at 50km/h on
  dry roads.
- A three-second gap will allow
  steering room at 70km/h on
  dry roads.
- Four seconds provides time
  and space to steer or slow
  down enough to avoid hazards
  when travelling on dry roads
  at 100 km/h.

Passing obstructions in built-up areas

- Limit overtaking in built-up areas
  to only what is necessary.
- Practise being patient and
  accommodating. It is useful to
  overtake in a built-up area only
  when passing obstructions or
  stopped traffic that is waiting
  to turn.
- Look well ahead and anticipate
  where traffic will stop so that you
  can move lanes or position in the
  lane to pass smoothly without
  disrupting the traffic flow.
- Do not overtake in or near an
  intersection or side road.
- Watch for the movements of
  other road users that may affect
  your decision to overtake.
- Passing and overtaking is
  prohibited in areas with solid
  white lines.

2C Maintaining proper speed & spacing
Check-list and log-sheet

| 2C Practice 1 Date | 2C Practice 2 Date | 2C Practice 3 Date |

Before moving on to the next session, you should be able to demonstrate 'green light' mastery in each skill.
Use this sheet to track progress by **ticking the circles** as shown.

✓ Skill preformed with competence, consistently showing mastery
○ Skill performed correctly but driver sometimes needs prompting
◔ Skill accomplished but driver sometimes forgets a check or step
◑ Skill completed with some help or a prompt from the mentor
◉ Skill cannot be completed or requires substantial help from mentor

Intersections

○○○○○	Checks mirrors, communicates and slows down correctly in preparation for the turn
○○○○○	Looks all around intersection to identify open, closed and changing areas
○○○○○	Changes speed or lane position to allow for closed or changing areas
○○○○○	Yields to other traffic and pedestrians as required
○○○○○	Stops completely when required in the proper position
○○○○○	Checks and communicates prior to changing position or direction

Safe gaps

○○○○○	Identifies and uses targets 15–20 seconds ahead
○○○○○	Maintains a three- to four-second following gap at all times
○○○○○	Constantly assesses the three- to four-second travel path option
○○○○○	Identifies open, closed and changing areas
○○○○○	Adjusts speed and space to make best use of open areas

Overtaking in built-up areas

○○○○○	Passes and overtakes only when necessary
○○○○○	Looks well ahead to anticipate where traffic will stop/ need to be avoided
○○○○○	Changes lane or position well in advance and smoothly
○○○○○	Chooses the safest passing place
○○○○○	Only overtakes where permitted

We have spent adequate time practicing the skills from session 2C and feel competent enough to move on to the next skill-development session.

Student driver's signature

Mentor's signature

Date

When all practice sessions 2 are complete, be sure to record this in the training record sheet in the blue section in the middle of the book so that the driving instructor will know that you are ready to progress to driving lesson 3.

Notes

3

Observations

In this session we will practise...

3A ■ Observational skills, turning and intersections
3B ■ Observational skills, bends, intersections and roundabouts

Introduction

Good all round observation is particularly important when turning and at intersections. By looking well ahead to the target area you can make sure that the area is 'open' and that moving there will allow you to progress. For observation to be fully effective you must be aware of everything that is happening in all surrounding areas, and not just where you intend to go. Good observation enables you to make a fully informed decision before you change position, direction or speed. Observation is more than just looking, it means taking in and processing information and understanding the implications.

- The pivot point is the point around which the vehicle moves in a turn.
- When a vehicle turns while moving forward, the pivot point is located in line with the driver in the middle of the vehicle between the two front seats.
- When turning in reverse, the pivot point is located to the rear of the vehicle in a position close to or just behind the centre of the back seats.
- The steering recovery point is reached when the vehicle is still at an angle but the wheels are pointed in the intended direction of the turn.
- Be a good observer, look 15 -18 seconds ahead to a target point on your intended course.
- During practice sessions, when you observe a hazard, say it out loud. This helps heighten your awareness of potential hazards.
- In the beginning, you will tend to go where you're looking, it's important to look well ahead, keep scanning and try not to focus too long on any one thing.
- Avoid focusing at length just in front of the vehicle, or looking directly at the road markings as this tends to cause weaving.

Left and right turns

- Practise (12 times or more) making left turns while moving forward.
- Practise making left turns from a standing start.
- Left turns should be rounded.
- Look to the target area before and during the turn.
- Line up the pivot point with the intended turn before turning the steering wheel.
- Find the recovery point and allow the steering wheel to slide back through your hands to return to a straight course following a turn.
- Maintain a 1-metre distance from the kerb when turning left.
- Practise making right turns while moving forward.
- Practise right turns from a standing start.
- Right turns should be squared off – i.e. don't 'cut' the corner.

3A Observational skills, turning and intersections

Skills
- Making smooth and controlled turns to the left and right (including identifying the pivot point and recovery point).
- Practicing awareness of where you're looking and establishing 'targets' to help maintain a steady course.
- Left and right turns at intersections.

Ideal location
- Start out in a car park or quiet neighbourhood and as competence and confidence grow, progress to more complex roads.
- Avoid task loading. By venturing onto busy roads too early, you will just add stress and detract from the key learning objectives and the practice session is in danger of turning into a survival exercise.

Recommended practice time
- Two one-hour sessions. Remember that this is a guideline. You may find that you need more or less time, depending on how you progress.

Additional reading
Instruction Guide
Lesson 3

Steer Clear Driver Education Manual
Scanning (p.148)

RSA Rules of the Road
Junctions (p.98)

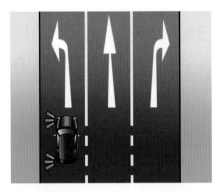

- Look around or across a corner to choose a clear path before starting a turn.
- Practise the correct use of mirrors, observation, speed and steering control.

Turning left at an intersection

- When approaching an intersection, scan all around it, checking for traffic, pedestrians and signals.
- Check your mirrors, use your indicator and slow down or stop if necessary.
- For left turns, aim for a left-lane position 1 metre from the kerb.
- When the pivot point of the vehicle is 1 metre past the beginning of the turn, turn the steering wheel to the left, steer around the corner until the recovery point, and then let the wheel slide through your hands so you can continue going straight.

- When turning left after stopping, wait for a gap in the traffic. Move forward and turn into the left-hand lane of the new road, looking well ahead to the target throughout the manoeuvre.

Right turns at intersections

- Approach the intersection with due care, making all the necessary checks and signalling your intentions to other road users.
- Stop 15cm to the left of the centre line and behind the stop line (if there is one).
- Keep the wheels straight.
- Only move into the centre of the intersection or box junction when the way ahead and the target area are clear.
- When there is a sufficient gap, turn right without hesitation.
- If there is more than one lane in the new road, select the one that matches the one you have come from – i.e., if coming from

the outside lane, stay in the outside lane.

- When you reach the recovery point, allow the steering wheel to slide back through your hands to the normal driving position.
- Choose a new target area in the lane ahead and accelerate gradually to suit the traffic flow.

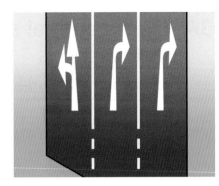

3A Observational skills, turning and intersections

Check-list and log-sheet

3A Practice 1	3A Practice 2	3A Practice 3
Date	Date	Date

Before moving on to the next session, you should be able to demonstrate 'green light' mastery in each skill.
Use this sheet to track progress by **ticking the circles** as shown.

✓ Skill preformed with competence, consistently showing mastery

○ Skill performed correctly but driver sometimes needs prompting

○ Skill accomplished but driver sometimes forgets a check or step

◐ Skill completed with some help or a prompt from the mentor

◯ Skill cannot be completed or requires substantial help from mentor

Turning basics

○○○○○ Observation and communication prior to beginning a turn
○○○○○ Gear selection and controlled speed through turn
○○○○○ Looking to target area prior to turning
○○○○○ Squaring right turns
○○○○○ Rounding left turns
○○○○○ Steering control throughout the turn

Observational skills

○○○○○ Looking to target area 15-20 seconds ahead
○○○○○ Observing all around by continually scanning while avoiding fixating
○○○○○ Correct interpretation of road signs and markings
○○○○○ Understanding and adhering to traffic signals

○○○○○ Observing all areas at junctions and intersections
○○○○○ Yielding to pedestrians and other traffic with due care
○○○○○ Observing the selected target area beyond intersections
○○○○○ Using good steering control and techniques
○○○○○ Preparing for a turn with good observation and communication
○○○○○ Selecting appropriate gaps and keeping a sufficient safety margin
○○○○○ Maintaining good speed control
○○○○○ Proceeds assertively and avoids undue hesitation

Vehicle positioning when turning

○○○○○ Selection of correct lane in preparation for turn
○○○○○ Selecting correct position within the lane before the turn
○○○○○ Maintaining a 1-metre separation from the kerb when turning left
○○○○○ Left of the centre line positioning in preparation for a right turn
○○○○○ Stopping behind the stop line where appropriate
○○○○○ Keeping the wheels straight while waiting to turn right
○○○○○ Entering the middle of a junction when a gap is about to open
○○○○○ Maintaining lane position throughout a turn

We have spent adequate time practising the skills from session 3A and feel competent enough to move on to the next skill development session.

Student driver's signature

Mentor's signature

Date

Practice Session 3

3B Observational skills, bends, intersections and roundabouts

Skills
- Using observational skills to identify the limit point and target areas when negotiating turns and bends.
- Adjusting speed and steering to control the vehicle on bends.
- Making neat and efficient left and right turns.
- Handling a variety of junctions and intersections.
- Entering and exiting roundabouts.

Ideal location
- You'll need some bends and a variety of junctions and roundabouts for these practice sessions.
  Begin at times when the traffic is light. When the ability improves, practise when the roads are busier.

Recommended practice time
- 3 one-hour sessions to practice the basics, continue practising these skills until competence is reached. Remember that this is a guideline. You may find that you need more or less time, depending on how you progress.

Additional reading
Instruction Guide
Lesson 3,

Steer Clear Driver Education Manual
Road Markings (p.57 -58)

RSA Rules of the Road
Junctions (p.98 - 111)

Balance and control in a bend

- Loss of traction and control is frequently caused by a combination of excessive speed and late braking while attempting to steer a vehicle around a bend.
- The amount of vehicle control available in a bend is affected by many factors; the vehicle's speed, braking, the load being carried, the curvature and tilt of the bend, the condition of the vehicle, the weather and the road.
- The vehicle is most stable when its weight is evenly distributed over all of its wheels and it is travelling in a straight line at a constant speed.
- Braking transfers weight to the front wheels, acceleration transfers the weight to the back, turning shifts the weight to the wheels on the outside of the curve: all three factors result in less traction by the opposing tyres. When two traction compromising factors come together, such as during braking and turning, the effect is even more destabilising.
- When traction is lost from the inner and rear tyres and correspondingly transferred to the front outside tyre (when braking and turning simultaneously), the momentum causes the vehicle to pirouette around the last remaining traction point, causing the vehicle to skid out of control.

Continue developing the observational skills needed for judging road position and for identifying the limit point and target areas. Identify and steer towards targets that are 15–20 seconds ahead of the vehicle. Picking targets helps to improve steering control and it also helps with identifying potential hazards in sufficient time to avoid them.

Control through bends

- When approaching a bend, look well ahead to the curve's apex and exit.

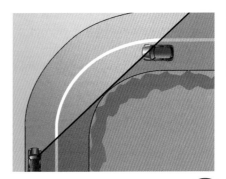

Choose the lane position that will afford you the best line of sight.

- Slow down to the posted speed limit – or slower – before starting the turn.
- Gradually apply the brake until you reach the apex of the curve.
- When you've passed the apex, begin accelerating to move out of the turn.

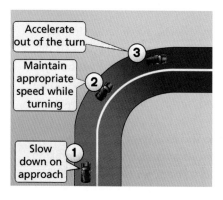

Accelerate out of the turn
Maintain appropriate speed while turning
Slow down on approach

Finding the safe speed for bends

- Match your speed through a bend to the speed at which the limit point moves away from you.
- The limit point in any driving situation is the furthest point ahead that you can see without interruption, you must at all times be able to stop safely within the distance that separates you from that point. If there is any doubt, slow down.

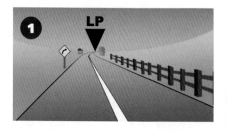

1 On approach to the bend look for the limit point, initially it will seem stationary. As the gap between you and the limit point gets shorter, adjust speed to allow safe stopping within that distance.

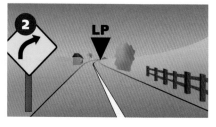

2 Gather as much information from the view ahead, signs, road surface, tree line, to access the curvature and severity of the bend.

3 As you get nearer to the bend and the view ahead opens, the limit point starts to move away at a constant pace. As you enter the bend match the vehicle's speed and gear selection to the speed at which the limit point moves away.

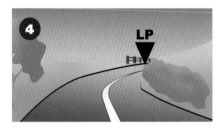

4 As you reach the apex of the curve and the bend starts to straighten out, the distance to the limit point begins to extend more quickly, this allows you to increase speed proportionately as the amount of steering decreases.

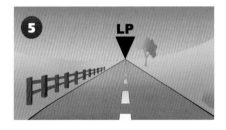

5 As you exit the bend continue to accelerate towards the limit point until you resume a comfortable driving speed for the conditions and within the regulations.

Junctions

■ Try to incorporate a variety of different junctions, intersections and roundabouts into the practice sessions.

■ Pay attention to the movements and needs of other road users.

■ Practice turning left and right at different types of junctions.

■ Remember to use the SIDE and MSM routines to guide how you make your observations and how you communicate your intentions to other road users.

■ When making right turns, practice 'squaring' the corner. Drive up to the turn and stop when your shoulder is in line with the target road. When the way is clear and after making checks and signals, move forward and turn right. Keep the turn close to 90° – do not cut the corner. Straighten up once you've reached the recovery point.

■ Left turns require the same checks and indications as you approach the turn. Slow down so that by the time you reach the turn you have almost stopped. Drive just past the turn until your shoulder is in line with the centre of the target lane. 'Rounding' the corner gives a smoother left turn and prevents the back of the car from swinging out into the adjoining lane.

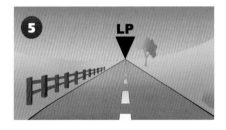

Practice Session 3

Roundabouts

- Start the roundabout practise with simple first-exit manoeuvres. Then travelling straight through and finally progress to taking the third or subsequent exits.
- When you have mastered basic roundabouts, take a trip as a passenger to a complex multi-lane roundabout – preferably one which is signal controlled

(if possible). Ask your mentor to talk through the manoeuvre pointing out the key points (observation, communication, positioning) so that you can observe and learn.

- When you are ready, practice driving with your mentor through the roundabout at a time when the traffic is not too heavy.

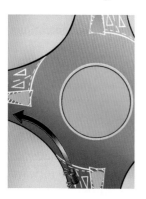
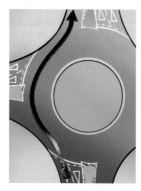
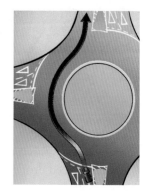

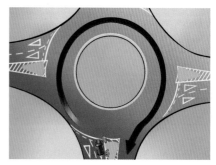

3B   Junctions and roundabouts
Check-list and log-sheet

| 3B Practice 1 | 3B Practice 2 | 3B Practice 3 |
| Date | Date | Date |

Before moving on to the next session, you should be able to
demonstrate 'green light' mastery in each skill.
Use this sheet to track progress by **ticking the circles** as shown.

✔️ Skill preformed with competence, consistently showing mastery

◯ Skill performed correctly but driver sometimes needs prompting

◯ Skill accomplished but driver sometimes forgets a check or step

◯ Skill completed with some help or a prompt from the mentor

◯ Skill cannot be completed or requires substantial help from mentor

Bends and curves

◯◯◯◯◯ Advanced observation of approaching bends

◯◯◯◯◯ Recognition and identification of helpful bend
severity information

◯◯◯◯◯ Adaptation of correct speed on approach to bends

◯◯◯◯◯ Control of speed and deceleration

◯◯◯◯◯ Adjusts speed to suit traffic flow while keeping a safe gap

◯◯◯◯◯ Recognition and use of limit point cues

◯◯◯◯◯ Speed and control through bend

◯◯◯◯◯ Acceleration and speed control coming out of bend

Interaction at intersections

⦿⦿○○○ Identification of open, occupied and traffic movement areas at intersections

⦿⦿○○○ Changing speed or position to accommodate the needs of others

⦿⦿○○○ Yielding to other traffic and pedestrians as required

⦿⦿○○○ Stopping completely in the proper position when required

⦿⦿○○○ Checking and communicating prior to changing position or direction

Roundabouts

⦿⦿○○○ Recognition of signs on approach to roundabouts

⦿⦿○○○ Slowing or stopping appropriately on approach

⦿⦿○○○ Selection of correct lane and positioning within the lane

⦿⦿○○○ Observation on approach and when using the roundabout

⦿⦿○○○ Use of the correct signals and communication at roundabouts

⦿⦿○○○ Resuming normal speed and road position after roundabouts

We have spent adequate time practising the skills from session 3B and feel competent enough to move on to the next skill development session.

Student driver's signature _____

Mentor's signature _____

Date _____

4

Town and city driving

In this session we will practise...

4A ■ Town and city driving
4B ■ Driving on dual carriageways and in rural areas

Introduction

Driving in built-up areas leaves little room for error. You must be able to make the correct decisions quickly by distinguishing between what's important and what's not – festive decor and shop windows should be ignored but pedestrian movement is something that you should be very aware of. The movements of pedestrians and cyclists can be difficult to predict, especially when there are large crowds or when the weather is bad. Unprotected pedestrians and cyclists will be badly hurt if hit by your vehicle. Slow down and give vulnerable road users ample consideration.

4A Town and city driving

Skills
- Scanning ahead.
- Constantly observing all around.
- Making decisions by using the SIDE rule.
- Coping with hazards particular to city driving.
- Dealing with distractions.
- Handling one-way streets.

Ideal location
- The goal of these sessions is to become comfortable with driving in urban areas. Start out in a town or city suburb and, as the learning progresses, move into heavier city traffic (if possible).

Recommended practice time
- Town and city driving can be very tiring for new drivers. Initially it may be more effective to limit these sessions to 30-40 minutes then progress to 50-60 minutes as you get more comfortable.

Additional reading
Instruction Guide
Lesson 4

Steer Clear Driver Education Manual
Scanning (p.148)
The SIDE rule and multiple hazards (p.155)
Sharing the road (p.260)
Keeping your cool (p.265)
Different road types, different challenges (go to section on urban and suburban roads, p.295)

Speed gives you less time to react and it causes a lot more damage.

Speed Kills

- A pedestrian or cyclist hit by a car travelling at 30km/h will be badly hurt, but in nine out of ten cases they will survive the impact
- On the other hand a pedestrian or cyclist hit by a car travelling at 60km/h has only a one in ten chance of surviving.

Driving decisively and using the SIDE rule

The SIDE rule is a method of remembering all the steps required to gather information and make informed decisions. Drivers who get into the habit of using the SIDE rule are less likely to omit a critical step when anticipating and avoiding possible hazards whenever they need to change direction or lane position.

S Scan ahead, behind (using mirrors) and to the sides for possible hazards and/or open areas.

I Identify possible problems and/ or opportunities.

D Decide what course to take or to avoid.

E Execute the manoeuvre after indicating and checking your mirrors again to make sure it is safe.

- Adjust your lane position to leave more room as you pass parked cars.
- Look well ahead to anticipate the actions and needs of other road users.
- Check upcoming intersections and entrances for traffic that is entering and crossing the roadway.
- Keep a lookout for pedestrians and anticipate what they may do.
- Anticipate the actions of people using public transport – for example, running to catch buses or alighting from them.

- Leave room for buses to re-enter the traffic flow.
- Check for vehicles using the bus lane before you attempt to make a left turn.
- Look well ahead and anticipate which lane you'll need for your intended route.
- Where possible, avoid blocking side roads and entrances when stopped in heavy traffic.
- Leave space between your vehicle and the one in front. You should be able to see it's tyres touching the road.

City-driving hazards

- Take care when passing vehicles parked at the roadside because their doors may open as you go by.
- Watch for pedestrians crossing between vehicles and in other places not designated for crossing.
- In wet weather, be alert for pedestrians running for cover.
- When a light turns green, check that the pedestrian crossings are clear before you proceed.
- In busy pedestrian areas, be alert for people who follow the crowd at crossings without checking the lights. Also, watch out for pedestrians who step off the pavement without looking for oncoming traffic.
- Leave room for trucks and delivery vehicles to load and unload cargo.
- Anticipate that delivery vehicles may make stops in unusual locations.
- Driving in congested city traffic can be stressful. Be patient and don't let others' aggressive driving antagonise you.
- When you spot a hazard and are preparing to stop, cover the brake but don't ride it.

One-way streets

- Plan ahead when driving in the city so that you can use one-way streets to your advantage.

- On a one-way street with multiple lines, be alert for traffic passing on both sides.

- Sometimes parking is permitted on both sides of the road. Leave room for vehicles pulling out from your right because they will have a restricted view of the roadway.

- Anticipate your exit and get into the correct lane before you plan to turn off a one-way street.

- When turning from a one-way into a two-way street, be sure to move over to the left.

- Some one-way streets allow more than one lane to turn at a junction. In this case, stay in your lane throughout the turn so that you don't impede other traffic.

- When there are two turning lanes and you are in the lane closest to the corner, you must make the turn – even if the middle lane allows traffic to turn or continue straight on. Obey the arrows in your lane.

- Take extra care where a bus lane runs in the opposite direction to the main traffic flow on a one-way street. (This is known as a contra-flow bus lane.)

4A Town and city driving
Check-list and log-sheet

| 4A Practice 1 Date | 4A Practice 2 Date | 4A Practice 3 Date |

Before moving on to the next session, you should be able to demonstrate 'green light' mastery in each skill.
Use this sheet to track progress by **ticking the circles** as shown.

✓ Skill preformed with competence, consistently showing mastery
○ Skill performed correctly but driver sometimes needs prompting
○ Skill accomplished but driver sometimes forgets a check or step
○ Skill completed with some help or a prompt from the mentor
○ Skill cannot be completed or requires substantial help from mentor

Decisive driving

○○○○○	Looks ahead to anticipate others' needs
○○○○○	Checks upcoming junctions and intersections well in advance
○○○○○	Adjusts lane position to accommodate other road users
○○○○○	Observes and anticipates pedestrian movements
○○○○○	Assists the movement of traffic by accommodating public transport vehicles
○○○○○	Checks for traffic in bus lane before moving to left
○○○○○	Moves to correct lane early in preparation for turns
○○○○○	Leaves enough distance from vehicle in front – should be able to see vehicle's tyres touch the road
○○○○○	Does not block intersections or side roads when stopped in traffic

City driving hazards

○○○○○ Recognises hazards of urban driving

○○○○○ Leaves room and is prepared to avoid doors being opened on parked cars

○○○○○ Checks for pedestrians crossing between vehicles

○○○○○ Checks pedestrian crossings are clear before proceeding

○○○○○ Leaves sufficient room from delivery vehicles to accommodate needs

○○○○○ Shows consideration for others' needs

○○○○○ Does not allow the pressure of aggressive drivers to influence own driving

○○○○○ Covers the brake but does not ride the pedal when hazards are identified

One-way streets

○○○○○ Is watchful for traffic passing on both sides

○○○○○ Gets into correct lane when preparing to turn off one-way street

○○○○○ Obeys arrows in lane when turning

We have spent adequate time practising the skills required to drive in built-up areas and feel competent enough to move on to the next skill-development session.

Student driver's signature

Mentor's signature

Date

4B Driving on dual carriageways and in rural areas

Skills
- Selecting the correct lane on a dual carriageway.
- Maintaining proper lane position on a dual carriageway.
- Changing from major to minor roads and vice versa.
- Dealing with hazards particular to driving in rural areas (e.g. animals, agricultural vehicles and blind bends).

Ideal location
- For the skills in this part of Module 4, you'll need to spend some sessions on dual carriageways and some in rural areas. Practise going from minor to major roads and vice versa. Where possible, the learner should also get some experience of driving on narrow, winding country roads.

Recommended practice time
- Two one-hour sessions. Remember that this is a guideline. You may find that you need more or less time, depending on how you progress.

Additional Reading
Instructor Guide
Lesson 4

Steer Clear Driver Education Manual
Different road types different challenges (P 292 -294)

220

Driving on dual carriageways

Main roads with a centre median allow for faster traffic movement and more lanes.

- Select the correct lane for your direction of travel – generally, it'll be the left lane (unless you are overtaking). On multi-lane roads, use signs or road markings to determine which lane is correct.

- Position your vehicle in the middle of the lane to create the most space on either side.

- Traffic moves more quickly on dual carriageways, so anticipate where you need to be in plenty of time and get into the correct lane by using the SIDE rule.

- Dual carriageways have intersections and junctions that allow traffic of all types to cross and enter the road. Pay attention to the movements of other traffic, and anticipate and accommodate other drivers' needs.

- In heavy traffic, keep a lookout for motorcycles travelling between the lanes of traffic.

- Check for buses and taxis using the bus lanes, especially when you wish to cross a lane to turn at a junction or into a side road.

- Remember to keep a two-second safe gap between you and the vehicle in front. Extend this gap if conditions deteriorate.

- Slow down if necessary to create a lateral space in the lane beside you. Where possible, avoid driving alongside another vehicle.

- If another vehicle is tailgating or driving too close behind you, allow them to pass if possible. If not, create more space to the front by slowing down a little. This will reduce the likelihood of you having to make a sudden stop or change of direction.

- Staying well back from trucks and other large vehicles will help prevent debris from hitting your windscreen. Staying back will also enable the truck driver to see you. (Remember that if you can't see the truck's side mirrors, the driver will be unable to see you.)

Negotiating road changes

- Anticipating road changes and preparing to adjust your speed will make for a smoother journey.
- When going from a dual carriageway to a smaller road, take note of the new speed limit and conditions and adjust accordingly.
- When going from a minor road to a major one, increase your speed while in the slip lane to match the traffic and conditions on the new road. Where there is no slip road, increase speed without delay to match the traffic flow; do not impede the other traffic.

Rural driving

- Looking ahead and observing the surroundings will give clues to the hidden hazards of driving in rural areas. Look for changes in the tree line or hedgerows to give advance warning of side roads, hills, dips and entrances.
- Pay attention to the observations you make. If you're unsure of what's up ahead, slow down.
- Telltale signs such as grass or fresh manure on the road should alert you to slow down and expect a hazard ahead.
- Give agricultural vehicles plenty of room to manoeuvre. Staying well back will help protect you should another vehicle approach from behind.
- It takes a tractor 10-15 seconds to enter or cross a rural road, your driving speed must take this into account and be ready to accommodate for their needs when travelling in the country.
- Have patience and overtake carefully only when you are sure it is safe.

- It is often safer to pass a dangerous right-hand turn and come back to it as a left-hand turn from the other direction. For example, if the junction were in a dip and stopping and waiting in the centre of the road to turn right would expose you to danger from behind.

- Watch for pedestrians and animals using the road. If you can't see around a bend, slow down in anticipation of oncoming traffic or hidden obstructions.

- Use your lights or horn to warn other drivers as you approach a very blind bend.
- Slow down as you approach towns, villages and community areas, even where traffic-calming zones are not marked.
- Recognise areas where traction may be compromised such as under shaded areas, or when there is mud, wet leaves, standing water or loose gravel on the road.

4B Driving on dual carriageways and in rural areas

Check-list and log-sheet

4B Practice 1 Date	4B Practice 2 Date	4B Practice 3 Date

Before moving on to the next session, you should be able to demonstrate 'green light' mastery in each skill.
Use this sheet to track progress by **ticking the circles** as shown.

✓ Skill preformed with competence, consistently showing mastery
◯ Skill performed correctly but driver sometimes needs prompting
◯ Skill accomplished but driver sometimes forgets a check or step
◯ Skill completed with some help or a prompt from the mentor
◯ Skill cannot be completed or requires substantial help from mentor

General

◯◯ ◯◯ Approaches vehicle with due care and awareness
◯◯ ◯◯ Gets into car and completes cockpit drill
◯◯ ◯◯ Checks mirrors and signals before manoeuvring
◯◯ ◯◯ Controls speed, acceleration and deceleration
◯◯ ◯◯ Adjusts speed to suit rural driving
◯◯ ◯◯ Uses mirrors correctly and frequently in normal driving
◯◯ ◯◯ Doesn't hesitate and moves decisively

Decisive driving

◯◯ ◯◯ Looks well ahead to gather information from tree and hedge lines
◯◯ ◯◯ Checks upcoming junctions and intersections well in advance
◯◯ ◯◯ Adjusts road position to accommodate other road users

○○○○○ Anticipates upcoming hazards

○○○○○ Shows consideration for agricultural needs

○○○○○ Anticipates and slows down in preparation for turns

○○○○○ Leaves enough space in front to protect rear when stopped unexpectedly

○○○○○ Recognises areas prone to poor traction

Driving on dual carriageways

○○○○○ Selects correct lane for intended route

○○○○○ Positions vehicle in centre of lane for maximum lateral space

○○○○○ Uses the SIDE rule to anticipate and make lane changes

○○○○○ Maintains two-second (or more) gap from vehicle in front

○○○○○ In heavy traffic, keeps lookout for motorbikes between lanes

Rural driving hazards

○○○○○ Slows down when approaching blind bends

○○○○○ Recognises dangers of hills and dips in road

○○○○○ Recognises the signs of hedge trimmings etc.

○○○○○ Slows down when entering villages

○○○○○ Allows others to pass or responds correctly to being passed

○○○○○ Anticipates the need to pass obstruction and does so smoothly

We have spent adequate time practising the skills required to drive on dual carriageways and in rural areas and feel competent enough to move on to the next skill-development session.

Student driver's signature

Mentor's signature

Date

Notes

5

Parking

In this session we will practise...

- Parking

Practice Session 5

Introduction

When choosing a place to park it is important that your vehicle will not obstruct, endanger, disturb or inconvenience other road users. Your parked vehicle must not block an entrance or obstruct the view of other road users. Considerate parking is essential for road safety. Parking on the path, opposite a white line, very close to a corner or close to a pedestrian crossing puts others at risk and is therefore illegal. If there are no designated parking spaces or where the road is too narrow, refrain from parking and find an alternative place that better suits the purpose.

5   Parking

Skills
- Driving straight into and reversing out of a parking space that's at an angle.
- Entering and exiting a perpendicular (bay) parking space.
- Parallel parking.
- Parking on a hill.

Ideal location
- Start out in a large open car park when it isn't busy. You'll need to practise entering and exiting parallel and perpendicular parking spaces, and bays that are at an angle. You'll also need to practice parking on a hill. It's better to practice all these skills in quiet areas where the traffic volume is low. Light plastic cones or other markers will help in creating artificial parking spaces.

Recommended practice time
- Practising parking skills is a valuable way to improve close manoeuvring skills. Be sure to take plenty of time to practice each of the parking procedures enough times to master the skills competently. Remember that this is a guideline. You may find that you need more or less time, depending on how you progress.

Additional reading
Instructor Guide
Lesson 5

Steer Clear Driver Education Manual
Communication (p.271)

RSA Rules of the Road
Parking (p.112)

Check for oncoming traffic and pedestrians and indicate your intentions in plenty of time before commencing a parking manoeuvre.

Show consideration for other road users when choosing a place to park. Your vehicle should not block an entrance or obstruct the view of other drivers. Parking on the footpath is illegal and dangerous. If the road is not wide enough for you to park safely, go to a place where it is.

Where there are no designated parking spaces or no other parking signs or markings, you must not park:

- opposite a continuous white line;
- within 5m of a corner;
- 15m before a pedestrian crossing or 5m after it;
- opposite another vehicle on a narrow road;
- in a bus or cycle lane, or in a taxi rank;
- in any place that would obstruct, endanger or disturb other road users.

Practise the various parking manoeuvres from the left and from the right at least 10–15 times – or until you feel competent.

Parking at an angle

- Locate a suitable free parking space. Check behind you before signalling and slowing down to stop about 1 to 1.5 metres away from the space.
- Parking spaces that are at an angle are usually designed for front-in parking – you drive straight into them instead of reversing.
- When approaching the space from the left, move forwards slowly until the white parking-space line that's nearest to you is aligned with the centre of the bonnet.
- Look to the centre of the space and turn sharply while moving slowly into it.
- Continue moving into the space until you reach the recovery

Practice Session 5

point. Then straighten up so that you are centred in the space.

- Stop when the front bumper is 15-20 cm from the end line or kerb.

- When parking in a space to the right, align the white parking-space line that's nearest to you with the steering wheel before beginning to turn sharply into the space.

- When leaving your parking space, scan your intended course and wait for a suitable gap in traffic if necessary.

- Place your foot on the brake, depress the clutch, indicate, select reverse gear and slowly begin reversing straight out of the space.

- When your seat is in line with the bumper of the vehicle next to you, start turning the steering wheel.

- Check the clearance of the bumper on the far side because it swings wider than the arc of the turn.

- When you are completely out of the parking space, stop, check all around, signal and shift gears in preparation to move off.

Perpendicular or bay parking

- Whenever possible, it is better to reverse into the parking space. This allows for a safer departure especially in a busy parking area or on a busy street.

- The first thing to do is get into a good starting position for the manoeuvre. As you drive up alongside the space, allow a 1m gap between the side of your vehicle and the end of the space. Align the rear passenger door with the parking-space line that was farthest from you as you approached the space.

- Check all around for obstructions. Turn the steering wheel sharply towards the parking space and reverse into the centre.

- Straighten up and stop 15-20cm from the line or kerb.

- To drive forward into a perpendicular space, stop 2 metres before the end of the space. Then move forward until your seat is aligned with the white parking-space line that's nearest to you as you approach the space.

- Steer sharply into the space and move forward at a controlled, slow speed.

- Centre the vehicle within the space and stop 15-20 cm back from the kerb.

- Leave sufficient room for vehicles parked on either side of you to open their doors.

Parallel parking

- You should always try to parallel park so that your car is facing in the same direction as the traffic flow. This will make exiting the parking space easier and safer.

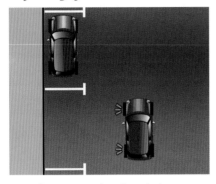

- Pull up, just ahead and about 1metre out from the vehicle parked in front of your chosen parking space.

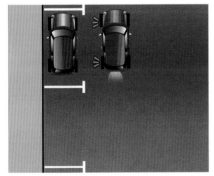

- Check all around you and reverse straight back until your wing mirror is in line with the rear bumper of the vehicle in front. Now turn the steering wheel sharply in the direction of the space.

- Reverse slowly and keep checking your clearance to the front and rear you should now be entering the space at a 45° angle. Stop when the front of your vehicle is clear of the vehicle in front. Turn the steering wheel one full turn towards the road to straighten up the wheels.

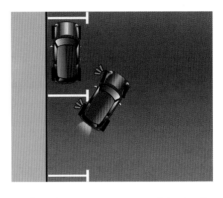

- Continue to reverse straight back slowly until you are close to the vehicle behind. At this stage you should be able to see the wheels of the vehicle in front touching the road.

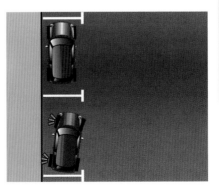

- Move forward and back as necessary to centre your vehicle within the parking space about 15cm from the kerb.

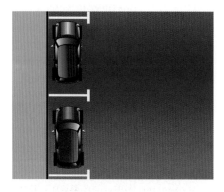

- Straighten the wheels, apply the parking brake and switch off the engine.
- Check the mirrors and over your shoulder before opening the door to get out.
- Lock the vehicle and walk around to the pavement side of the vehicle facing oncoming traffic and keeping a good lookout as you go.

Parking on a hill

- When parking facing uphill, engage the parking brake and leave the car in first gear (or 'drive' if your car is an automatic). When facing downhill, engage the parking brake and leave the car in reverse gear.

- Turning the front wheels will prevent the car from accidentally rolling into traffic:
  - When facing downhill, turn the wheels towards the kerb.
  - When facing uphill, turn the wheels away from the kerb.
  - When facing uphill on a road without a kerb, turn the wheels towards the edge of the road.

Moving off from your parking space

- Check your mirrors and over your shoulder before beginning to move off. Switch on the indicator and if the way is clear, move forwards slowly while turning the steering wheel.
- Start in first gear but once you're moving, change up the gears as you accelerate and move out into your chosen lane.
- When exiting a parallel parking space, start by moving back

position on a hill, leave extra time and space for manoeuvring, changing gears and controlling the parking brake.

- Whenever possible, it is better to reverse into a parking space. This will allow you to drive straight out of the space, giving you a better view of any hazards and obstructions.

within the space to allow more room to clear the vehicle parked in front.

- In built-up areas, watch out for cyclists travelling alongside rows of parked cars. If necessary, open the window and look out to make sure the way is clear.

- When moving off from a parking

- Take extra care in busy car parks, particularly in shopping areas, because pedestrians and children are often distracted and do not pay sufficient attention to manoeuvring vehicles.

- When reversing in car parks, be alert for other vehicles manoeuvring at the same time.

5   Parking

Check-list and log-sheet

5A Practice 1 Date	5A Practice 2 Date	5A Practice 3 Date

Before moving on to the next session, you should be able to demonstrate 'green light' mastery in each skill.
Use this sheet to track progress by **ticking the circles** as shown.

✓ Skill preformed with competence, consistently showing mastery
○ Skill performed correctly but driver sometimes needs prompting
○ Skill accomplished but driver sometimes forgets a check or step
○ Skill completed with some help or a prompt from the mentor
◑ Skill cannot be completed or requires substantial help from mentor

Parking

○○○○○ Selecting an appropriate parking space

○○○○○ Checking mirrors and signals before slowing to a stop

○○○○○ Controlling speed throughout the manoeuvre

○○○○○ Reversing into parking space whenever possible

○○○○○ Leaving adequate clearance from obstacles and other vehicles

○○○○○ Centres the vehicle within the space

○○○○○ Check mirrors and over shoulder before opening the door

○○○○○ Prior to moving off, checking all around and choosing a safe gap

Angle parking

○○○○○ Checking front and rear, signalling intention and slowing to a stop

○○○○○ When approaching space, allows adequate gap and aligns with appropriate parking-space line

○○○○○ Constantly checking front, rear and corners while moving slowly

○○○○○ Steers tidily into space and centres approx. 15cm from end

○○○○○ Exits parking space with due care and attention

Perpendicular parking bays

○○○○○ Checks front and rear, signals intention and slows to a stop

○○○○○ Positions car approximately 2m from space or other vehicles before starting turn

○○○○○ Steers at a slow, controlled speed into target area

○○○○○ Centres vehicle within space

○○○○○ Stops vehicle approximately 15cm from kerb or end line

○○○○○ Exits the parking space slowly with due care and attention

Parallel parking

○○○○○ Checks front and rear, signals intention and slows to a stop

○○○○○ Stops alongside of vehicle that is in front of space

○○○○○ Reverses until wing mirror is in line with rear of other vehicle

○○○○○ Maintains adequate space while turning sharply into space

○○○○○ Checks front and rear clearance frequently

○○○○○ Centres & straightens vehicle close to kerb in the space

○○○○○ When leaving, reverses back to maximise front clearance

○○○○○ Checks over shoulder and signals before pulling out

○○○○○ Rejoins traffic flow carefully & in control

○○○○○ Gets up to speed without delay and does not hamper other traffic

We have spent adequate time practising the skills from Session 5 and feel competent to progress to the next skill-development session.

Student driver's signature

Mentor's signature

Date

Notes

6

Emergency braking

In this session we will practise...

6A ■ Emergency braking
6B ■ Avoiding skids

Introduction

The necessity to brake hard usually comes as a result of failing to leave sufficient space or failing to anticipate what may happen in a given situation. While there will be emergencies when immediate braking is required, for the most part harsh braking it can be avoided by staying focused on the driving task, looking well ahead, maintaining a safe gap and driving at a safe speed. In anticipating what is likely to happen consideration should be given for traffic volume, your speed, pedestrian activity, the weather and the overall driving environment.

6A Emergency braking

Skills
Reversing
- Understanding the factors that govern how quickly a vehicle stops.
- Knowing the difference between conventional and antilock braking systems.
- Stopping safely.
- Using hazard lights correctly.
- Dealing with brake failure.

Ideal location
- Find a suitable location such as a large, empty car park to practise emergency stops. If possible practise the procedures in a vehicle with antilock brakes and also in one with conventional brakes.

Recommended practice time
- One hour. Remember that this is a guideline. You may find that you need more or less time, depending on how you progress.

Additional reading
Instruction Guide
Lesson 6

Steer Clear Driver Education Manual
Momentum, braking, slowing, stopping (p.44)
Breakdowns & personal safety (p.98)
Managing breakdowns (p.102)
Anticipating and managing driving hazards (p.150)
Controlling Deceleration (p.222)
Stopping time and distance (p.243)

RSA Rules of the Road
(P.48), (p.87), (p.126)

To avoid having to brake hard or late:
- Stay focused on the driving task.
- Be prepared by looking well ahead.
- Maintain a generous safe gap (remember the two-second rule).
- Anticipate what may happen given the traffic volume, pedestrian activity, the weather, the road conditions and the type of environment in which you're driving.
- Always drive at a speed that allows you to stay in control of your vehicle.

Factors affecting stopping distance

Several factors influence the amount of road you cover before coming to a full stop (stopping distance). In normal driving, a number of these factors will be working at the same time.

- Factor 1: Your speed. The faster you're travelling, the more time and space you will need to stop. For example, if your car is travelling at 50km/h on a dry, straight road, you'll need 25 metres to stop. If you double that speed, you almost triple the stopping distance to 70 metres.

- Factor 2: The condition of the road. You'll get the best traction and thus the best stopping distance on a dry road with a good surface. However, if the road is wet, icy or muddy, or if the surface is brand new with only a sub surface, the

traction will not be as good. For example, if you're travelling at 50km/h on a wet, straight road, you'll need 30 metres to stop. At double the speed, you'll need more than four times this distance – that's 125 metres.

- Factor 3: The condition of your tyres, both tread and pressure. If your tyres have poor tread and/or are not correctly inflated, the traction will be seriously compromised, increasing your stopping distance. A tyre with (1.6mm) the legal minimum tread

can take up to five times longer to stop than a new tyre.

- Factor 4: Your vehicle's load. The greater the load your vehicle is carrying, the greater the stopping distance.
- Factor 5: The direction in which your vehicle is travelling when you brake. Braking is more effective when the vehicle is travelling in a straight line than in a turn. When turning, the traction is working to counter the centrifugal force and keep the vehicle on the road as it changes

direction. This means there is less traction available for braking. If you brake hard in a turn, your vehicle is more likely to skid.

Common dashboard warning lights

Adjust your driving style as the conditions require. If the road is wet, icy or muddy, if visibility is poor, or if your vehicle is heavily laden, slow down and leave a generous safe gap. This will give you the greater stopping distance you need.

Stopping safely

- Avoid harsh or late braking. Even in an emergency situation, your braking action should be as smooth and gradual as possible to help avoid skidding.
- Find out which type of braking system your vehicle has – is it antilock or conventional? This is important to know because each system needs to be operated differently in an emergency.
- Antilock brakes have an

electronic system that prevents the brakes from locking up when you brake hard. This system temporarily releases and then re-engages the brakes automatically before they lock up. To come to an emergency stop, press hard on the brake until the vehicle stops. You will feel the pedal shudder as the antilock system releases and re-engages the brakes.

- Because conventional brakes don't have a system to prevent them from locking up, you need to use them differently in an emergency. To avoid a skid, you must prevent the wheels from stopping completely. Press the brake pedal gently at first and then apply more pressure gradually. When you feel the brakes begin to lock, ease off the pedal and then press down again. You might need to use this pumping action several times until the vehicle stops.

- Knowing how to use both types of brakes is important because you may be driving a vehicle with a different brake system when you hire or borrow a vehicle in the future.

Always drive at a speed that allows you to stay in control of your vehicle. This will dramatically reduce your chances of having to attempt an abrupt stop.

Using the hazard lights

- Many motorists are in the habit of using their hazard lights to say 'thank you'. Although common practice, it is not legal and it is best avoided as it creates a potential hazard. Give a 'thank you' wave instead.

- Save the hazard lights for situations when you need to send out an urgent warning. For example, if you're driving on a motorway but must slow down suddenly because of a tailback ahead, use the hazard lights to warn the drivers behind you.

- In situations where you must pull over to the side of the roadway in an emergency, switch on the hazard lights to alert other drivers to your presence.

- Don't use the hazard lights to sanction an illegal or dangerous manoeuvre. Switching on the hazard lights does not make it OK to double-park or obstruct traffic.

Brake failure

Most drivers are not prepared for brake failure and wouldn't know how to respond if the worst happened. Rehearse the following procedure and memorise it so that you'll know what to do if your brakes fail. Remember, though, that the brakes should not fail in a vehicle that has been properly maintained.

- Slow to a stop by easing off the accelerator and gearing down.
- Gradually apply the handbrake.
- While slowing down, steer to avoid obstacles. Allow plenty of time to steer around obstacles; don't wait until the last second, when you'll be forced to swerve.
- Hold the steering wheel firmly and don't panic.

Maintaining a generous safe gap at all times will give you more room to manoeuvre in the unlikely event of brake failure.

Leaving the roadway in an emergency

At some point in your driving career, you may need to pull off the road quickly – for example, if you feel unwell or if a problem arises with your vehicle. Review and practise the following procedure.

- Remember to 'Control, Choose and Communicate': ensure that you have the vehicle under control, decide on a course of action and communicate your intentions to other motorists.
- Grip the steering wheel firmly. Look for a suitable place to pull over and then indicate. You may also choose to put on your hazard lights to let other drivers know that you are in difficulty.
- Park as far away from the traffic stream as you can.
- Get out of the car on the side farthest away from the road, even if this means you have to climb over the passenger seat.
- If it is safe, put out a warning triangle to alert other drivers to your presence.
- If you're waiting for roadside assistance, do not wait in the car. Do not stand behind the vehicle

because you might block other drivers' view of your tail lights. Much worse, if another vehicle ran into the back of your car, you would be crushed in the collision.

- You may run into trouble on a road that has no hard shoulder – a winding country road, for example. If you can, drive on to see if you can find a safe place to pull over, such as a driveway. If you can't continue driving, put on your hazard lights and stop the car. Do your best to warn following traffic that your vehicle is stopped in the roadway. You could get out of the car and put out a warning triangle, or put on a reflective vest/jacket and walk up the road to flag drivers down. Proceed with great care. Call for assistance as soon as possible.

6B Avoiding skids

Skills

- Recognising the conditions in which skids are more likely to occur.
- Understanding the effect tyre tread and pressure have on traction.
- Avoiding skids.
- Driving out of a skid.

Ideal location

- A wide open space such as an empty car park is best for practicing controlled skid recovery.
- If you can, arrange to take a lesson at a 'skid school'. These schools have a closed course and specially adapted vehicles so drivers can experience what different types of skid feel like and learn how to regain control over a skidding car.

Recommended practice time

- One hour. Remember that this is a guideline. You may find that you need more or less time, depending on how you progress.

Additional reading

Instruction Guide
Lesson 6

Steer Clear Driver Education Manual
Momentum, braking, slowing, stopping (p.44)
Tyre pressure (p.87) and changing a tyre (p.88)
Error correction (p.232)

RSA Rules of the Road
Tyres (p.31)

The roads can be particularly treacherous during the first light rainfall after several days of dry weather. The rainwater combines with the oils and dirt particles that have accumulated on the road surface in the dry spell, giving rise to a very slick mixture. If you're out driving during or after the first rainfall, slow down.

Causes of skids

A skid is a loss of contact between your vehicle's tyres and the road. As you might expect, skids are more likely when traction is compromised in some way. Many factors can affect traction:

- The condition of the roadway, whether it's wet, icy, muddy or oily. Water, dirt, oil, leaves and loose chippings all reduce the amount of grip between the tyres and the road. Also, road surfaces that are brand new or very worn provide less grip.
- The condition of your vehicle's tyres – both their pressure and tread. You'll learn more about this in the next section.

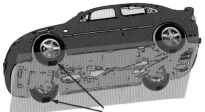

Applying the brakes and slowing shifts weight forward and reduces rear tyre traction

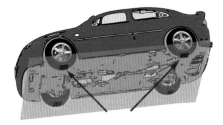

Traction is pitched towards the side.

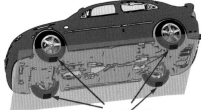

Normal traction distributes weight fairly evenly between all four wheels for traction

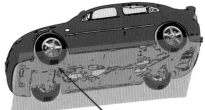

Braking and cornering at the same time transfers traction to the outside front wheel.

- Excessive speed, particularly when you try to change direction. If you try to turn too abruptly at high speed, the vehicle's momentum may overcome the tyres' traction. The result can be a rear-wheel or 'fishtail' skid, where the rear of the car slides out of control. The worst scenario is when all four tyres lose traction: the vehicle continues moving in its original direction, completely out of control. It may even spin.
- Excessive braking. When you brake abruptly, the vehicle's momentum may overcome traction – particularly on a slippery road. But harsh braking can cause a skid even when road conditions are good.
- Excessive power/acceleration can cause you to lose control or the wheels to spin, losing traction and power.

In most cases, skids occur when the vehicle is travelling too quickly for the conditions.

Skids and tyre tread & pressure

Give yourself the best possible traction under the conditions by ensuring that your tyres are properly inflated and in good condition.

- The law requires that you have a minimum of 1.6mm of tread – that's approximately the thickness of a €2 coin. Remember that this is the minimum. It's better to have a tread of 5-6mm.
- Correctly-inflated tyres have up to three times more contact and grip with the road than over- or under-inflated tyres.
- Get into the habit of checking your tyres whenever you refuel. For tips on checking your tread depth, go to Module 9.

Your best defence against skids

- When there is water, ice, mud or oil on the road, give yourself the best possible traction under the conditions by SLOWING DOWN.
- Never take a bend at speed. Slow down as you approach the bend.
- Your driving style should always be measured and cautious; you should always avoid abrupt or harsh manoeuvres. But taking extra care in poor conditions.

What to do if your vehicle skids

If you are able to recognise the signs of a skid immediately, then you'll be able to react quickly, improving your chances of getting the vehicle back under control. Review and memorise the following procedure. If possible, try to get some practice at a 'skid school'.

- At the onset of a skid, your vehicle will feel as if it is 'skating' or 'sailing' along the road. You may feel this sensation on some or all of the wheels.
- Remain calm.
- Take your feet off the brake and accelerator pedals. (Do not brake hard, try to accelerate, or wrestle with the steering wheel; this will make the situation worse.)
- Turn the steering wheel gently in the direction of the skid. For example, if the rear of the car is skidding to the left, steer to the left. Try to point the front of the car in the direction in which the car is skidding.
- You may need to brake to avoid a collision. If your vehicle doesn't have ABS brakes, pump the brakes to prevent them from locking up.
- These measures should be enough to stop a rear-wheel skid quite quickly. In a four-wheel skid, the vehicle may slide a little farther.

- As you regain control, don't yank the steering wheel to get the car back on course. You will risk flipping the car. Steer gradually. (This is especially important in vehicles with a high centre of gravity, such as SUVs, which are more prone to rolling.)
- Pull over as soon as you can. Skids are frightening and you will need time to calm down before you can return to normal driving.

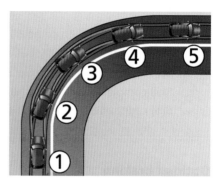

1 Car enters corner too quickly.
2 Rear wheels loose traction, tail end of car fishtails, car skids to the left.
3 Correct the skid by easing of the power and steering left.
4 Traction regained.
5 Control regained.

6 Emergency braking and skid avoidance

Check-list and log-sheet

| 6 Practice 1 | 6 Practice 2 | 6 Practice 3 |
| Date | Date | Date |

Before moving on to the next session, you should be able to demonstrate 'green light' mastery in each skill.
Use this sheet to track progress by **ticking the circles** as shown.

✓ Skill preformed with competence, consistently showing mastery
○ Skill performed correctly but driver sometimes needs prompting
○ Skill accomplished but driver sometimes forgets a check or step
○ Skill completed with some help or a prompt from the mentor
● Skill cannot be completed or requires substantial help from mentor

Optimal braking

○○○○○ Identifies all factors affecting stopping distance

○○○○○ Slows down and increases safe gap to allow for poor road or weather conditions

○○○○○ Maintains ample safe gap and avoids harsh or late braking

○○○○○ Describes difference between antilock and conventional brakes

○○○○○ Applies antilock or conventional brakes correctly to come to an abrupt stop

Hazard Lights, brake failure and pulling off the road

○○○○○ Uses hazard lights only as warning signal

○○○○○ Describes correct procedure for dealing with brake failure

○○○○○ Communicates intentions before pulling off road

○○○○○ Parks vehicle away from traffic stream

○○○○○ Takes reasonable measures to warn following traffic of stopped vehicle's presence

Preventing skids

○○○○○ Lists various road conditions in which skids are more likely

○○○○○ Describes how excessive speed in a turn can result in a skid

○○○○○ Describes how harsh braking can lead to skidding

○○○○○ Explains influence of tyre tread and pressure on likelihood of skids

Responding to a skid

○○○○○ Recognises onset of skid

○○○○○ Describes correct response to skid

○○○○○ Explains importance of avoiding over-steering when recovering from skid

We have spent adequate time practising the skills from session 6 and feel competent enough to move on to the next skill-development session.

Student driver's signature

Mentor's signature

Date

Practice Session 6

Notes

7

Adverse driving conditions

In this session we will practise...

7A ■ Accommodating emergency vehicles and mobile phone use
■ Night driving
7B ■ Adverse weather conditions
■ Freezing conditions

Introduction

Just as it is important to begin driving practice in a low stress environment on dry fine days in daylight, it is also important to practice driving in less favourable conditions and at night. By this stage you should be fairly comfortable with basic vehicle manoeuvring skills and you should be reasonably relaxed when driving. You should also be ready, by now, to increase the complexity of the driving task. In this session we introduce some more challenging driving situations to better prepare you to deal with more realistic everyday driving events.

7A Accommodating emergency vehicles and mobile phone use

Skills
- Emergency services interaction.
- Mobile phone use.
- Driving within the range of your headlights.
- Dealing with oncoming headlights and recovering from glare.
- Overtaking at night and using reflective road markings.

Ideal location
- Practise mobile phone use in a suburban area when traffic is light.
- Practise night time driving in a familiar and secluded area.

Recommended practice time
- Devote specific time to the proper use of mobile phones.
- Practise dealing with emergency vehicles as the opportunity arises.
- Spread night driving throughout the mentoring process.

Additional reading
Instructor Guide
Lesson 7

Steer Clear Driver Education Manual
Attention, Alertness (p.114), First Aid (p. 328)
Risk Management, Emergency Procedures (p.316)
Fatigue and Drowsiness (p.130) Night Driving (p.306)

RSA Rules of the Road
Other safety responsibilities (p.39)
Emergency services vehicles (p.175)
Driving at night (p.50), Tiredness & fatigue (p.136)

Yielding for emergency vehicles

- Maintain a constant awareness of your surroundings. That way you'll be quicker to recognise when an emergency vehicle is approaching. Check your mirrors frequently and scan ahead.

- When an emergency vehicle is approaching from behind, look all around and select a safe place to pull over to allow the vehicle to pass.

- Check your mirrors and signal before continuing on your way because other emergency vehicles may follow – or inconsiderate drivers may attempt to grab the opportunity to move ahead.

- Often, an emergency vehicle approaching from the opposite direction may need to travel on your side of the road to overtake vehicles on the other side. To make room for the emergency vehicle on your side of the road, check your mirrors, signal and pull over to the side.

- Observe how other drivers respond and make way for the emergency vehicle. Follow suit, if it is safe to do so. For example,

you may notice that all the drivers behind you are pulling off to the right to allow the emergency vehicle to pass on the inside. Do the same if the way is clear.

Resuming normal driving after an emergency vehicle passes

- When the emergency vehicle has passed, look out for other vehicles behind it; for example, an ambulance may be following a fire engine. There may be several vehicles, so remain vigilant.

- When the way is clear you may continue on your way but leave at least 150m behind the emergency vehicle in case the driver needs to stop suddenly.

- Take care when pulling back out after yielding for emergency vehicles because some drivers may get back on course more quickly than others.

- Get back into your normal lane position and build up speed with caution.

- Remember that you and other drivers may be distracted by thoughts of the emergency.

Passing the scene of a collision

- Slow down and pass the scene of a collision with due care.
- Give emergency vehicles a wide berth. Emergency personnel need ample room to work; they may be totally absorbed in the task of providing emergency care and be unaware of your presence.
- Watch for instructions from emergency-services personnel and look out for temporary signs.
- Do not stop unless directed to do so or if you are first on the scene and can offer valuable assistance.
- If you must stop, park in a place that will not cause further disruption or danger.
- You may have to drive onto the hard shoulder, between two lanes or into the centre median to avoid a collision scene. Be prepared to wait or give way.
- It is dangerous to focus your attention on the scene of a collision as you pass by. It diverts your attention from the task of driving in a situation where others may also be distracted. It can easily lead to another crash and usually results in unnecessary delays for following traffic.

Safety is paramount. Mobile phone calls are low priority while driving – you can ignore a call or text and easily attend to it at a later time when it's safe to do so.

Mobile phones

It is illegal to make or take a call unless you're using a 'hands-free' set. But even then, being involved in a phone conversation is distracting and dangerous. It takes your attention away from the complex task of driving.

Talking on a mobile phone is different from talking to a passenger or listening to the radio. Passengers know what is going on around the vehicle and they allow for breaks in the conversation. But the person you're talking to on the phone doesn't make such allowances. This means you have to be more attentive to the conversation, and less attentive to your driving.

Switch off the phone when you're driving or learn to ignore a ringing phone until you're in a safe place to answer it. Never attempt to read or write texts while driving

It is best to avoid using a mobile phone while driving. No call is as important as your life.

Stopping to make a call

- If you feel you must make a call, pull well off the road and park in a safe location before picking up the phone.
- Stopping on the hard shoulder is illegal. It is an unsafe place to use a mobile phone because collision records show that on average, vehicles stopped on the hard shoulder get hit within 15 minutes of stopping.
- Continue to pay close attention to your surroundings and to the traffic while on the call. Check your mirrors and keep a good lookout throughout the call; don't get lulled into a false sense of security just because you are inside the vehicle.
- If you must take a call on the hands-free set while driving, remain vigilant to your surroundings and to the traffic while you're on the phone. Keep the call short.

Re-entering the traffic flow after a call

- Finish the call and put down or switch off the phone before attempting to re-enter the traffic flow.
- You must return your complete attention to your driving before moving off. Put the call aside for now.
- If a call or text has been emotional or distressing, you may need to take a break or find a way to calm yourself before continuing to drive.
- No matter what the call was about, you must put it behind you and concentrate on your driving. Your life and the lives of those around you depend on it.

Practice Session 7

255

7   Night driving

Driving after dark presents extra hazards, especially for inexperienced drivers.

When it's dark, you see less colour and contrast, which affects your depth perception. This means it's more difficult to estimate the speed of an approaching vehicle or how quickly you're closing a gap.

Your eyes must constantly readjust as you pass from areas with streetlights to areas that are in darkness.

Night driving often coincides with times when you'd normally be sleeping, which can make it difficult to stay alert.

In the evening you are more likely to encounter other road users who are tired or those who have been drinking, so extra care is needed to avoid them.

Remember, be sure that all your lights are on and working. Carry spare bulbs and replace failed bulbs immediately. It's dangerous and against the law to drive if any of your lights are not working.

Driving within the range of the headlights

- The law states that 'a driver must only drive at a speed that enables him to stop within the distance he can see to be clear'. This is especially important at night. You must ensure that your stopping distance is no longer than the area illuminated by your headlights.
- Slow down and increase your safety margin.
- Street lighting helps you to see the surroundings better, but take care because shadows and the dark gaps between lights can easily obscure hazards.

- Posted speed limits are calculated for optimum daylight conditions. At night, however, you'll often need to slow down to decrease your stopping distance so that it's within the range of the headlights.

- Turn down the dashboard lights and refrain from using lights inside the vehicle because these will severely impair your night vision.

- To check your stopping distance, count the seconds that elapse between the instant you spot an object (such as a road sign) with your light beams and the instant you pass it. On secondary and rural roads, allowing a six-second interval will give you a safer stopping distance. Practice using this method. If you don't reach six, you need to slow down.

- Other vehicles' lights in the distance can fool you into thinking you're getting a clear view of what's up ahead. Do not rely on other vehicles' lights.

- Dirt on the inside or outside of the windscreen will severely hamper your vision, so get into the habit of cleaning your windows frequently.

- Dirty headlights can reduce headlight effectiveness by as much as 75%. Clean your headlights as often as you clean your windscreen.

- Beware of others driving without lights in built-up and well-lit areas.

- Slow down when approaching bends and turns. Your headlights point straight ahead, so you can't see to the sides or what lies around the bend.

Oncoming headlights and glare

- Look slightly to the left to avoid being 'blinded' by the lights of oncoming vehicles, but glance back frequently at the road ahead to ensure the way is clear. Use the left side of the road as a guide to maintaining your position.

- Keep the oncoming vehicle in your peripheral vision.

- If necessary, slow down until you can see clearly again. It takes time for your eyes to adjust after being blinded by bright lights.

- Smudged and dirty windows and mirrors amplify glare, so keep them clean.

- Reduce the glare from following vehicles by adjusting your rear-view mirror for night time driving.
- Dip your own headlights when there is oncoming traffic to avoid dazzling other drivers.

Overtaking at night

- Overtaking at night demands extra care and plenty of room. Be sure the way forward is clear and that it will remain so until you complete the manoeuvre. This isn't always easy to judge. Be patient and wait for the right time. Don't get killed because you don't want to be inconvenienced.
- Switch on your high beams only after you've pulled past the vehicle that you're overtaking.
- When another car overtakes you, leave your lights on high beam until the overtaking driver draws level with you. This gives the overtaking driver a better view of the road. Dip them as the car passes and pulls back into lane in front of you.

Reflective road markings

- Colour-coded 'cat's eye' reflectors, reflective delineator posts and other reflective road markings make night driving easier when you understand their meaning. **The closer reflectors are to each other, the greater the potential hazards.** Cat's eyes in the centre of the road are placed 24 metres apart; at intersection and slip roads, they are 12 metres apart; at bends and dangerous areas, they are placed every 6 metres.

- **White cat's eyes** are used to indicate the centre of the road, divisions between lanes and also the edges of cross hatchings.
- **White delineators** (reflectors on short posts) mark the grass verge where there are no intersections.
- **Yellow cat's eyes** appear on the left-hand side of the road (broken yellow lines by day) and left of the centre medians of motorways (white unbroken line by day).
- **Green cat's eyes** or **green delineators** indicate approaching side roads, slip roads and lay-bys. Green reflective delineators are

also placed in the centre median where a junction is approaching on your right.

- **Red delineators** are posted on the far left-hand side of the centre median of a right-hand junction.
- Bright **amber flashing lights** warn of roadwork hazards ahead.
- Construction cones with **white reflective bands** and topped with rotating **amber reflectors** warn of road-works. Slow down and pass with care.

Bridges and tunnels

- Take extra care crossing bridges in windy conditions. Vehicles crossing bridges and fly-overs are more exposed and subject to the effects of cross winds.
- In freezing temperatures bridges and over-passes freeze sooner than surrounding roads. Pay extra attention to the road surface, the look of the surface and a change in the sound of your vehicle on the road should alert you to the presence of ice.
- When you notice frost on grass verges or frozen puddles expect ice patches on the road especially on elevated road surfaces.
- Get into the appropriate lane in good time on the approach to a tunnel and stay in the same lane throughout. If not already

on switch on your lights before entering the tunnel.

- Reduce speed as necessary to provide an adequate safety margin of at least 3 seconds whilst in the tunnel. Avoid travelling directly alongside other vehicles, as a staggered position gives you some lateral space for manoeuvre should it be necessary in an emergency.

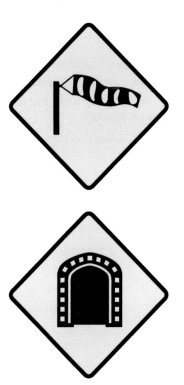

7A Emergency vehicles / mobile phones / night driving /bridges & tunnels

Check-list and log-sheet

<table>
<tr><td>7A Practice 1
Date</td><td>7A Practice 2
Date</td><td>7A Practice 3
Date</td></tr>
</table>

Before moving on to the next session, you should be able to demonstrate 'green light' mastery in each skill.
Use this sheet to track progress by **ticking the circles** as shown.

✓ Skill preformed with competence, consistently showing mastery

◯ Skill performed correctly but driver sometimes needs prompting

◯ Skill accomplished but driver sometimes forgets a check or step

◯ Skill completed with some help or a prompt from the mentor

◯ Skill cannot be completed or requires substantial help from mentor

Emergency situations

◯◯◯◯◯ Keeps a constant awareness for emergency traffic

◯◯◯◯◯ Passes or is passed by emergency vehicles at or near an accident scene

◯◯◯◯◯ Manoeuvres safely to allow emergency vehicles to pass

◯◯◯◯◯ Manoeuvres around the accident scene safely and cautiously

◯◯◯◯◯ Keeps a safe distance back from emergency and other vehicles

◯◯◯◯◯ Can describe what to do in the event of an emergency

◯◯◯◯◯ Rejoins traffic safely once past the scene or once the emergency vehicle has passed

Mobile phone use

◐○○○○   Selects a safe place to pull off the road to make a phone call

◐◐○○○   Checks well ahead to the target stopping area before commencing pulling over

◐◐○○○   Uses MSM before pulling over

◐◐○○○   Checks to the side and over the right shoulder before pulling over

◐◐○○○   Describes the correct procedure and numbers for making an emergency call

◐◐○○○   Rejoins traffic flow after making brief stop

Night driving

◐◐○○○   Drives at a speed that would allow stopping within the distance that can been seen to be clear

◐◐○○○   Does not overdrive the headlights

◐◐○○○   Dips headlights for oncoming traffic and when following

◐◐○○○   Looks to side away from dazzling headlights

◐◐○○○   Glances back momentarily to path of travel

◐◐○○○   Adjusts dash lights and mirror angles to lessen glare at night

◐◐○○○   Checks well ahead and into unlit areas for hazards

Bridges and tunnels

◐◐○○○   Adjusts speed to accommodate for extra wind on fly-overs and bridges

◐◐○○○   Gets into correct lane and stays in it throughout tunnel

◐◐○○○   Keeps an added safety margin in front and to the sides in tunnels

We have spent adequate time practising the skills in Session 7 and feel competent enough to progress to the next skill-development session.

Student driver's signature

Mentor's signature

Date

7B   Adverse weather conditions

Skills
- Keeping control of your vehicle in high winds.
- Coping with reduced visibility when it rains.
- Compensating for reduced traction on wet roads.
- Getting out of a skid.
- Responding to aquaplaning and driving through flooded areas.
- Driving in freezing conditions.
- Driving in fog.
- Coping with glare and reduced visibility in very bright sunshine.

Ideal location
- Take the opportunity to practice driving in rainy and blustery weather. Your usual practice zone will be fine – if possible, try to include a variety of roads (urban and rural). It is best to find an open, empty area such as a car park for the first practice sessions in freezing conditions.

Recommended practice time
- Driving in adverse conditions can be very tiring for inexperienced drivers – multiple short practice sessions may be more beneficial than longer sessions, use good judgment. A total of at least one hour should be given to practicing each type of driving condition.

Additional reading
Instructor Guide
Lesson 7

Steer Clear Driver Education Manual
(p.37), (p.243), (p.296), (p.301), (p.305)

RSA Rules of the Road
Stopping distances for cars (p.94)

Slowing down for the weather

Wind, rain, snow, ice, mist, fog and even sunshine present different driving challenges. Slowing down and increasing your safety margin gives you more time to detect and respond to hazards. The worse the weather conditions get, the more you need to slow down to keep your vehicle under control.

High winds

- Strong gusts of wind have a greater effect on motorcycles, bicycles, trucks and trailers than they have on cars. Be alert for vehicles getting pushed into your path. Leave extra lateral space when overtaking or when being passed.

- Wind that is blocked momentarily by an obstacle (such as a building) can hit you suddenly when you get past it. If you feel a loss of control in circumstances like these, slow down immediately to reduce lift, to increase traction and to improve your road holding so that you can regain control.

Rain

The hazards of driving in the rain include:

- reduced visibility,
- reduced road holding,
- compromised steering,
- increased stopping time and increased stopping distance.

When it rains, the volume and density of traffic often increases and there are extra problems associated with pedestrians and cyclists rushing to avoid the elements.

Dealing with reduced visibility when it rains

Rainy weather interferes with your ability to see other road users and with their ability to see you:

- The distance you can see is shortened because of water droplets in your line of sight.

- Mist rising off a warm road or spray from the wheels of other vehicles will obscure your view even more.

- Cool rain falling on warm

windows causes them to mist up on the inside, compounding the problem.

- Rain clouds obscure the sunlight and make the road darker – especially close to dawn and dusk.
- All drivers will have the same problems, which means that in rainy weather, everyone on the road will not see as well as they would in dry conditions. You can take steps to improve your vision and visibility, but it is physically impossible for it to be as good as it is on a clear, sunny day.

Take these measures to compensate for the reduced visibility of rainy weather:

- Use your wipers and window washing fluid to keep the outside of the windscreen clear.
- Turn on your dipped headlights to make yourself more visible.
- Keeping the inside of your windscreen clean will reduce interior condensation. Use the heater to clear the windows and mirrors.
- Stay well back from other vehicles so you don't have to contend with their spray on your windscreen as well as the rain.
- Use extra caution when overtaking in the rain – but note that overtaking may only be appropriate on dual carriageways or motorways. Switch your wipers to the fastest setting before you start to pass because the vehicle in front may have been acting as a barrier against the rain while you were behind it. Faster wiper speed will also deal with the added spray that will wash across your windscreen as you go by.
- Stay alert and keep scanning. Turn the radio down or off so that you are better able to hear what's going on around your vehicle.

Reduced traction on wet roads

Water on the road acts as a lubricant resulting in reduced tyre traction. You are more likely to lose control or skid in wet conditions. When the road is wet, you can easily lose control at speeds that would be fine on a dry road. These measures will help you cope with reduced traction on wet roads:

- Slow down. Remember, the slower you go, the more control you have because you maximise traction and minimise the forces trying to overcome traction.

- Take care of your tyres. Be sure you have adequate tread; the tread design forces water away from your tyres to help maintain traction. Proper inflation is also important for this reason.

- Be extremely careful when there is a light rain after a long dry spell. The small amount of water combines with accumulated oil, debris and dirt on the road surface, resulting in a particularly slick mixture.

- Aquaplaning can occur when the tyre tread cannot eject water from under the tyres quickly enough. With a thin layer of water between your tyres and the road, you have no traction, the steering becomes unresponsive and braking causes you to skid. If this happens, immediately take your foot off the accelerator. Once you slow down enough, you should regain traction.

- Prevent aquaplaning by slowing down and avoiding accumulated water patches. If you must drive through standing water, slow down even more.

- Regardless of speed, it takes far more time and distance to stop when the road is wet. Slow down and allow at least twice as much stopping distance as you would in dry weather. The two-second rule becomes the four-second rule. Begin decelerating and braking lightly sooner than you normally would.

Floods

Where possible, avoid driving through any significant flooding. It is generally a much safer alternative to turn around and use another route or to wait for the water to drain. If you must drive across a flooded road, these guidelines will help:

- Do not cross a flooded area if you can't determine how deep it is. If you're unfamiliar with the road, it's better to wait and watch another vehicle go through. If there's little traffic, you may be able to pull off the road safely and inspect the flooded area on foot.

- Do not attempt to cross a flooded area with high water flow, even if it looks shallow. Do not drive through water that reaches just below the centre point of your wheels unless you're in a vehicle that is specially equipped for such conditions.

- Stop as you approach the flood, scan the area, and then proceed slowly if you deem it safe to do so. Stay in low gear to keep the engine speed up – this helps keep water out of the exhaust.

- Stay where the water is shallowest. On a level road, this is normally in the centre where the high point of the camber is. On a sloped road, it is on the uphill side.

- After leaving the water, drive slowly and gently test your brakes to be sure they're dry and working properly.

7   Freezing conditions

- Use winter-grade windscreen wash during the winter to prevent ice from forming on your windscreen. (It will also help protect the reservoir from cracking.) Be sure that you have adequate antifreeze in the engine's cooling system. Carry a windscreen de-icer or scraper and clear all the windows and lights before driving.

- Be sure that your tyres are correctly inflated and that they have the minimum tread required by law.

- Warm up the engine according to the manufacturer's guidelines, if necessary.

- Drive more slowly to increase your safety margin.

- Watch closely for signs of ice. Look for ice on windows, on cars and on puddles and grass verges. Listen to how the road sounds; a change may indicate the presence of ice. If you have trouble walking to your car due to ice, you can assume it will be a problem on the road.

- Be especially careful when crossing bridges and overpasses because these areas freeze more quickly than roads at ground level. This is because cold air passes over and under them, taking away heat more rapidly.

- When conditions warm up and the ice melts, watch out for parts of the road that are in shade. These may retain ice long after the rest of the road has thawed.

- Melting ice has even less traction than solid ice.

- Be particularly careful if a light rain falls in sub-freezing temperatures because this can form black ice. Black ice is a very thin but slick ice patch that is difficult to see.

- Slow down and speed up gradually and with caution in icy conditions. Sharp manoeuvres of any kind tend to cause skidding and loss of control. If you find yourself skidding, take your foot off the accelerator and turn gently in the direction of the skid.

Driving in snow

To stay safe in snowy conditions, it's better to avoid driving if at all possible. If you do have to drive, the following measures will help you cope with snow:

- Slow down. Assume there is ice under the snow and give yourself the same safety margin you would allow on ice – or greater.

- Dress in warm clothing and pack the following in your car: a mobile phone, rug, shovel, scraper, brush and some emergency food and drink if you'll be in a rural or isolated area.

- Clear snow from all windows and lights before setting out.

- Drive in the ruts left by other vehicles to help your traction.

- If you get caught in a snow storm, slow down gradually. Refrain from overtaking, unnecessary lane changes or sudden movements. Drive

carefully with dipped headlights on, increase your stopping distance and look as far ahead as possible. Turn off the radio because driving in snow requires your full attention. If conditions are very bad, you should get off the road and park in a safe place. If you're within a couple of kilometres of home, the best choice may be to leave the car safely parked and walk.

- If you get stuck in a snow storm somewhere hazardous and cannot leave the vehicle, turn on your hazard lights and use your engine sparingly to stay warm. Open the window slightly for ventilation.

Driving in fog

Loss of visibility is the main hazard in fog; it's hard to see and to be seen. If the fog is very bad, the prudent measure is to wait until it lifts. If the fog sets in while you're driving, however, you need to deal with it, at least until you can pull over somewhere safe. Here are some ways to stay safe while driving in fog:

- Slow down. Stay well back from other vehicles. If you can see their lights clearly, you're probably too close. Be aware that the vehicle ahead will displace the fog, and create the illusion that visibility is better than it really is.

- Turn on your dipped headlights. Don't use high beams because the light reflects off the water droplets that make up the fog, creating glare.
- Don't speed up in the clear patches between fog banks. There may be something hidden just inside the next fogged area.
- Use the road lines and reflective markings to maintain your lateral safety margin.
- Drive at a speed that allows you to stop safely within the distance you can see clearly.
- Slow down gradually and give ample warning to following traffic that may be too close or that may not be able to see your brake lights.
- If you have fog lights, use them. They won't obscure other drivers' view if the fog has reduced visibility to 100 metres or less. It is inappropriate and hazardous to use fog lights when there is no fog or in any conditions that

interfere with another driver's ability to see, so be sure to turn them off when the fog clears. You may find it helpful to alternate between the high beams and fog lights as the fog density changes.

■ If conditions deteriorate and you feel that you are not in control, find a safe place to stop well off the road and wait for conditions to improve.

Dealing with bright sunshine

■ Lower the sunshade or put on sunglasses.

■ If sunlight is obscuring your view, it's doing the same to other drivers. It is more difficult for others to see your indicators or brake lights. Also, when the sun

is low and behind you, it will be hard for oncoming traffic to see ahead.

■ Be vigilant for pedestrians who are usually unaware that the dazzling sunlight conceals them. More often, they think they're plainly visible because the sun is shining brightly.

■ Slow down as you would in other adverse conditions, because this gives you a greater safety margin.

7B Adverse weather conditions
Check-list and log-sheet

7B Practice 1 Date	7B Practice 2 Date	7B Practice 3 Date

Before moving on to the next session, you should be able to demonstrate 'green light' mastery in each skill.
Use this sheet to track progress by **ticking the circles** as shown.

- ✓ Skill preformed with competence, consistently showing mastery
- ○ Skill performed correctly but driver sometimes needs prompting
- ○ Skill accomplished but driver sometimes forgets a check or step
- ○ Skill completed with some help or a prompt from the mentor
- ○ Skill cannot be completed or requires substantial help from mentor

Poor weather conditions

○○○○○	Slows down to accommodate for poor weather conditions
○○○○○	Increases following gap in bad weather
○○○○○	Keeps windows, mirrors and lights clean and clear
○○○○○	Anticipates the effects of wind and rain when passing or being passed

Rain

○○○○○	Cleans windows and mirrors before driving
○○○○○	Drives in a position well clear of spray and debris from other traffic
○○○○○	Drives with lights on in adverse weather conditions
○○○○○	Adjusts window wiper speed in anticipation of extra load when overtaking
○○○○○	Anticipates and allows for erratic pedestrian movement in rain

○○○○○ Factors in extra driving time to lessen stress in adverse conditions

○○○○○ Remains calm and alert in congested traffic situations

○○○○○ Navigate around or through an area of standing water

Hot and cold conditions

○○○○○ Recognise the tell tale signs of frost and ice

○○○○○ Takes time to prepare vehicle for driving in freezing conditions

○○○○○ Slows down sufficiently in snow or ice

○○○○○ Prevents or recovers from an aquaplaning situation

○○○○○ Correctly uses fog lights

○○○○○ Maintains an adequate speed and following distance in fog

○○○○○ Deals correctly with low or dazzling sunlight situations

We have spent adequate time practising the skills required to drive in sbuilt up areas and feel competent to progress to the next skill development session.

Student driver's signature

Mentor's signature

Date

Notes

8

Dual carriageways and motorways

In this session we will practise...

8A ■ Dual carriageways and motorways
8B ■ Changing lanes, overtaking and leaving motorways

Introduction

Motorways allow traffic to move long distances without interruption; ramps and fly-overs enable traffic to cross unhindered. Divided lanes allow traffic to travel more safely in opposite directions, lessening the possibilities of head-on or side-on impact collisions. Learner drivers are not permitted to drive on motorways, but it is important that you know how to use them. Simulated motorway driving practice can take place on high grade dual carriageways or as an attentive and engaged passenger in a vehicle being driven on a motorway by your mentor.

8A Dual carriageways and motorways

Skills

- Entering a motorway or dual carriageway.
- Maintaining the best lane position.
- Monitoring and adjusting your safety margin.
- Enabling other drivers to merge and diverge safely.
- Co-operating when another driver overtakes.
- Changing lanes and overtaking.
- Approaching and leaving toll booths.
- Using exit ramps to leave the motorway.
- Adjusting to new road conditions after motorway driving.

Ideal location

- Start out on dual carriageways and primary roads with motorway like conditions in preparation for driving on the motorway. Observe as a passenger, good motorway driving practices being demonstrated by the mentor.

Recommended practice time

- Two one hour sessions. Time spent as a passenger in a car travelling on a motorway where the mentor is demonstrating good motorway driving practice, is also recommended.

Additional reading

Instruction Guide
Lesson 8

Steer Clear Driver Education Manual
(p.230), (p.239), (p.267), (p.292), (p.142), (p.144)

RSA Rules of the Road
(p.43), (p.44), (p.119), (p.88)

Limited-access primary roads and motorways use a system of on ramps and off ramps for accessing and exiting the main road. This makes joining the traffic flow safer. On motorways, elevated interchanges remove the dangers of road-level junctions, enabling traffic to travel at higher speeds more safely.

Entering a motorway or dual carriageway

- Entry ramps have three parts: the entrance ramp itself, the acceleration lane and the merge area.

- While on the entrance ramp, look to the road ahead and glance to the sides to assess the traffic flow, speed and available gaps.

- In the acceleration lane, speed up to match the speed of the traffic flow and switch on the right indicator.

- When the white line or edge of the traffic separation island becomes a broken line, you may begin to merge if there is an adequate gap.

- Adjust your speed so that you can move into the best available gap.

- When you've established your new lane position, turn off the indicator and adjust your speed if necessary.

- Adopt an appropriate travelling speed to suit the conditions.

Optimum lane position

- The normal driving position is in the centre of the lane. Practise driving in this position by looking to the target area well in advance, 15–20 seconds ahead.

- The centre position offers the most options and clearance from other traffic.

- Practise moving to the right of the lane when overtaking.

- Adopt a left-side lane position to maximise space when being overtaken by large vehicles.

- When preparing to take a left exit, leave a safety margin of about 20cm from the left side line. Occasionally it will be necessary to straddle a lane line to avoid an obstruction; use this position cautiously and for as little time as possible.

- You are entitled to use the hard shoulder temporarily but only in an emergency, not in the course of normal driving or exiting the motorway.

Safety margins

- You have the most control over the space or gap you leave in front of your vehicle. New drivers should aim to leave at least three seconds to allow time for making decisions and taking action. Three seconds gives you time to steer or brake to avoid hazards when travelling at moderate speeds.

- Practise making speed adjustments to maintain a three-second gap and to stay comfortably in the traffic flow. (You can adopt the standard two-second gap later, when you have gained sufficient experience.)

- Practise dropping back whenever other vehicles cut into your safety margin.

- While it should be unusual to have tailbacks or stoppages on a motorway, road-works and heavy traffic congestion make motorway slowdowns reasonably common.

- If you have to stop unexpectedly, for example if a tailback forms due to a collision up ahead, turn on your hazard lights to warn following traffic that you have stopped.

- When you stop, you should be able to see where the rear wheels of the car in front of you meet the road.

Lateral space

- Avoid driving beside other vehicles on a multi-lane road. Practise staying slightly behind or slightly ahead of other vehicles to gain more options.

- Practise dropping back or adjusting your lane position when other vehicles enter your lateral space.

- Pass vehicles only when the way ahead is clear. Don't get stuck in a compromised position.

Anticipating and accommodating the needs of others

- Road signs, overpasses and green cat's eyes should alert you to upcoming slip lanes for getting on and off the motorway.

- When approaching or passing motorway entry and exit ramps, keep a lookout and adjust your position and speed if necessary to facilitate other vehicles entering or leaving the road.

- When you see a vehicle trying to join the motorway from a slip road, move over to the overtaking lane if it is safe. Alternatively, adjusting your speed may also assist incoming traffic to merge safely.

Being overtaken

- Be prepared to adjust your speed and position to accommodate overtaking vehicles.

- If a vehicle cuts in too close after passing you, slow down to avoid debris from its wheels.

- Moving to the left lessens the effect of spray and dirt from large passing vehicles in rainy conditions.

- Assisting other drivers who want to pass is far safer than hindering or competing with them.

8B   Changing lanes, overtaking and leaving motorways

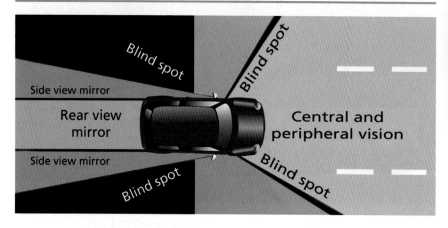

Observing blind spots and to the rear

- Check the rear-view and side mirrors frequently – every 7-10 seconds.
- Be aware that objects viewed in mirrors are much closer than they appear.
- Check to the sides and over your right shoulder to ensure your blind spots are clear.
- Make sure you don't move the steering wheel when you turn your head to look around.

Changing lanes

- Practise changing lanes on a dual carriageway or multi-lane road.
- Practise anticipating the needs of other drivers and accommodating them by changing lanes where necessary.
- Anticipate and get into the required lane in good time in preparation for turns.
- Check to the rear and sides for traffic flow and gaps.
- When you've identified a target area, communicate your intended manoeuvre by indicating.
- Check again to the rear, the sides and over your right shoulder.

- Accelerate gently while gradually steering towards the new lane position.
- Adopt the optimum lane position in the new lane.
- Choose a position with the greatest lateral space.
- Return to the left-hand lane when you have completed your manoeuvre and when it is safe to do so.
- Complete all the rear-view and blind-spot checks before moving back into the left-hand lane.
- Remember to move back into the left-hand lane gradually and to slightly accelerate to allow for the greater distance covered during the diagonal phase of the manoeuvre.

Overtaking

- Practise overtaking stationary or slow-moving vehicles.
- First ensure that you're in an area where overtaking is permitted, and that the manoeuvre will be safe.
- Look to the target area and ensure that it's clear before commencing the manoeuvre.
- Check your mirrors and blind spots.

- Indicate to let other drivers know that you're about to overtake.
- Move out gradually in plenty of time to leave sufficient room from the obstruction or the vehicle you're overtaking. Avoid erratic movements and lane changes.
- When two lanes are available, move fully into the overtaking lane.
- Completely clear the obstruction or vehicle before you indicate your intention to move back into your lane.
- Check your mirrors. The vehicle/obstruction you've passed should be fully visible in the rear-view mirror before you return to your original lane position.
- When overtaking larger vehicles in bad weather, be prepared for extra rain and wind when you pass the relative shelter of the vehicle.

Toll booths

- When availing of a toll road, think ahead and prepare by having money ready to cover the charge.

- If you don't have the money to hand in advance, do not attempt to find it when you're approaching the toll area. It is much safer to look for the correct change when you've stopped in the booth area.

- Get into the correct lane well in advance as you approach the booths. Refrain from jumping from one lane to another.

- If you're joining the back of a queue at a toll station, leave a gap the length of a car until at least two vehicles have stopped behind you. Check your mirrors and be ready to respond if the vehicle behind you looks unlikely to stop in time.

- It is an offence – and it's dangerous – to cross a solid white dividing line between lanes in a toll-booth area.

- Watch for other drivers who may be 'lane hopping'. Be courteous to drivers who have inadvertently found themselves in the wrong lane and who need to move over.

- When you've paid the correct toll and you get the green light, move off without delay.

- Be careful as you leave the toll area where many lanes merge.

- If you plan on using a toll road often, investing in a prepaid token will save you time.

- Prepaid toll tags will become the norm shortly, they can be purchased on line or by telephone; using them will be more efficient and less costly than paying cash.

Leaving the motorway

- Plan well ahead so that you can anticipate when you will arrive at the exit of your choice. Knowing the number of the exit or road you wish to take will help.

- Junction signs with road numbers are posted approximately one kilometre before the exit.

- Signs with destinations and place names are posted half a kilometre ahead of the exit.

- Blue 'countdown' signs with

white bars are posted at 300m, 200m and 100m prior to the beginning of an exit ramp.

- Exit ramps have three parts: the approach, which begins at the 100m countdown sign; the slip road (the exit ramp itself), where you should slow down; and the merging or stopping area where the exit ramp joins the next road or junction.

- When you see the 300m-to-exit signpost, check your mirrors, signal and prepare to move over into the slip lane as you pass the 100m sign.

- Maintain speed until you have left the travelling lane and are fully within the slip lane. Then check your mirrors again and slow down to the posted speed limit.

- Gear down and adjust your driving to suit the new road conditions when you leave the motorway travel lane. You may need to decrease your speed several times.

- Look well ahead and anticipate the need to come to a stop if necessary.

- If the slip road has a curve or sharp bend, slow down in plenty of time so that you'll remain in control.

- When there is more than one lane on the exit ramp, choose the lane that will set you up for the turn you need to make at the end of the ramp.

- If you miss the exit, continue on to the next one. Never attempt to cut into a slip lane at the last second or to reverse along the hard shoulder back to an exit ramp.

Adjusting to a new environment after leaving a motorway

- When you leave the motorway, be alert for other types of road users such as pedestrians and cyclists.

- On the motorway, junctions and intersections consist of exit ramps and overpasses. But off the motorway, junctions and intersections are at road-level and must be handled differently. Keep this in mind as you leave the motorway.

- When the background colour of road signs changes from blue to green or black, it means that you are no longer on the motorway and that the motorway rules do not apply. This may occur when a motorway becomes a dual carriageway. Even though the dual carriageway is of similar size to the motorway, it may have intersections and reduced speeds. The dual carriageway may also be open to traffic that would not be allowed on the motorway (e.g. slower-moving vehicles and cyclists).

- When you've been driving at high speed on the motorway, it can be difficult to judge your speed on the new road. Travelling at 60km/h feels like 40km/h or less after 120km/h.

8 Dual carriageway and motorway driving

Check-list and log-sheet

| 8 Practice 1 Date | 8 Practice 2 Date | 8 Practice 3 Date |

Before moving on to the next session, you should be able to demonstrate 'green light' mastery in each skill.
Use this sheet to track progress by **ticking the circles** as shown.

✔ Skill preformed with competence, consistently showing mastery
○ Skill performed correctly but driver sometimes needs prompting
○ Skill accomplished but driver sometimes forgets a check or step
○ Skill completed with some help or a prompt from the mentor
◐ Skill cannot be completed or requires substantial help from mentor

Entering the motorway

○○○○○ Approaches from slip road with due care and awareness
○○○○○ Matches speed to merge seamlessly with traffic
○○○○○ Checks mirrors and signals before manoeuvring
○○○○○ Adjusts speed to suit traffic flow and chooses safe gap to merge
○○○○○ Uses mirrors correctly, checks over right shoulder
○○○○○ Moves decisively onto the motorway at appropriate angle

Optimum lane position

○○○○○ Selects the optimum lane position for driving straight ahead
○○○○○ Selects the correct lane position to avoid an obstruction
○○○○○ Adopts the best lane position when being overtaken
○○○○○ Looks well ahead to anticipate and make adjustments

Safety margins

⦿⦾⦾⦾⦾ Maintains a three-second following safety margin

⦿⦾⦾⦾⦾ Monitors movements of other vehicles and allows for their needs

⦿⦾⦾⦾⦾ Stops well back from other vehicles stopped in traffic

⦿⦾⦾⦾⦾ Approaches tailback traffic queues cautiously

⦿⦾⦾⦾⦾ Stops at least two car lengths behind the last vehicle in a queue

⦿⦾⦾⦾⦾ Monitors following traffic and uses hazard lights when stopped

⦿⦾⦾⦾⦾ Closes gap to queue after following vehicles have stopped

Space management

⦿⦾⦾⦾⦾ Has good spatial awareness, checks mirrors & ahead frequently

⦿⦾⦾⦾⦾ Maximises lateral lane space when being overtaken

⦿⦾⦾⦾⦾ Maximises lateral lane space when overtaking

⦿⦾⦾⦾⦾ Adjusts lane position to maximise lateral space in heavy traffic

⦿⦾⦾⦾⦾ Anticipates and prepares for effects of weather conditions when overtaking or when being overtaken

⦿⦾⦾⦾⦾ Accommodates other drivers who want to pass or change lanes

⦿⦾⦾⦾⦾ Adjusts following gap to accommodate overtaking vehicle

Observing blind spots and to the rear

⦿⦾⦾⦾⦾ Is fully aware of presence of following traffic

⦿⦾⦾⦾⦾ Checks mirrors frequently, every 7-10 seconds

⦿⦾⦾⦾⦾ Checks all areas before manoeuvres

⦿⦾⦾⦾⦾ Keeps steering wheel steady when checking blind spots

Changing lanes

○○○○○   Checks to ensure that the target area is free to enter or exit

○○○○○   Checks blind spots before indicating or beginning to manoeuvre

○○○○○   Indicates correctly in good time

○○○○○   Moves to new lane at gradual angle over 4-5 broken line marks

○○○○○   Chooses lane position with optimum spacing from other traffic

○○○○○   Anticipates and prepares for upcoming exits

○○○○○   Anticipates the needs of other drivers and adjusts accordingly

○○○○○   Drives in the left-hand lane as a rule and only uses the right-hand lane for overtaking, avoiding obstructions and aiding the general flow of traffic

Overtaking

○○○○○   Chooses safe and appropriate places to overtake

○○○○○   Checks target area before commencing overtaking manoeuvre

○○○○○   Moves completely into overtaking lane when passing

○○○○○   Moves into overtaking position at a smooth and gradual angle

○○○○○   Accelerates gradually when changing lanes to compensate for extra distance covered

○○○○○   Checks rear, side views before indicating

○○○○○   Ensures that vehicles just passed are fully visible in rear-view mirror before attempting to pull back into lane

○○○○○   Returns to left lane once overtaking is complete

○○○○○   Leaves an adequate and considerate safety margin to the rear when returning to the lane in front of the vehicle just passed

Practice Session 8

285

Toll booths and leaving the motorway

○○○○○	Approaches toll with care, selects correct lane well in advance
○○○○○	Exits toll area keeping good observation, speed and position
○○○○○	Gathers information from advance signs in preparation for exit
○○○○○	Correctly prepares to take exit from motorway
○○○○○	Maintains speed, visual checks and signals to take exit
○○○○○	Once on slip road slows to appropriate speed
○○○○○	Chooses correct lane position for change of direction at next junction

We have spent adequate time practising the lane changing and overtaking skills from session 8A/8B and feel competent enough to progress to the next skill development session.

Student driver's signature

Mentor's signature

Date

When all practice sessions 8 are complete, be sure to record this in the training record sheet in the blue section in the middle of the book so that the driving instructor will know that the you are is ready to progress to driving lesson 9.

9

Vehicle maintenance and navigation

In this session we will practise...

- Maintaining care of your vehicle
- Navigation

Introduction

Vehicles that are cared for properly are more dependable and efficient. Replacing worn parts is less costly than breakdowns and repairs, saving you money in the long run. Well kept vehicles are more likely to perform as expected, which is particularly important in emergency situations. Knowing how to carry out routine maintenance and deal with minor breakdowns is an essential element of being a responsible driver. This session introduces everyday maintenance skills and will help you to avoid expensive problems and deal with minor problems, like a flat tyre.

9　Maintaining your vehicle

Skills
- Light maintenance and changing light bulbs.
- Checking oil level, window-washer fluid and wipers
- Brake fluid and coolant levels.
- Tyre tread, pressure and wheel changing.
- Safety restraints and seat adjustment.
- Maps, route planning and information services.

Ideal location
- Go outside, roll up your sleeves and spend some time looking at the vehicle inside, outside and under the bonnet.
- Practise navigation first at home and later as you are driving.

Recommended practice time
- Ensure sufficient time is spent to get familiar with the routine checks and maintenance by actually doing the checks and changing a wheel and various light bulbs.
- While you can learn the basics of navigation in half an hour, putting it into practice is best done while driving around.

Additional reading
Instruction Guide
Lesson 9

Steer Clear Driver Education Manual
Routine checks (p.79), Basic maintenance (p.82)

RSA Rules of the Road
Lights and reflectors (p.32), Windscreens and mirrors (p.34)

Taking care of your vehicle

Safe, happy and incident-free driving is all about prevention and risk management. Keeping your vehicle well maintained will help avoid breakdowns and unexpected mechanical problems. Vehicles that are not well maintained cannot be relied on to perform as expected and may let you down – not just in an everyday driving situation but, worse, in an emergency.

Keeping a service log

A service log is a great asset in keeping your car roadworthy. The kilometres slip by faster than you realise, and it's easy to forget to check your brakes or change the oil. The owner's manual in your vehicle has a maintenance-log section for recording services and repairs. If you keep it up to date, you'll know in advance when the next service is due. You'll also have fewer service-related problems because you'll know when to get worn parts replaced before they become a problem. Replacing a timing belt, at a regular service, for example, can be as much as ten times less expensive than replacing and repairing the damage caused by a timing belt that fails while driving. When the time comes to sell your vehicle, a good service record will reassure any prospective buyer and help to enhance the resale value.

Maintaining the lights

Driving at night or at other times when visibility is poor hampers your ability to see and be seen. Even the cleanest and brightest headlights will not compensate fully for the conditions but they provide the best visibility under the circumstances.

Dirt on your windscreen and on your headlights can reduce your ability to see by as much as 75%, so it is imperative that you keep them clean. If your windscreen needs cleaning it is likely that your lights do too. Headlights that don't have integrated washers will need to be cleaned by hand regularly. Get into the habit of doing this every time you fill up with fuel and any time you have been driving in a particularly dirty environment such as behind a truck or through a construction area.

Broken or faulty lights are extremely dangerous for you and for other road users:

- When only one headlight is working, you could be mistaken for a motorcycle and be hit by an oncoming vehicle that has not left sufficient room for you, or you might fail to see a pedestrian or obstruction at the side of the road if the inside headlight is broken.

- If one or more bulbs are not working properly, the remainder of the bulbs tend to be too bright, causing glare and dazzling oncoming drivers.

- If your indicators are broken, you won't be able to communicate your intentions correctly to other drivers.

- Malfunctioning or broken brake lights are particularly hazardous, because following traffic will have no idea that you are stopping or slowing until it may be too late to respond.

- Get into the habit of checking the reflection of your lights in shop windows or in the rear of the vehicle in front when you're stopped in traffic.

- Once a week or every time you refuel, check the light bulbs by walking around the vehicle with the lights switched on. Get someone to help you check the brake lights.

Most manufacturers and auto stores now carry model-specific and generic bulb kits so that you can have a complete bulb replacement set in your vehicle at all times. In most European countries, the law states that drivers must carry and be able to replace a full set of lights in their vehicle. It is an offence – and it's very dangerous – to drive a vehicle with defective lights.

Replacing light bulbs

- When you realise that you have a blown bulb, turn off the lights before attempting to replace the bulb. If you don't know how to change the bulb, check the owner's handbook for instructions.

- In general, you access headlight bulbs from behind the light, which you can get to by opening the bonnet.

- The headlight bulb is usually the largest socket visible from the back; it has three wires connected to it. To access the bulb you must first remove the cover from the back of the headlamp unit. You now need to release a clip or spring to release the bulb. As you remove the old bulb, note how it fits into the socket. Take care not to touch the glass of the new bulb – hold it through its wrapper or a cloth. (This is because grease from your fingers can create uneven heating, causing the new bulb to fail prematurely.) Once the bulb is in place, reposition the spring/clip and insert the bulb back into position. Then lock the whole lot back into the lamp socket.

■ The side lights are located in the same area as the headlights and usually have two wires coming out of the plug. A twist-and-pull action usually releases the bulb and socket together.

■ Indicator bulbs vary from one vehicle to another but most are the bayonet type that require a slight push in and twist, similar to a household bulb.

■ To save on replacement costs, expensive coloured indicator lenses have been replaced with low cost coloured bulbs. After a certain amount of use the paint fades and cracks and the orange colour is no longer effective, when this happens it is time to replace the bulb.

■ To change the rear bulbs, you usually need to remove an access panel where all the bulbs are mounted together. Remove the bulbs from the front of the mounting by using the gentle press-in-and-twist method.

■ When you have replaced a bulb, make sure it's working properly.

Checking the oil level

■ It is normal for engines to consume some oil. Older engines tend to consume more oil than newer ones; if your engine uses a lot of oil it needs to be checked by a mechanic. You should be in the habit of checking your oil every 500km and before you begin a long trip.

■ To check the oil level, park on level ground and switch off the engine. Wait for about 3-5 minutes to allow the engine to cool a little and for the oil to settle back into the oil pan.

■ Have a cloth ready and remove the oil dipstick. Wipe the end clean and then reinsert it all the way. Remove it again and check the level on the min/max mark on the dip stick. The oil should not be below the minimum level or above the maximum level. If the level is low, top it up with the appropriate grade of oil (check the owner's manual). Top up in small amounts and keep an eye

on the level because overfilling can lead to increased internal pressure and can result in serious engine damage.

- Over time, oil loses its lubrication properties and needs to be changed to ensure the longevity of your engine. See your owner's manual for details of how often the oil and oil filters need to be changed (usually this is between 8,000 and 16,000km). Oil and filters are best changed in a service station where any waste products can be disposed of correctly, without harming the environment.

Fuel

- As a general rule, keep the fuel level above the halfway mark. Always fill up the petrol or diesel tank before embarking on a long journey, especially if travelling to unfamiliar areas or before using a motorway.
- Pull up close to your chosen fuel pump on the same side as your vehicle's fuel filling point. If there is more than one pump available, drive forward to allow other vehicles to access the other pumps. Switch off the engine.
- Do not smoke while filling up because fuel fumes are highly flammable and can ignite easily.
- Using a mobile phone is not advisable because filling fuel is a potentially dangerous activity which requires your full attention.
- Petrol is a known carcinogen which means that it causes cancer. To avoid inhaling petrol or diesel fumes, stand upwind of the pump. Place the petrol nozzle fully into the filling point on your vehicle and squeeze the pump handle to begin the flow. The handle should click off automatically when the fuel tank is full. Allow the nozzle to drip into the tank before removing it and putting it back into the pump holder.
- If you spill or splash petrol, wipe it up immediately. Make sure you remove petrol-soaked clothes before coming close to naked flames or cigarettes.

Window washer fluid

- You'll be able to see the amount of water in the window washer reservoir by looking at it from the outside. Top it up if necessary. You can use ordinary water but washer fluid is better for cleaning and it doesn't freeze.

- Winter-grade washer fluid has a lower freezing point which is very useful in winter time. Ordinary water freezes at a higher temperature, expanding and cracking the reservoir and lines. Ordinary water will be ineffective in freezing conditions in any case, because it will freeze the moment it's sprayed onto the windscreen.

- Summer-grade washer fluid has special additives for removing squashed bugs from your windscreen.

- In some vehicles, the rear window washer fluid needs to be filled separately. Check your owner's manual.

- From time to time it may be necessary to clean out the small opening in the washer spraying nozzle. Use a paper clip or something similar.

Windshield wipers

- Wiper blades that do not clear your windshield properly or wipers that are split or cracked need to be replaced. Check for damaged wipers by lifting the wiper off the windscreen and inspecting it. If you notice that the wipers are leaving streaks on

the windscreen, then it's time to replace them.

- Remove damaged wipers by lifting the wiper arm away from the glass to an upright position. Turn the blade to a 90° angle to release it from the arm. Replace with a compatible new blade (available from your car dealer or motor accessory shops). New wiper blades usually have fitting instructions on the box.

- In older vehicles, the arm spring may not be pressing the blade against the glass, which means the arm will need to be replaced. Most motor factors are helpful with these kind of minor repairs; if you have difficulty following the instructions supplied with the replacements, ask for help.

- In winter the blades may freeze and get stuck to the windshield. Don't try to force them loose or you may damage the mechanism. Use a defroster or heat up the windshield with the defroster inside. A few minutes' patience will prevent a lot of bother later.

Brake fluid

Check the brake fluid level by looking at the level between the minimum and maximum marks on the reservoir. If you are losing brake fluid, you need to get this checked by a service technician without delay.

Coolant

Engine coolant is made up of 1/3 anti-freeze and 2/3 water and it also contains corrosion inhibitors to protect your engine. It's essential to keep the coolant at the correct level. Check the manufacturer's guidelines.

- Insufficient coolant can result in the engine overheating. In older vehicles, it is not unusual to have to top up the coolant on a regular basis.
- You can check the coolant level through the reservoir. The minimum and maximum indicator lines are marked on the outside of the container.

- Do NOT attempt to open the coolant reservoir or the radiator when the engine is hot. Extremely hot liquid can escape under pressure and cause severe burns. If you find that you have to fill up the coolant frequently – for example, every two months – your engine may have a leak. Get a mechanic to check.

Maintaining sufficient tyre tread

Taking good care of your tyres and replacing old or worn ones is essential for effective control. Tyres that are well maintained and properly inflated are less likely to skid.

By law, the minimum tyre tread considered necessary to provide sufficient traction is 1.6mm (less than the thickness of a €2 coin). But it's worth remembering that it is the bare minimum. New car tyres have 6mm or more of tread and provide at least double the grip and stopping ability of worn tyres.

Tyres are made of rubber which grips the road, providing traction and control. The grooves and treads are necessary to displace water and other debris and allow for maximum grip between the rubber and the road. It's easy to check

the condition of your tyres. If the wear-indicator marks are exposed between the treads then the tyre is worn i.e. if the little rubber knobs are flush with the outside tread then the tyre needs replacing.

To ensure that the tread depth is greater than 1.6mm:
- Use a tread gauge if available or…
- Place a coin into the groove between the treads.
- Move your thumb and finger up so your nails touch the edge of the tyre. Grasp the coin at that point and withdraw it.

- Now compare the amount of coin exposed beyond your fingers to the 2mm thickness of a €2 coin. Anything close and your safety is compromised.

Check all the tyres including the spare on a regular basis. A good habit is to check your tyres every time you fill up the fuel tank. You should also have your tyres checked by a tyre service centre at least once a year. Many offer free balancing services and will rotate the tyres front to back and diagonally for a small fee. This will help you to get a longer and more effective life from your tyres.

Maintaining the correct tyre pressure
At best, when correctly inflated, only a small area of each tyre is in contact with the road – less than the area of a €50 note on the average saloon car. When a tyre is over-inflated, only the centre of it touches the road, like a ball on a flat surface. An under-inflated tyre only touches the road at its sides, because the centre of the tyre is arched upwards. Get down on your hands and knees in front of a vehicle with low tyre pressure and you'll see the problem clearly.

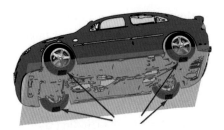

Tyre contact points

When tyres are under or over-inflated, traction can be reduced by fifty to seventy percent, added to this, incorrectly inflated tyres do not perform as required in cornering or stopping manoeuvres. Furthermore, they'll cost you money: soft tyres use at least two extra tanks of fuel per year, and they wear out more quickly so will need to be replaced more frequently.

To adjust your tyre pressure:
- Check the owner's manual or the tyre pressure chart which is usually on the back of the fuel door or on the frame of the driver's door. The correct pressure depends on the load you plan to carry.
- Remove the dust cap from the inflation valve and push the end of the air pump nozzle onto the valve. This enables you to check the current tyre pressure on the gauge.
- Add air by fully depressing the lever on the inflation mechanism.

- To release air partially depress the lever.
- Quickly pull the air pump off the valve. A little air will escape as you do so. Replace the valve's cap.

Regular tyre pressure checks will ensure maximum fuel efficiency and tyre life.

Changing a wheel

Practise changing a wheel in a suitable area, before you have to do it in earnest. That way, you will be prepared and far less anxious if and when you get a flat. On the trial run, you may discover that cable ties need to be cut or that your wheels have a locking mechanism that is quite tricky to figure out even when you are not under pressure. You may even discover that the necessary wheel-release tools are hard to locate or absent in second-hand vehicles. It's better to find out in advance rather than on a cold wet night at the side of the road with a car full of passengers. Take the time to practise it now and sort out any potential problems.

To change a wheel:
- Park the vehicle in a safe location. Turn off the engine and apply the parking brake. Shift into first gear or into the park position in an automatic.
- If you are attempting to change

the wheel at the side of a road, put on your reflective jacket and place your safety triangle at least 50m back from the vehicle.

- Take out the spare wheel, brace, jack, gloves and wheel chocks, if you have them. (If not, try to find some suitable stones to use instead.)

- Place the spare tyre under the vehicle close to the flat. This will provide a buffer if the jack slips.

- To stop the vehicle from moving while you work, place the chocks or rocks on either side of the wheel opposite the flat tyre.

- Use one of the car's floor mats to kneel on.

- If there is a hub cap on the damaged wheel, remove it. You may need to use a special tool or cut a plastic cable tie.

- Use the wheel brace to loosen the nuts on the wheel. Do this before lifting the vehicle with the jack; otherwise, the wheel will spin, making it impossible to loosen the nuts. You may need to put your foot on the wheel brace or use an extension bar if you are having difficulty getting the nuts to loosen. Some vehicles have a special locking nut to prevent theft – you should find the key or unique opening device with the jack and brace or in the glove box.

- Open the jack and place it under the vehicle at the jacking point nearest to the flat tyre. Ensure that the jack is level and on firm ground.

- Open the jack by unscrewing or pumping it until the vehicle and the wheel are raised above the ground. Give yourself room to work. Note that the spare will be slightly larger than the flat because it is fully inflated.

- DO NOT PUT ANY PART OF YOUR BODY UNDER THE VEHICLE WHILE IT IS RAISED UP ON THE JACK.

- Remove the nuts completely and place them to one side. Remove the flat and mount the spare without delay. Hand-tighten the nuts back in place.

- Lower the vehicle on the jack and then tighten all the wheel nuts with the brace.

- Replace the hub cap. Put the wheel chocks, jack, brace, warning triangle and the flat wheel back into the vehicle.

- Wipe your hands, put the floor mat back into the vehicle and prepare to resume your journey.
- If the spare is a compact temporary wheel, do not exceed the stated speed. Go to a garage as soon as possible to have the regular tyre repaired or replaced.
- If carrying a spare wheel is not practical, e.g., on a motorcycle, you can use a chemical tyre inflation aerosol to make a temporary repair. This may also be used in an emergency when it would not be safe or practical to change a flat.

Safety belts and other safety restraints

- The safety belt keeps you in place in the event of sudden slowing or stopping. The powerful and dangerous energy of your body's momentum is dissipated into the vehicle through the safety belt, preventing you from flying forward and colliding with the windshield.
- The safety belt also supports good posture and seating position which helps you to stay alert, especially on long journeys or after a day's work. Practise adjusting your safety belt and seating position to find the most comfortable and secure arrangement.

- Check that all of the safety belts can run freely in and out. Be sure that there are no twists, worn or frayed areas. If the shoulder height can be adjusted, the belt should pass over your shoulder – not over your neck or forearm. Always adjust and lock the adjustment mechanism fully in place before commencing driving. Never attempt to adjust it while driving.
- To check the inertia tension mechanism, pull sharply on the belt. It should lock up if it is working properly. Safety belts that have been activated and stretched in the event of a collision will need to be replaced because the activation tensioners may no longer be reliable.
- In vehicles with drop-down seat backs (which are used for carrying loads), make sure that the safety belts are not snagged or obstructed.
- As the driver, you are responsible for ensuring that all seat belts and safety restraints in the vehicle are in good working order and that they are suitable for each passenger. Be sure that you know how to adjust all restraints correctly, especially when there are children on board.

Mirrors

- Clean mirrors are vital for safety. Check your mirrors every time you drive – never begin a journey with dirty mirrors. Mist and rain stays on dirty wing mirrors for longer and even the smallest spots tend to distort images and cause glare when the sun or lights are reflected in the mirrors.

- During your cockpit drill, quickly check that all the mirrors are correctly adjusted to give you the best view to the sides and rear. This is especially important after parking in a confined space or public car park where you may have adjusted your side mirrors for parking. The mirrors may also have been knocked out of place by pedestrians passing by.

- As part of your routine vehicle checks, gently grip the mirrors and try moving them to see if they are securely mounted.

- Cracked or broken mirrors distort images and could mask or obscure a hazard. Replace damaged mirrors without delay.

Seats

- As part of your cockpit drill, shift your weight around in your seat to check that it's properly anchored and locked into position. After any reconfiguration or movement of the other seats in the vehicle, check them to ensure that they are correctly secured in position.

- The head restraints have two main functions. First, they help prevent spinal injuries (such as whiplash) in the event of sudden impact. Second, in a sudden stop, they prevent unsecured objects, that are flying forwards, from hitting you in the back of the head. For the best effectiveness, the restraint should be in line with the back of your head and the middle of the restraint at the same level as your ears. The restraint should just clear the back of your head when you are seated correctly. Remember that it is a head restraint, not a head rest. (These guidelines apply for the driver and passengers.)

- In vehicles fitted with WIPS (whiplash injury prevention) safety systems, make sure that nothing is placed directly behind the backs of the front seats – anything obstructing the back of the seat will render the WIPS ineffective. WIPS safety systems are designed to prevent whiplash when a vehicle is hit from behind. The back of the seat immediately reclines and helps to dissipate energy away from the occupant's spine.

- In vehicles with drop-down seat backs for ease of loading, make sure that the backs are properly secured after use.

- In general, adjust the seat and head restraint so that you are comfortable, safe and have the best possible vantage point. Make sure that your seating position is far enough back from the steering column so that your knees are free to move about but not so far that you have difficulty fully depressing the pedals.

- Ensure that the steering wheel is at least 20cm-25cm from your chest when you're seated in the driving position. If there is an airbag in the steering wheel, tilt the wheel so that the bag is aimed at your chest and not at your face.

9   Navigation

Map reading

- Look at a map or road atlas of your local area and study the legend (or key) to learn what the various colours and symbols mean.

- To practise route-planning, identify your present location on the map and find an efficient route to another location – e.g. the nearest hospital or airport.

- For a longer journey, write down the names of large towns and road identification numbers en route. Sometimes it's easier to find a destination by identifying a larger destination further along the same route. For example, when travelling from Cork to Clane in Co. Kildare, it would be prudent to follow the Dublin route signs most of the way until you reach Naas in Co. Kildare. You can then switch to the local road information as you get close to the destination.

- Use a road atlas to identify primary, secondary, rural and urban roads. Consider how the various road types might affect your journey (e.g. speed limits and traffic volumes). You should also be able to identify other useful road safety or journey-related information such as rest stops or places where you can refuel and get something to eat.

- With practice, you will be able to use the information on the map to estimate the distance and time required to get from one location to another.
- On a city map, identify parking areas and one-way streets.
- Plan a trip and prepare for your journey by calling AA Roadwatch to check for traffic advisories (you can also find advisories in the newspaper). Check on the Internet for traffic information in your destination or en route. Practicing this now will make you aware of the information available from these services; it will come in handy when you do set out on a long trip.

GPS

In vehicles fitted with GPS (global positioning system) and RDS (radio data system) navigation systems, read the owner's manual before you set out on a journey. Try not to rely on the devices too much and don't let yourself get distracted by technology while driving. Even if you have a GPS device, it's still worth bringing a map or road atlas along on your journey, just in case the GPS fails.

Planning a journey

When you're travelling long distances or on unfamiliar routes, allow plenty of extra time for your journey. This will prevent you from getting stressed if there are any delays. It will also enable you to take a break when you're tired.

9   Maintaining your vehicle
Check-list and log-sheet

9 Practice 1	9 Practice 2	9 Practice 3
Date	Date	Date

Before moving on to the next session, you should be able to demonstrate 'green light' mastery in each skill.
Use this sheet to track progress by **ticking the circles** as shown.

✓ Skill preformed with competence, consistently showing mastery
○ Skill performed correctly but driver sometimes needs prompting
○ Skill accomplished but driver sometimes forgets a check or step
○ Skill completed with some help or a prompt from the mentor
○ Skill cannot be completed or requires substantial help from mentor

Maintaining lights

○○○○○ Habitually checks lights (e.g. when filling up with fuel)
○○○○○ Can locate and access lights at both front and rear of vehicle
○○○○○ Correctly identifies headlights and side lamps
○○○○○ Removes blown bulb using push-and-twist action
○○○○○ Uses cloth/wrapper to protect replacement bulb from grease
○○○○○ Checks that replaced bulb is working

Oil level

○○○○○ Parks on level ground to check oil level
○○○○○ Locates oil reservoir
○○○○○ Allows engine to cool slightly before commencing the check
○○○○○ Cleans dipstick before checking oil level
○○○○○ Tops up oil using appropriate grade

Windshield wipers and washer fluid

OO○OO   Recognises signs of aging/damaged wiper blades and wiper arms

OO○OO   Replaces wiper blade correctly

OO○OO   Uses defroster to release wiper blades frozen onto windshield

OO○OO   Locates washer-fluid reservoir

OO○OO   Understands function of different types of washer fluid

OO○OO   Understands limits of water as a washer fluid

Brake fluid and coolant

OO○OO   Identifies brake-fluid reservoir and assesses level correctly

OO○OO   Locates coolant reservoir

OO○OO   Allows engine to cool completely before checking coolant level

OO○OO   Understands both functions of coolant

Tyre tread and pressure

OO○OO   Performs quick visual check of tread depth

OO○OO   Uses inflation gauge or 'coin test' for assessment of tread depth

OO○OO   Uses visual check to estimate if tyres are under- or over-inflated

OO○OO   Consults owner's manual or tyre pressure chart to determine correct pressure for intended load

OO○OO   Uses air pump to gauge and adjust tyre pressure

Changing a tyre

OO○OO   Chooses safest possible location for changing tyre

OO○OO   Places safety triangle 50m behind vehicle

OO○OO   Places spare tyre under vehicle, close to flat, as extra buffer

OO○OO   Secures vehicle using chocks or rocks

OO○OO   Loosens nuts before raising vehicle on jack

OO○OO   Identifies jacking point nearest to flat tyre

○○○○○ Drives within limits of compact spare (if applicable)

Safety belts, seats and mirrors

○○○○○ Checks that all safety belts run freely and are
not damaged

○○○○○ Adjusts shoulder height correctly (if applicable)

○○○○○ Checks inertia tension mechanism by pulling sharply
on belt

○○○○○ Positions head restraint for maximum protection in event
of collision

○○○○○ Positions steering wheel 20-25 cm from chest

○○○○○ Tilts steering wheel to aim airbag at chest rather than face

○○○○○ Checks that mirrors are securely mounted

Map reading and route/journey planning

○○○○○ Identifies different road types on a map

○○○○○ Uses map's legend (or key) to identify landmarks

○○○○○ Traces one or more routes from starting point
to destination

○○○○○ Identifies key points along route

○○○○○ Estimates distance and time required for journey

○○○○○ Uses resources such as AA Roadwatch, newspapers and
web sites for traffic information

○○○○○ Uses city map to identify parking facilities and
one-way streets

We have spent adequate time practising the skills from session 9 and feel
competent enough to progress to the next skill development session.

Student driver's signature

Mentor's signature

Date

(10)

Vehicle loading

In this session we will practise...

- Vehicle loading
- Trailers and towing
- Interacting with large vehicles

Introduction

Congratulations! Now that you have reached the final practice session, you are well on your way to becoming a competent driver. The skills you have learned and practised will stand to you for life. However; only time and experience that will teach you everything you need to know about the dangerous environment of our roads. Even after you pass your driving test the learning never stops. In this session, we concentrate on the best practice for transporting people and cargo, and how to share the road with large or heavily-loaded vehicles.

10 Vehicle loading

Skills
- Stowing cargo.
- Roof rack/box safety.
- Adjusting for laden weight.
- Loading and towing trailers.
- Restricted views of HGVs.
- Manoeuvring and accommodating work vehicles.

Ideal location
- Spend time looking at the best ways of stowing cargo in the vehicle. If possible, bring some items with you (e.g., a bicycle, large box or shopping bags).
- If you have access to a trailer, practise loading, attaching and towing it. If you don't have a trailer, go to an auto store and spend some time discussing loading and towing.
- Conduct large vehicle interaction in urban and suburban areas.

Recommended practice time
- Allow adequate time to become fully familiar with the different ways to load and stow cargo properly.
- Take a drive with two or three extra passengers in the back to see how the vehicle's handling is affected by the extra load.

Additional reading
Instructor Guide
Lesson 10

Steer Clear Driver Education Manual
(p.276), (p.310), (p.229)

RSA Rules of the Road
(p.38), (p.39), (p.48), (p.41)

Carrying passengers and cargo inside your vehicle

For this practice session, it's a good idea to ask some family members or friends to come along as passengers. Although the correct techniques for carrying loads and passengers are covered in the lessons with your instructor, it's important to get some real-world experience. Having passengers on board will clearly illustrate the effects of passenger weight on how the vehicle handles, and the resulting need to adjust driving style, tyre pressure, lights and speed.

- It is your responsibility to ensure that your vehicle's cabin is not overloaded. Consider using a roof box or a trailer for larger loads.
- Loose items become lethal projectiles in the event of a sudden stop. You must stow and secure them properly to protect you and your passengers.
- Stow loose items in a secure position in the boot or on the floor of the vehicle. The ideal place is in the boot.
- When you must carry articles in the vehicle's cabin, stow them as low as possible and secure them with the seat belt (or find another way to tie them down).
- Do not place items on the dashboard or over airbags.

- If your vehicle has a cargo net, make sure that you have fitted it correctly. If it's not properly secured, it won't stay in place in the event of a collision. Check the owner's manual for the anchoring points.

Securing passengers and pets

- As the driver you are responsible for ensuring that everyone in your vehicle is secure and properly restrained. Even though adults can be independently penalised for not wearing safety belts in your vehicle, any unrestrained person, object or pet has the potential to do massive damage in the event of a sudden stop or collision. Insist that everyone in your vehicle wears the correct restraint properly.
- As the driver you are directly responsible for ensuring that all children under 17 are securely restrained in child safety seats and/or with the appropriate safety belts. Take time to familiarise yourself with the correct use of child safety restraints.
- Rear-facing infant seats must not be used in the front seat of vehicles with active front airbags. In any case, it is safest to install

all child seats in the rear. Fit an extra rear-view mirror to monitor children in the back.

- Unsecured pets are an unnecessary distraction when you are driving but, much worse, they can become deadly missiles in the event of a sudden stop or impact. Most vehicles have luggage tie-down points in the boot or other suitable tie-down areas in the rear; you can attach a dog's lead to these or use them to secure a cat's box. A secured pet will also be unable to dash out onto the road and cause an accident when you open the door at the end of your journey.

Loading a roof rack or roof box

Even if you don't plan on using a roof rack or box at this time, knowing how to use each one correctly will likely serve you well in the future. If you don't have a roof rack/box readily available, you

could enlist the help of a friend who has one or go to your local motor factors or service centre and get expert help and advice there.

- Loading cargo on top of your vehicle raises the vehicle's centre of gravity. The higher the centre of gravity, the less stable the vehicle is. You must adjust your driving style to compensate; the first thing to do is **slow down**.
- Check that the roof rack is securely attached to the vehicle every time you use it.
- Use straps or good rope with well tied knots to secure items onto the rack.
- After you've travelled a short distance, stop and check the security of the load because cargo often settles or moves in transit. Re-tighten the straps if necessary.
- Larger items that overhang the front or rear of the vehicle should also be secured to the tie-down points under the front/rear bumper to prevent wind lift.
- If you're using a waterproof covering, fasten it securely so

that it will withstand the intense wind pressure that occurs at higher speeds.

- If items fall from your vehicle, you are responsible for any damage caused.
- Stop to retrieve fallen items only if it is safe to do so.
- Never stop on a motorway to retrieve lost cargo. Get off the motorway at the next exit and phone the Gardaí.

Adjusting tyre pressure, lights and driving style in a laden vehicle

- When your vehicle is heavily loaded, you must increase the tyre pressure to ensure correct traction and control. You'll find the appropriate pressure value in the owner's manual or pressure chart (usually found inside the driver's door).

- If your vehicle has a light-levelling switch, adjust the angle of the headlights to suit the load you're carrying. (When the vehicle is weighed down with cargo, the headlights' beam will be higher, so you need to tilt the lights downwards to avoid dazzling other drivers.)
- Carrying heavier loads – whether passengers or cargo – affects how the vehicle handles. You'll need to slow down and corner more gradually when driving a laden vehicle.
- When your vehicle is full of passengers and/or cargo, your view can be blocked. Take extra care when carrying out manoeuvres (such as a three-point turn or merging).
- Overloading can have a drastic effect on how the vehicle handles, compromising control and safety.

A vehicle's centre of gravity and stability are affected by many factors including: acceleration, deceleration, turning, the tilt of the road and the load being carried. Whether extra weight comes from carrying passengers or goods it can dramatically alter how the vehicle handles in different conditions, additional weight therefore must always be taken into account to maintain safety when driving.

Trailers and towing

A full driving licence entitles you to tow a trailer. Even if you don't plan to tow a trailer in the near future, take some time to study the proper loading, mounting and towing techniques. The skills you learn may eventually come in handy.

Loading a trailer

- Before hitching up the trailer, make sure that it is correctly balanced. Weight should be placed over the axle.
- The gross weight of the trailer must not exceed the vehicle's towing capacity. Check the owner's manual.
- As a rule, the weight of the trailer should not exceed 85% of the weight of the vehicle. Depending on your driving licence, the combined weight of the vehicle and trailer may not exceed a certain value. Check your licence and the **Rules of the Road** for

details. For example, the EB licence permits 3,500kg or less; the EC1 permits 1,200kg or less.

- Ensure even weight distribution so that when coupled to the vehicle, the nose of the trailer is in line with the vehicle's tow hitch. The trailer must not lift the back of the vehicle up or push it down excessively.
- Check that the load on the trailer is securely tied down in more than one place. The load should not be able to shift forwards, backwards or to the sides.
- Boats and other tapered loads should be secured at the narrowest point. If you secure them elsewhere, make sure that the ties will not slip to the narrowest point and come loose. Securing two tie-down straps together across the wider part of the load may help to prevent slippage.

When a ball hitch and trailing equipment are attached to your vehicle, the vehicle's crumple zones and occupant safety features are severely compromised. If possible, choose a detachable system. This will reduce the injury risk to occupants if the vehicle is hit from the rear.

Attaching a trailer

- Once the coupling is placed over the ball, release and then secure the locking mechanism. Pull it up to check that it's secure.
- Attach the breakaway cable or chain to both the vehicle and the trailer.
- Attach the lights cable and check to see if the indicators and lights are working. If possible, adjust the angle of the vehicle's headlights to account for the extra weight.
- Check the tyre pressure and treads of the trailer. Carry a spare wheel or a chemical inflator on long journeys. Check that the axle and wheel connections are well lubricated, especially on trailers that are not used often.

- If the trailer has a braking system, ensure that it's working.
- Retract the jockey wheel and secure it in the up position.
- Once the load and the trailer are secured, make a short trip and then pull over in a safe place to check all tie downs again.
- When towing a caravan, ensure that all windows, doors and vents are closed. Check that all fuel supplies (e.g. gas bottles) are turned off and well secured.

Towing a trailer

- When you're satisfied that the trailer and load are secure, check your mirrors and blind spots. If necessary attach a mirror extension.
- Remember that a trailer affects your vehicle's centre of gravity and therefore its stability.
- Take extra care when towing. You will require a larger turning circle, a greater stopping distance and more time to build up speed. Allow more space and time to stop and slow down, and brake earlier than usual. Allow three

times more time/distance for overtaking than you otherwise would.

- Trailers affect your ability to see clearly so keep this in mind before you begin a manoeuvre.
- Practise in a quiet area until you feel comfortable.
- Use your mirrors frequently to check the trailer and other traffic.
- The maximum speed limit for towing trailers is 80km/h or less on minor roads.
- Travel in the left lane at all times unless the way is blocked or in exceptional cases (for example, on a motorway where the speed limit is below 80km/h).
- Avoid towing a trailer on very windy days. If you must travel, take extra care.
- Be considerate and allow other vehicles to pass if you are causing a tailback.
- If the trailer begins to 'snake', slow down by easing off on the accelerator. Allow the steering wheel to twitch a little. Where possible use the engine to slow the vehicle down. Do not try to stabilise the trailer by zigzagging or by making sharp steering corrections.

Being towed is potentially a very dangerous procedure and should only be undertaken by experienced drivers.

Being towed

Only resort to being towed in exceptional circumstances.

Most insurance policies now include a 24 hour breakdown service that should be availed of in the case of vehicle breakdown.
To locate your vehicle's towing points, check the owner's manual and then take a look at the vehicle's underside. Some vehicles have a detachable screw-in eye bolt which has a reverse thread. Be familiar with the towing points – it's an important part of your preparation for safe motoring.

The use of a towing bar is much safer than using a flexible rope or strap.

Interacting with large vehicles

- You can help truck and bus drivers by being aware of what they can and cannot see. When driving near an oversized vehicle, keep well back to enable the driver to see you.
- In general, if you can't see the bus or truck's mirrors, the driver won't be able to see you.

- Drivers of buses, trucks and other large vehicles may not be able to see what's directly in front of them; close beside them; or for a considerable distance behind them. Stay out of these areas when possible or clear them quickly if you must enter.
- When reversing, large vehicles are required to make a sound signal as a warning. However, it

is not safe to rely on sound alone. Observe the vehicle's movements and tail lights.

Following large vehicles

- Stay well back to get a better view of the road ahead and to avoid any dirt or spray thrown up by the large vehicle's wheels.
- Adjust your driving style and allow a greater safe gap when following large vehicles. Trucks, buses and so on require a greater stopping distance than cars or other smaller vehicles.
- Try to leave as much space as possible when passing or being passed by a large vehicle. Be prepared to be buffeted by wind after passing.

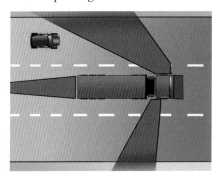

Loading and unloading commercial vehicles

- Don't be taken by surprise – anticipate when commercial carriers may need to stop or unload their cargo.
- Don't park too close to a commercial vehicle that may need room to unload goods or passengers.
- When passing a large vehicle that has stopped, leave room to allow for doors that swing outwards or for personnel to walk around the vehicle.
- Be considerate and allow buses to re-enter the traffic flow. This will help the traffic move better for everyone.
- Leave plenty of space behind or to the side of vehicles that are adapted for disabled access.

Large vehicles and corners

- Leave enough room for large vehicles to get around corners.
- Large vehicles may need to pull over to the right to make a left turn or to the left to make a right turn.
- Never pass a large vehicle on the inside when it is attempting to manoeuvre.
- Large vehicles turning into minor roads or commercial areas may need to approach the turn from the other side of the road. You may need to stop to accommodate their needs.
- If a truck is joining the minor road you're on, you may need to move over to accommodate it.
- If a large vehicle is turning into a junction that you are leaving, do not attempt to pull out in its shadow. Another vehicle may be overtaking the truck/bus and fail to see you.
- Leave extra room when pulling out from a junction in front of a large vehicle. They do not have the same ability to slow or stop as lighter vehicles do.

10 Loading, towing and interacting with large vehicles

Check-list and log-sheet

10 Practice 1 Date	10 Practice 2 Date	10 Practice 3 Date

Before moving on to the next session, you should be able to demonstrate 'green light' mastery in each skill.
Use this sheet to track progress by **ticking the circles** as shown.

✓ Skill preformed with competence, consistently showing mastery
○ Skill performed correctly but driver sometimes needs prompting
○ Skill accomplished but driver sometimes forgets a check or step
◑ Skill completed with some help or a prompt from the mentor
◓ Skill cannot be completed or requires substantial help from mentor

Loading cargo inside the vehicle and on the roof

○○○○○ Secures items inside vehicle using safety belt or other tie-down
○○○○○ Positions and secures cargo net correctly (if applicable)
○○○○○ Secures load on roof rack/box
○○○○○ Checks and adjusts tyre pressure to suit load

Securing passengers and pets

○○○○○ Ensures that all passengers are properly restrained
○○○○○ Fits and secures child-safety equipment (e.g., car seats)
○○○○○ Adjusts driving style to account for passenger weight
○○○○○ Restrains pets travelling in vehicle

Practice Session 10

Attaching, loading and towing a trailer

⬤⬤ ⬤⬤ Attaches and secures trailer

⬤⬤ ⬤⬤ Connects and checks trailer's lights

⬤⬤ ⬤⬤ Checks and adjusts tyre pressure to suit load

⬤⬤ ⬤⬤ Adjusts driving style when towing

Positioning with respect to large vehicles

⬤⬤ ⬤⬤ Anticipates any manoeuvres necessary on encountering a large vehicle

⬤⬤ ⬤⬤ Adopts a safe following position behind a large vehicle

⬤⬤ ⬤⬤ Prepares to overtake a large vehicle in good time

⬤⬤ ⬤⬤ Chooses to stay behind or selects good overtaking location

⬤⬤ ⬤⬤ Leaves adequate room before resuming left-lane position after overtaking

Accommodating large vehicles

⬤⬤ ⬤⬤ Passes loading or unloading vehicles with due care

⬤⬤ ⬤⬤ Anticipates and accommodates needs of public transport vehicles

⬤⬤ ⬤⬤ Leaves sufficient space when pulling out in front of large vehicles

⬤⬤ ⬤⬤ Allows for effects of weather on larger vehicles

We have spent adequate time practising the skills from session 10 and feel ready to take the driving test!

Student driver's signature

Mentor's signature

Date

Acknowledgements

Acknowledgements: The Irish Drivers Education Association is indebted to all those who have contributed to the research, development and production of the Steer Clear Driving Skills Manual and Logbook. Since the beginning of the project, we have received encouragement and support from countless individuals and organisations within Ireland and abroad and for this we are very appreciative and would like to say a big thanks to all of you.

Development, consultation and review: David Baddeley (Volvo Irl.) Michael Byrne (RSO-DCC) Ron Christie (RACV), Des Cummins (DIR), Trish Daly, John Dusch (MVA) Conor Faughnan (AA), Steve Garrod (DIAmond), Tom O'Connor (Motor Distributors Ltd) Prof Ray Fuller (TCD), Peter Laub (IVV), Dave Leahy (BBWA), Larry Lonero (AAAFTS), Sorcha McDonagh, Bob Montgomery, NCT Deansgrange, Nicole O'Neill, Dan Rohan (DEHLG), Prof Peter Russell (IMTD, IVV), Denise Sweeney, Forbes Zigers (NRA)

Editing team: Máire Daly, Mark Loughran, Sorcha McDonagh, Brian Murphy, Monica Schaefer, Denise Sweeney

Director of operations: Brian Murphy

Design and production: Anneke Calis and Tani Pratchayaopak (Tanika Design), Dave Leahy (Big Bad Wolf Animation), Mark Loughran (Identikit Design Consultants), William Siddall

Author and editor: Monica Schaefer

Road Signs

Regulatory Signs

These signs indicate the existance of a road regulation and show the course that you, the driver, must follow. They can also show the action you are permitted to take, or action you are forbidden to take.

Speed Limit
50 km/h

Speed Limit
60 km/h

Speed Limit
80 km/h

Speed Limit
100 km/h

Speed Limit
120 km/h

Stop Sign

Yield Right
of Way

Yield Right
of Way

No Entry

No Left
Turn

No Right
Turn

No U
Turn

Parking
Permitted

Parking
Prohibited

Turn
Left

Straight
Ahead Only

Keep
Left

Keep
Right

Pass Either
Side

Turn Left
Ahead

Turn Right
Ahead

School
Wardens Sign

Weight
Restriction

Axel Weight
Restriction

Height
Restriction

Parking
Weight
Restriction

Pedestrian
Zone

Clearway
Stopping or
Parking
Prohibited

Cycle and
Pedestrian
Track

Approaching
a Bus Lane

Bus Lane

Contra Flow
Bus Lane

Speed Limit
entering Town
or Village

No
Overtaking

Pedal Cyclists
only

Pedal Cyclists
Access only
for vehicles

No Entry
except
for Trams

Tram Lane

Road Signs

Warning Signs

These signs give advance warning of a hazard. They are diamond shaped with black symbols / letters on a yellow background.

Junction ahead with road or roads of equal importance

Junction ahead with road or roads of less importance (the latter being indicated by arms of lesser width)

Staggered junction ahead with roads of less importance.

Staggered junction ahead with roads of equal importance.

Merging and / or diverging traffic ahead

Dangerous bend ahead with junction or junctions

Dual carriageway with junction

Warning of major junction with dual carriageway

Advanced warning of major junction ahead

 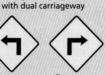

Roundabout ahead

Mini roundabout

Dangerous corner ahead

Dangerous corner ahead

Dangerous bend ahead

Series of dangerous bends ahead

Series of dangerous corners ahead

Road Signs

Warning Signs *continued*

These signs give advance warning of a hazard. They are diamond shaped with black symbols / letters on a yellow background.

Two-way traffic ahead

Road narrows dangerously

Road narrows ahead

Road narrows on left side

Road narrows on right side

Dual-carriageway ends

Road divides ahead

Steep ascent

Steep descent

Sharp depression

Sharp rise ahead

Series of bumps or hollows

Tunnel ahead

Unprotected Quay ahead

Slippery stretch of road ahead

Low flying aircraft

Tramway Crossing ahead

Level Crossing ahead Unprotected

Level Crossing ahead protected by gates

Level Crossing ahead with lights and barriers

Crosswinds

Aire Leanaí
CAUTION CHILDREN

School Children crossing ahead

School ahead

Pedestrian crossing ahead

Possibility of riders on horseback

Risk of wild deer

Low Bridge ahead

Motorway Signs

Motorway ahead

NO L-drivers,
Vehicles under 50cc.,
Slow vehicles (under 30 mph),
Invalid-Carriages,
Pedal-cycles,
Pedestrians,
Animals.

Motorway ahead

Entry to Motorway

Approaching end of Motorway

End of Motorway

Countdown markers for Motorway sliproad at 100m intervals

Road Signs

Warning signs for Roadworks

These are the same shape as ordinary warning signs but are orange coloured instead of yellow

Roadworks
ahead

Road narrows
on left side

Traffic crossover
ahead

Traffic Lights
ahead

Manual traffic
control ahead

Two way
traffic

Road narrows
ahead

Left Lane
closed ahead

Inside Lane
closed ahead

Middle Lane
closed ahead

Outside Lane
closed ahead

Lane closed
Deviate to right

Mid lane closed
Deviate to right

No Through
Road

MAJOR ROAD WORKS AHEAD
Major Road
Works ahead

Móroibreacha Bóthair Romhat
Móroibreacha
Bóthair Romhat

Bóthar Dúnta ROAD CLOSED
Road Closed

DETOUR 400m
Detour Ahead

DIVERTED TRAFFIC →
Direction of
Diverted Traffic

Information signs

These signs show direction, distance and route number etc. They also show facilities and places of interest.

N6

Áth Cliath
DUBLIN
An Longfort
LONGFORD
N4
Advance
Direction Sign

Gaillimh   km
GALWAY   94
Sligeach
SLIGO   29
(Dún na nGall
DONEGAL   49)
Route Confirmation Sign

↑ R430 Mainistir Laoise
ABBEYLEIX
Advance Direction Sign

Baile Bachaille   km
BALLYBOUGHAL 5
R129
Direction Sign

P ♿ ➤
Car Park with
access facilities

Alternative route
for high vehicles

Naomh Caoimhín
ST. KEVINS
3 km

km Tearmann Éan
2 BIRD SANCTUARY

← Dolmain
DOLMEN

Tourist Information signs showing route and distance

← Áth Cliath M7
DUBLIN
Luimneach →
LIMERICK M7
Motorway Advance
Direction Sign

H 100m
Hospital
Distance Sign

321

Other publications you might find helpful

AA Driving Test – Pass First Time
Automobile Association

AA How to be an Expert Driver
Automobile Association

Car Basics
Kevin Elliot

Clever Car Buying
Eddie Cunningham

Colour Lesson Plan... Visuals
Theory First

Drive The DVD
Yorkshire Shire Oak

Essential Teaching Skills
Chris Kyriacou

Get It – The Irish Driving Test
Brian O'Leary

Is Your Car Safe?
Vivian Foley

It's No Accident
Lisa Lewis

Know Your Traffic Signs – UK
Department of Transport

Learn to Drive
Robert Davies

Passing the Test
Dominic McGinley

Practical Teaching Skills for Driving Instructors
J. Miller and M. Stacey

Rules of the Road
Road Safety Authority

The Driving Instructor's Handbook
J. Miller and M. Stacey

The Driving Test in Ireland
Des Cummins

The Essential Police Driver's Handbook
Phillip Coyne

The Highway Code
Automobile Association

The Highway Code – For Northern Ireland
Department of Environment

The Official Driver Theory Test
Road Safety Authority

The Official DSA Guide to Hazard Perception
Driving Standards Authority

Vehicle Maintenance for Women
Charlotte Williamson

What If? The Official Guide to Boosting Driver Awareness
Driving Standards Authority

Useful web links

An Garda Síochána	**www.garda.ie**
Automobile Association (AA) Ireland	**www.aaireland.ie** **www.aaroadwatch.ie**
Auto Trader Magazine	**www.autotrader.ie**
Car Buyers Guide	**www.cbg.ie**
Driver Theory Test	**www.dtts.ie**
Driving Test	**www.drivingtest.ie**
European Road Safety Charter	**www.paueducation.com**
Irish Drivers Education Association	**www.steerclear.ie**
Motor Tax Office	**www.motortax.ie**
Mapping Websites	**www.maps.live.com** **www.googlemaps.com**
National Car Testing	**www.nct.ie**
National Roads Authority	**www.nra.ie**
Penalty Points Information	**www.penaltypoints.ie**
Road Safety Authority	**www.rsa.ie**
Royal Automobile Club	**www.rac.co.uk**
Society of the Irish Motor Industry	**www.simi.ie**
Steer Clear	**www.steerclear.ie**
UN Make Roads Safe Campaign	**www.makeroadssafe.org**
Weather information	**www.meteireann.ie**

RSA Driving Test Report Form

No. 000000

DRIVING TEST REPORT

1. Passed your Driving Test

Having passed your driving test you should nevertheless continue to pay particular attention to the faults marked overleaf without neglecting other aspects of your driving.

2. Failure of your Driving Test

Failure of the test arises where you incur any of the following:

1 or more grade 3 faults;

4 of the same grade 2 faults for a single aspect;

6 or more grade 2 faults under the same heading; or a total of

9 or more grade 2 faults overall.

Up to a maximum of 4 grade 2 faults may be recorded for any single aspect.

3. Grading of faults

Faults are graded as follows:

Grade 1 (Green Area) Minor Fault, Grade 2 (Blue Area) More Serious Fault, Grade 3 (Pink Area) Dangerous/Potentially Dangerous faults or total disregard of traffic controls.

Grade 1 faults do not affect the rest result.

A combination of 3 or more unanswered or incorrectly answered questions on the Rules of the Road/ Checks, constitutes a grade 2 fault. (Checks include doors closed safely, the headrest, mirrors, seat and seat-belt adjustments, and for motorcyclists, the helmet, gloves, boots and protective clothing).

3 or more hand signals not demonstrated correctly constitutes a grade 2 fault.

3 or more Secondary Controls not demonstrated correctly constitutes a grade 2 fault. (Secondary controls include temperature controls, fan, air vents, rear-window heater, wipers, windscreen washer, light switches, air intake control, rear fog light and air conditioner, if fitted).

Not operating a Secondary Control as required during the practical test can also constitute a fault.

4. Technical Checks – all categories

Inability to describe a check on 3 or more of the following constitutes a grade 2 fault:

The tyres, lights, reflectors, indicators, engine oil, coolant, windscreen washer fluid, steering, brakes and horn. Where necessary, the bonnet should be opened and closed safely. For motorcyclists the checks can also include the chain, and the emergency stop-switch, if fitted.

For categories C1, C, D1, D, EC1, ED1, and ED technical checks include the following as appropriate to the category:

The power assisted braking and steering systems, the condition of the wheels, wheel nuts, mudguards, windscreen, windows, wipers, air-pressure, air tanks, suspension, engine oil, coolant, windscreen washer fluid, the loading mechanism if fitted, the body, sheets, cargo doors, cabin locking, way of loading and securing the load, and checking and using the instrument panel and tachograph.

For categories D1, D, ED1 and ED technical checks include controlling the body, service doors, emergency exits, first aid equipment, fire extinguishers and other safety equipment.

5. Coupling/Uncoupling includes

a) Checking the coupling mechanism and the brake and electrical connections,

b) Uncoupling and recoupling the trailer from/to its towing vehicle using the correct sequence. The towing vehicle must be parked alongside the trailer as part of the exercise.

Parking in relation to categories EB, C1, C, EC1, and EC includes parking safely at a ramp or platform for loading/unloading.

Parking in relation to D1, D, ED1, and ED includes parking safely to let passengers on or off the bus.

6. Motorcyclists

Safety glance means looking around to check blind spots as necessary.

7. Preparing for your next Driving Test

In Preparing for your next test you should pay particular attention to the items which have been marked. Further information on these and other aspects of the test are contained in the booklet entitled "Rules of the Road" which is available at book shops and in the leaflet "Preparing for your Driving Test" which is issued with the acknowledgement of your application.

8. Note

Items on which faults occurred during your driving test are marked overleaf. The driver tester is not permitted to discuss the details of the test.

Údarás Um Shábháilteacht Ar Bhóithre
Road Safety Authority

Oifigí Rialtais, Béal an Átha, Co. Mhaigh Eo / Government Offices. Ballina, Co. Mayo.
locall: 1890 40 60 40 fax: (096) 78 287 website: www.drivingtest.ie

Reproduced with kind permission
from the Road Safety Authority

NAME OF APPLICANT:

DATE: DAY | MONTH | YEAR | **REG. NO.**

FAULTS	GRADE 1	GRADE 2	GRADE 3	FAULTS	GRADE 1	GRADE 2	GRADE 3
1. RULES/CHECKS				**11. MAINTAIN REASONABLE PROGRESS AND AVOID UNDUE HESITANCY WHEN**			
2. POSITION VEHICLE CORRECTLY AND IN GOOD TIME				MOVING OFF			
ON THE STRAIGHT				ON THE STRAIGHT			
ON BENDS				OVERTAKING			
IN TRAFFIC LANES				AT CROSS JUNCTIONS			
AT CROSS JUNCTIONS				AT ROUNDABOUTS			
AT ROUNDABOUTS				TURNING RIGHT			
TURNING RIGHT				TURNING LEFT			
TURNING LEFT				CHANGING LANES			
STOPPING				AT TRAFFIC LIGHTS			
FOLLOWING TRAFFIC				**12. MAKE PROPPER USE OF VEHICLE CONTROLS**			
3. TAKE PROPER OBSERVATION				ACCELERATOR			
MOVING OFF				CLUTCH			
OVERTAKING				GEARS			
CHANGING LANES				FOOTBRAKE			
AT CROSS JUNCTIONS				HANDBRAKE			
AT ROUNDABOUTS				STEERING			
TURNING RIGHT				SECONDARY CONTROLS			
TURNING LEFT				TECHNICAL CHECKS			
4. REACT PROMPTLY AND PROPERLY TO HAZARDS				COUPLING/UNCOUPLING			
REACTION				**13. ADJUST SPEED TO SUIT/ON APPROACH**			
5. USE MIRRORS PROPERLY, IN GOOD TIME AND BEFORE SIGNALLING				ROAD CONDITIONS			
MOVING OFF				TRAFFIC CONDITIONS			
ON THE STRAIGHT				ROUNDABOUTS			
OVERTAKING				CROSS JUNCTIONS			
CHANGING LANES				TURNING RIGHT			
AT ROUNDABOUTS				TURNING LEFT			
TURNING RIGHT				TRAFFIC CONTROLS			
TURNING LEFT				SPEED LIMIT			
SLOWING/STOPING				**14. COMPLY WITH TRAFFIC CONTROLS**			
6. ALLOW SUFFIENT CLEARANCE TO				TRAFFIC LIGHTS			
PEDESTRIANS				TRAFFIC SIGNS			
CYCLISTS				ROAD MARKINGS			
STATIONARY VEHICLES				PEDESTRIAN CROSSING			
OTHER TRAFFIC				GARDA/SCHOOL WARDEN			
OTHER OBJECTS				BUS LANES			
OVERTAKE SAFELY				CYCLE LANES			
7. GIVE CORRECT SIGNALS IN GOOD TIME				**15. YIELD RIGHT OF WAY AS REQUIRED**			
MOVING OFF				MOVING OFF			
OVERTAKING				OVERTAKING			
CHANGING LANES				CHANGING LANES			
AT ROUNDABOUTS				AT JUNCTIONS			
TURNING RIGHT				AT ROUNDABOUTS			
TURNING LEFT				TURNING RIGHT			
STOPPING				TURNING LEFT			
CANCEL PROMPTLY				**16. REVERSE**			
HAND SIGNALS				COMPETENTLY			
BECKONING OTHERS				OBSERVATION			
MISLEADING				RIGHT OF WAY			
8. MOTORCYCLES				**17. TURNABOUT**			
SAFETY GLANCE				COMPETENTLY			
U-TURN: CONTROL/OBS.				OBSERVATION			
SLOW RIDE				RIGHT OF WAY			
PARK ON/OFF STAND				**18. PARKING, LOADING/UNLOADING/PASSENGER STOPS**			
WALK ALONGSIDE				COMPETENTLY			
9. COURTESY				OBSERVATION			
10. ALIGHTING				RIGHT OF WAY			

Application for a driving test

For Office use only

APPLICATION FOR A DRIVING TEST

BEFORE COMPLETING THIS FORM PLEASE READ THE INFORMATION PROVIDED OVERLEAF

YOU CAN NOW APPLY AND PAY FOR YOUR DRIVING TEST ONLINE – PLEASE VISIT www.drivingtest.ie

When you have the application form completed, please forward it along with the correct fee to the address given below. If you do not receive an acknowledgement within two weeks, please contact the Department to confirm your application.

Driver Testing Section, Road Safety Authority,
Government Offices, Ballina, Co. Mayo.
Tel: (096 78289 / LoCall (1890) 40 60 40 / Fax: (096) 78290
Web: www.drivingtest.ie Email: drivingtest@rsa.ie

1. Please state the category in which you wish to be tested (*a list of the categories and a description of the type of vehicle which they cover is at 1 overleaf*)

   (Please note that you may apply for a test in respect of one category only)

2. Have you previously undergone a driving test?

   ☐ Yes
   ☐ No

   If, YES, please give the approximate date of the test

   D D M M Y Y Y Y

3. Please nominate the Centre at which you wish to be tested. (*A list of Centres is given at 2 overleaf*).

4. What is your date of birth?

   D D M M Y Y Y Y

5. Please indicate any date (e.g. a particular day each week) or periods when you will be **UNAVAILABLE** to undergo the test e.g. exams, holidays, etc.

6. Do you have any physical disability, which requires you to drive a specially adapted vehicle?

   ☐ Yes   ☐ No

7. Any other relevant information about your application.

8. Please list the telephone numbers (including local codes) at which you may be contacted.

   HOME   WORK

9. Please give your full name and address (BLOCK CAPITALS)

   Mr/Ms, etc

   Surname

   First Name(s)

   Address

10. I wish to apply for a driving test and I declare that the information which I have furnished is correct.

    SIGNAURE OF APPLICANT _____

    DATE _____

326

Reproduced with kind permission
from the Road Safety Authority

1. LICENCE CATEGORIES OF MECHANICALLY PROPELLED VEHICLES

CATEGORY	VEHICLES IN CATEGORY
A1	Motorcycles with an engine size of 51 – 125cc and/or a speed capability over 45 km/ and with a power rating not exceeding 11 kW.k with or without a sidecar
A	Motorcycles with or without a sidecar
B	(Cars and Light Vans) Vehicles with passenger accommodation for not more than 8 persons and having a design G.V.W. not over 3,500 kg.
C1	(Large Vans and Light Trucks) Vehicles with passenger accommodation for not more than 8 persons and having a design G.V.W. over 3,500 kg, but not mover 7,500 kg.
C	(Trucks) Vehicles with passenger accommodation for not more than 8 persons and having a design G.V.W. over 3,500 kg.
D1	(Minibuses) Vehicles in Category D with passenger accommodation for more than 8 persons.
*EB	Vehicles in Category B with trailer attached.
*EC	Articulated Trucks and Trucks in Category C with a trailer attached.
*EC1	Vehicles in Category C1 with trailer attached – the combination must not exceed 12,000 kg.
*ED	Vehicles in Category D with trailer attached.
*ED1	Vehicles in Category D with trailer attached – the combination must not exceed 12,000 kg.
M	Two wheeled vehicles with an engine size not exceeding 50 cc and/or a speed capability not more than 45 km/h.
W	Work vehicles and land tractors with or without a trailer attached.

* To be eligible for a provisional licence/test in these categories, you must be the holder of a full licence for the drawing vehicle. "Passenger accommodation" means seating accommodation for passengers in addition to the driver. "Design G.V.W". means design gross vehicle weight (i.e. maximum permissible laden weight).
In the case of motorcycles a sidecar is not permitted for test purposes (except in the case of a disabled person).

2. TEST CENTRES
There are five driving test centres in Dublin at Churchtown, Rathgar, Finglas, Raheny and Tallaght. Other centres are located in Athlone, Ballina, Birr, Buncrana, Carlow, Carrick-on-Shannon, Castlebar, Cavan, Clifden, Clonmel, Cork, Donegal, Dundalk, Dungarvan, Ennis, Galway, Gorey, Kilkenny, Killarney, Kilrush, Letterkenny, Limerick (2), Longford, Loughrea, Mallow, Monaghan, Mullingar, Naas, Navan, Nenagh, Newcastle West, Portlaoise, Roscommon, Shannon, Skibbereen, Sligo, Thurles, Tipperary, Tralee, Tuam, Tullamore, Waterford, Wexford and Wicklow.

As far as possible your test will be arranged for the centre you nominate. You should note, however, that tests for Categories C, EC, EC1, D, ED and ED1 are conducted only at a limited number of centres in cities and large towns. Consequently, if you apply for one of those tests at a centre where it is not conducted, you will be given an appointment for the centre nearest to you where it is conducted. If you are applying for a test in Categories W (Tractor) or A1 and M (Small Motorcycles), you may request to have the test conducted at a town nearer to you than any of the above centres and every effort will be made to conduct your test in that town. You can view a site map for each test centre, along with waiting times for each centre, on our website at www.drivingtest.ie.

3. PROVISIONAL LICENCE REQUIREMENTS
To undergo a Driving Test, you must hold a Provisional Licence covering the category in which you wish to be tested. In certain circumstances, eligibility for a Provisional Licence is conditional on the applicant already holding a full Driving Licence for a smaller/lighter vehicle. Consequently, before you apply for the test, you should ensure that you hold the correct Provisional Licence. Eligibility for a third or subsequent Provisional Licence for any category of vehicle is dependent on you having undergone a driving test within the previous two years or providing evidence of a forthcoming driving test appointment in respect of the vehicle category in question. **If you have any doubt about your eligibility for a Provisional Licence you should enquire immediately with your local Motor Taxation Office**. The telephone numbers of Motor Taxation Offices can be located under the "Local Authorities" heading of the telephone directory.

4. FEE
Please note that your application must be accompanied by the fee appropriate to each category of test. These are set out hereunder AND ARE NON-REFUNDABLE AND NON-TRANSFERABLE. Payment should be made by postal order, money order or cheque. These should be crossed and made payable to the Road Safety Authority. PLEASE DO NOT SEND CASH. Applications accompanied by an incorrect fee will be returned. (For administrative reasons, no refunds will be made in respect of €2 or less in excess of the fee for the category concerned).

Categories A, A1, B, EB, M and W	€38
Categories C, C1 and D1	€63
Categories EC, EC1, ED and ED	€76

5. CANCELLING YOUR DRIVING TEST
10 DAYS NOTICE of cancellation must be given, otherwise the fee is forfeit. A limit of two cancellations applies to appointments issued on foot of this application. Any further cancellations will result in forfeiture of the fee.

6. OTHER INFORMATION
An Irish language version of this form is available. Any person who completes this form in Irish or who completes the Irish Language version will have their test conducted in Irish. If you have difficulty communication in English or are deaf you are permitted to have an interpreter with you for the oral test. This person must not be a relative or your driving instructor and may not accompany you on the practical test.

If you need to do your test urgently and if you are willing to be tested at short notice, please submit appropriate supporting evidence. The availability of tests at short notice is dependent on the number of applicants who cancel, consequently the Authority cannot guarantee an early test to all urgent applicants.

Additional information on the Driving Test is available in the booklet entitled "Rules of Road" which can be purchased at bookshops or through the Government Publications Sales Office.

> THIS ROAD SAFETY AUTHORITY IS COMMITTED TO THE CONTINUOUS IMPROVEMENT OF ITS SERVICES AND WELCOMES COMMENTS,. IF YOU WISH TO MAKE A FORMAL COMPLAINT PLEASE WRITE TO THE CUSTOMER SERVICE OFFICER, DRIVER TESTING SECTION, ROAD SAFETY AUTHORITY, GOVERNMENT OFFICES, BALLINA, CO MAYO.

Notes